HARROD AND HIS TRADE CYCLE GROUP

Also by Warren Young

INTERPRETING MR KEYNES: the *IS–LM* Enigma

Harrod and his Trade Cycle Group

The Origins and Development of the Growth Research Programme

Warren Young

MACMILLAN

First published 1989

Published by
THE MACMILLAN PRESS LTD
Houndmills, Basingstoke, Hampshire RG21 2XS
and London
Companies and representatives
throughout the world

Printed in Hong Kong

British Library Cataloguing in Publication Data
Young, Warren, L.
Harrod and his Trade cycle group: the origins
and development of the growth research
programme.
1. Great Britain. Economic growth. Effects of
trade cycles on research projects
I. Title II. Harrod, Roy (Roy Forbes), 1900–1978
III. Growth Research Programme in Economics
338.9′0072041
ISBN 0–333–47019–2

For Professor James Meade and in memory of
Sir Roy Harrod

Contents

Acknowledgements

This book is dedicated to Sir Roy Harrod and Professor James Meade, whose fundamental contributions over 50 years ago changed the course of economic inquiry and brought about the growth research programme in economics. I want to thank Lady Harrod and Professor Meade for allowing me to cite from the Harrod-Meade correspondence in the Meade papers.

The Harrod papers are now held at Chiba University of Commerce, Ichikawa, Japan. They comprise, after the Keynes papers, perhaps the richest store of material for the history of economic thought this century. I wish to express here my deepest gratitude to Professor Y. Hayakawa, the President of Chiba University of Commerce, Y. Harada, the Chairman of the Board of Directors, Y. Tojo, the Director, General Affairs, and Professor R. Iwaki, Librarian of Chiba University of Commerce, for permission to cite at length from the Harrod papers, and also for their kind hospitality and assistance during my stay in Ichikawa.

In addition, my Japanese friends, Professors T. Nagashima and K. Iwai of Tokyo University, Professor N. Masuda of Toyama University, and Professor K. Kakihara of Chiba University, were of great help during my all-too-brief stay in Japan.

I was only able to get to Ichikawa, however, due to the kindness and co-operation of my former colleagues at the Victoria University of Wellington, New Zealand, where I spent the academic year 1987 as a visiting senior lecturer in economics. Financial assistance for my research efforts was provided by the internal research fund, and the Economics group research fund, Victoria University of Wellington, and the economics research fund of the Reserve Bank of New Zealand. I am most grateful for their assistance, and I wish to thank in this regard Professor S.H. Franklin, Dr L. Evans, Dr G. Wells, and also Mr P. Nicholl, Deputy Governor of the Reserve Bank of New Zealand.

I also want to again thank Professor S. Dennison for providing me with material from the Robertson papers, and for his kind permission to cite at length from the letters of Professor Sir Dennis Robertson. I also want to thank Maurice Allen for permission to cite from his letters to Harrod, and Professor Liz Durbin, for both sending me copies of letters from the papers of her father, the late Evan Durbin, and permission to cite from them here.

I also want to thank Professor H. Hagemann and the Faculty of Economics, University of Bremen, for inviting me to present material contained in this book at their seminar in July 1988, and Professors L. Jonung and B. Hansson of the Department of Economics, University of Lund, for inviting me to the 'Conference on the Stockholm School after 50 years', where material on Harrod and Lundberg was presented in August 1987.

The following individuals acted – sometimes even without knowing it – as 'intellectual sounding boards' for my sometimes incoherent ideas and interpretations, and I want to thank them for putting up with me: Professor Sir John Hicks, Professor Paul Samuelson, Professor Robert Clower, Professor William Baumol, Professor Don Patinkin, Professor Ralph Turvey, Professor Axel Leijonhufvuud, Professor Wynne Godley, Professor Frank Hahn, Professor Kenneth Arrow, Professor Hans Brems, and last but not least, Professor James Meade himself. Dr Charles Hitch also greatly assisted my efforts in understanding the crucial importance of Professor Meade's early work – both published and unpublished.

I also want to thank my former colleagues at the Victoria University of Wellington for actively assisting the development of my ideas on the subject of this book: Professor David Sheppard, Professor Bryan Philpott, Professor Barbu Niculescu, Dr Graeme Wells, Dr Geoff Bertram, Dr Lew Evans, Dr John Zanetti, Dr Mohammed Khaled, Dr Neil Quigley, Mr Bob Buckle, and Mr Bob Stephens. All put up with my constant 'Eureka!', until I really found the 'missing links'.

The impetus for this research emanated out of previous work I had done on Harrod, and long and fruitful conversations with Drs Geoff Harcourt and Peter Clarke of Cambridge University. I also want to thank in this context the Master of my college, Churchill, Professor Sir Hermann Bondi, and the college registrar, Miss M. Beveridge, for their kindness in arranging accommodation during my visits to the Faculty of Economics and Politics at Cambridge over 1985–8.

The friendship and support of Dr David and Mrs Suzette Pearson, and Mr Don Stewart, enabled me to get through the watery Wellington, N.Z. spring after my family had returned to a warmer clime. The hospitality of Dr David and Mrs Margaret Toase in Cambridge, and Mr Sam and Mrs Miri Klibansky in London, also helped me through the long separation involved in trying to conduct research away from one's family. And it is thus my wife Sara and daughters Shani and Natalie who deserve the most thanks, for allowing me to spend so much time away from home, again, engaged in 'hagiography'.

Preface

Sir Roy Harrod has been described as second only to Keynes amongst economists in terms of the originality of his contributions to modern economic thought. Even the renowned economist and Nobel Laureate, Sir John Hicks, noted his own long-standing intellectual debt to Harrod in his Nobel Lecture, when he acknowledged the fact that Harrod's work, in essence, provided him with many fertile ideas which he further developed in the course of his own distinguished career.

Harrod was instrumental in discovering and developing – both on his own and with the assistance of others, as in the case of Keynes – some of the most fundamental and profound concepts in modern economics. These include the notion of the marginal revenue curve, the IS–LM approach to Keynes's *General Theory*, the dynamic extension of the Keynesian system, and he is universally recognised as the father of modern growth theory in economics.

In fact, if Keynes was considered by the economics profession to be the 'sorcerer', then Harrod was his very independent minded 'apprentice'. Indeed, Harrod tried to go further than Keynes by expanding his scope. However, while Harrod ventured into areas of economic theory that Keynes left untouched, he also continuously tried to integrate and reconcile Keynes's views with the 'mainstream' of economic thought. Thus, the relationship between Keynes and Harrod, and even more so, the relationship between Harrod and the Cambridge 'Keynesians', was never like that between Keynes and his Cambridge 'disciples', as Robertson called them. Although reproached and admonished by Keynes many times over their disagreements regarding Keynes's *General Theory* approach, Harrod never became discouraged. Rather, he remained adamant in his attempt to dynamise and thereby, in his view, generalise Keynes, and also to integrate Keynes's *General Theory* approach with mainstream theory as he understood and interpreted it.

Now, although Harrod's published work on the trade cycle, growth, and dynamics only appeared between 1934 and 1939, he actually began to think about these problems during the 1920s. After taking his degree at New College, Oxford, and having been elected a teaching fellow at Christchurch, he spent two terms, during 1922–3, working with and under the supervision of Keynes at Cambridge.

Upon his return to Oxford, Harrod wrote a number of essays on the trade cycle, growth, and distribution over the period 1924–33, which, although never published, must be dealt with in the context of the evolution of his economic thought. This early work, along with the later input he received from what he called his Trade Cycle group and others – such as Robertson – during the mid-1930s, assisted him both in formulating his ideas as published in *The Trade Cycle* (1936a), and in the transition to his theory of growth and dynamics, as manifest in his 'Essay in Dynamic Theory' (1939a).

While much has been written about the issues emanating from Harrod's mainstream contributions in the field of economic growth and dynamics, with some work also recently appearing on other specific aspects of what can be called 'Harrodian economics' – and a systematic treatment of Harrod's economic world view and detailed survey of his many contributions to economic thought is long overdue – up to now, all analyses of Harrod's contributions have been based upon either published and secondary sources, or limited to the Keynes-Harrod correspondence as published in Keynes's collected writings. The material to be presented in this book, however, is based upon previously unpublished essays, manuscripts, and correspondence found in the Harrod and Meade papers, and therefore throws entirely new light on the origins and development of his ideas.

In the introduction to the book, the key questions and issues to be dealt with are presented, and the necessity for reassessment, reconstruction, and retrospective appraisal of the origins and development of Harrod's contribution outlined. In the first chapter, Harrod's unpublished early work on the trade cycle, growth, and distribution – initially set off by Keynes's *Tract*, and subsequently influenced by the *Treatise*, as will be seen – are surveyed. These include an essay on the trade cycle and income distribution (1924), a memo on the effect of falling prices on employment (1926a), an essay on the trade cycle (1926b), and an essay on the political economy of the trade cycle (1933b). In this context, Harrod's published work – such as his book *International Economics* (1933a), and critiques of Robertson (1927) and Pigou (1934a) – is placed in the perspective of correspondence between Harrod and Robertson, and Harrod and Keynes respectively, and also in that of his evolving approach to the trade cycle and growth.

In the second chapter the intellectual background to the development of the growth research programme is set out by focusing on the interests of individuals and groups in Oxbridge over the period

1930–39. While the activities of the 'Cambridge Circus' (1931), the subsequent 'General Theory group' (1934–6), and the Oxford Economists Research Group (OERG) have been documented, this chapter deals with the significance of the early and ongoing work of the members of what Harrod called his 'Trade Cycle group'. This is done by focusing on the degree of cross-fertilisation and exchange of ideas between Oxford-based economists such as Harrod, Meade, Allen, Fraser, and Hitch, and their Cambridge counterparts such as Robertson, Kahn, and Joan Robinson. In this context, almost totally forgotten volumes such as Meade's *Rate of Interest in a Progressive State* (1933), and various editions of his *Economic Analysis and Policy* (1936b; 1937; 1938; American version edited by Hitch), along with Fraser's *Economic Thought and Language* (1937) – in addition to critical evaluations of contemporary works on the trade cycle and economic methodology by Allen and Fraser, for example – are seen to provide a background for Harrod's ongoing interest in the problems of the trade cycle and growth.

In chapter 3, Harrod's progress in explaining the trade cycle and economic growth is dealt with by focusing on the years 1934–5, during which he was engaged in defending the position he took in his paper on credit expansion and economic advance published in *Economica* (1934d). Over this period he became involved in both public debate and private correspondence on the issues he raised in this paper with Robertson, Haberler, Bode, Kaldor, and Kahn. The first section of the chapter deals with the 1934 exchanges between Harrod and Robertson – both public and private. The second section presents the public debate and private correspondence between Harrod and Haberler, Bode, and Kaldor on his 1934 paper. The third section focuses on the correspondence between Harrod and Kahn on the issues that emerged from his 1934 paper. Finally, this chapter also deals with the 1934 League of Nations memorandum sent by Haberler to Harrod for comment, and which became the basis for Haberler's book *Prosperity and Depression* (1936). The previously unknown but important correspondence between Harrod and Haberler on this forms the final section of this chapter.

Chapter 4 focuses upon the central role of Harrod's book *The Trade Cycle* (1936a) in the evolution and development of his thought. The correspondence between Harrod and Robertson on the draft manuscript of the book over the period 1936–7, and Harrod and Henderson during 1936, is dealt with, as is the crucial influence of Meade, and also of Allen, on the book's development. In addition, this chapter deals with both the place of the 1936 Oxford Conference, and the role of what Harrod called his 'Trade Cycle group' in the development of his approach, and also shows the previously unknown early contribution of Meade (1936a) to Harrod's approach and to the growth research programme as a whole. Finally, the impact of the various critiques and reviews of the book upon Harrod – ranging from that of Keynes to those of Robertson, Hawtrey, Robinson, Tinbergen, Haberler, and Hansen, among others – is evaluated.

In chapter 5 the transition from Harrod's book on the trade cycle (1936a) to his 'Essay in Dynamic Theory' (1939a) is dealt with, focusing especially on a number of influences which may have assisted him in formalizing the analysis of growth and dynamics he actually presented, on his own account, in his 1936 work. This includes the impact of Cassel, Kalecki, Lundberg, Tinbergen, Lange, Hawtrey, Robertson, Robinson, and Durbin upon Harrod's thought; the correspondence on the draft of the 'Essay' between Harrod and Keynes, and the previously unknown exchange on it between Harrod and Robertson; and finally, the contribution of Marschak – described by Harrod at the time as the Oxford Institute of Statistics' 'Tinbergen' – to the development of Harrod's growth and dynamic theory. In this context, Marschak's previously unknown, but crucial detailed 'remarks' and diagram (1939), based upon the draft of Harrod's 1939 'Essay' – which was found in the Harrod papers – are presented and analysed.

In the final chapter conclusions regarding Harrod's approach are presented in the perspective of an overview of specific problems involved in its origins, development, central message, and core concepts. These include the issues of antecedents and precedence as they relate to Cassel, Lundberg, and Domar; the relationship between Harrod's work and that of Meade, Hicks, and Solow; the notions of warranted and optimum growth, systemic instability, *'Treatise Saving'*, and the 'knife-edge', and what Harrod's central message really was; and finally, the role Harrod's approach actually played in catalysing the Harrod-Meade growth research programme in economics.

WARREN YOUNG

Introduction: Key Questions and Issues, Myths and Missing Links

In March 1939 Roy Harrod published his, now classic, 'essay in dynamic theory'. Over the past 50 years much has been written about the approach Harrod outlined in this essay and its place in the development of economic inquiry and in his thought. Harrod's 1939 essay is considered by many observers not only to be a turning point in the evolution of modern economics, but in Harrod's thought itself. However, while the 1939 essay *did* constitute a breakthrough in economics, whether or not it represented a *new* direction in Harrod's thought – or was the outcome of the direction in which he was moving over the previous 15 years of his life – is another matter indeed.

In December 1964, 25 years after the publication of his 1939 essay, Harrod focused on the need for what he called 'continuing conceptual refurbishment [CCR] . . . in relation to dynamic economics'.[1] But the relevance of, and necessity for CCR has wider scope and application here. Indeed, it is necessary for the study of the origins and development of core concepts in modern economic inquiry such as Harrod's approach, and also for dealing with problematic aspects of the evaluation of his approach and the growth research programme that emanated from it. Now, in light of the controversial nature of Harrod's approach, and the debates surrounding it that have gone on amongst economists since its inception 50 years ago, the following *key* questions may be asked:

   (i) What is Harrod's approach to growth and dynamics?
  (ii) What is the nature of Harrod's growth equation system and what lies behind it?
 (iii) What are the origins of Harrod's approach and how did it develop?
 (iv) What catalysed Harrod's approach to the trade cycle, growth, and dynamics?
  (v) What brought about the transition from Harrod's initial concern with the trade cycle to his focus on growth and dynamics?

1

  (vi) Were there antecedents to Harrod's approach and, if so, how is his work related to them?

 (vii) Are there any missing links in the development of Harrod's approach.

(viii) Who actually influenced Harrod's approach?

  (ix) What is the central message of Harrod's approach?

   (x) What was the overall role of Harrod's approach in the evolution of the growth research programme?

The specific issues raised by each of these key questions will be outlined in detail below. Suffice it to say, however, that up to now most of these questions and the issues they raise have never been adequately dealt with. This is because all existing interpretations of Harrod's approach have, until now, been based upon a narrow range of secondary sources and anecdotal accounts of its origins and development. The object of this work, on the other hand, is to provide comprehensive answers to these questions based upon primary material found in the Harrod papers and a wide range of previously overlooked sources – both published and unpublished.

A. HARROD'S APPROACH TO THE TRADE CYCLE, GROWTH, AND DYNAMICS – TAUTOLOGY, OR THE DYNAMISATION OF KEYNES?

What is Harrod's Approach to Growth and Dynamics?

Harrod's growth equation system, and what many observers call the 'Harrod-Domar model', is familiar to all economists. Generations of students have been introduced to Harrod's approach via the equation

$$G = \frac{s}{C} \tag{1}$$

where G is the actual rate of growth of income (Y), that is $\Delta Y/Y$, s is the saving-income ratio, that is, total saving (S) divided by income (S/Y) and C is the incremental capital-output ratio, that is $\left(\dfrac{\Delta K}{\Delta Y} \right)$, or, as Harrod puts it, 'the value of capital goods required for the production of a unit increment of output'.

Moreover, they have been shown how this equation 'reduces' to the identity $S = I$, that is, savings equal to investment, by the algebraic rearrangement of its terms as follows:

$$\frac{S}{Y} = \frac{\Delta Y}{Y} \cdot \frac{\Delta K}{\Delta Y} \tag{2}$$

where K is equal to I, so that

$$\frac{S}{Y} = \frac{I}{Y} \tag{3}$$

and $S = I$. $\tag{4}$

Students are then told about Harrod's ideas regarding what he called 'warranted', 'expected' and 'natural' growth rates, and thereby introduced to what has been termed the 'knife-edge problem' by some observers. The problematic aspects of inherent instability and entrepreneurial behaviour in Harrod's proposed system are then dealt with, and the ostensible 'rigidity' and 'eccentricity' of Harrod's approach usually emphasised and contrasted to the more 'pliable', 'relevant' and 'useful' neoclassical approach to growth and dynamics.[2]

Harrod's approach, when presented in this manner, appears to be little more than an equational system based on special self-evident definitions, or, in other words, tautology. But, one must also emphasise here that for Harrod – as for others, such as Keynes and Fisher – tautology meant self-evident truth. As Harrod noted in 1968, this 'need not be regarded as a belittling description'. Rather, as he wrote in 1934, and again in 1936, while 'theory divorced from observation is mere definition or tautology', he went on to say 'this may be very useful' in economic inquiry 'especially in checking up on fallacies' or for expressing implicit statements and solutions in the process of what Leontieff called 'implicit theorizing'. As early as 1936, however, Harrod did qualify the use of such an approach when he wrote that 'those theorists who seek to make economics more scientific by eschewing the uncertainties, which are necessarily attached to empirical methods, are in fact taking the path which leads away from science to pure scholastic'.[3]

In his 1956 book *Foundations of Inductive Logic*, Harrod cited Whitehead on the problem of fundamental equations that are based on definition, that is, tautology. The example given by Whitehead involved the definition of force 'as the product of mass and accelera-tion'. According to Whitehead 'the difficulty' involved in this 'is that the familiar equation of elementary dynamics' in physics, that is, $F = ma$, becomes by this definition $ma = ma$. On Whitehead's view 'it is not easy to understand how an important science can issue from such premises'.

Harrod went on to resolve Whitehead's 'dilemma' by showing that two elements were actually involved with 'the alleged definition' in the case of $F = ma$. These were, on his view, 'the definition itself' and 'the hypothesis that force has further properties which can be re-vealed by experiment and which are not logically entailed' as a result of its definition, that is, the entity F has properties extending beyond its description. As a result of focusing on the 'self-evident' character of the Harrodian approach to growth and dynamics, then, most observers have overlooked the fact that, while it is based upon a set of definitional relationships whose 'truth is assured by the . . . pro-cess of assigning definitions' – as Hutchison observed in 1935 when dealing with tautologies and the nature of economic theory – the overall properties of the economic system it represents depend upon the fundamental relationships Harrod postulated between the equa-tional components, rather than their definitional context. In other words, while Harrod's equational-definitional system may be based upon tautology, as he recognised, this does not detract from its analytical power any more than does the equational-definitional system represented by $F = ma$, for example, detract from its power when used as one of the basic equations of dynamics in physics.[4]

Where, then, does the tautology in Harrod's approach come from? Is it the outcome of the $S = I$ identity, or is it due to Harrod's linking the process of saving to that of growth, and equating 'the supply of and demand for saving'? And, for that matter, where did Harrod initially and explicitly make the linkage? Now, in his 1936 book *The Trade Cycle*, Harrod wrote

Saving necessarily involves growth; for an increase in the amount of capital goods involves an increase of productive power. In order to determine an equilibrium volume of saving, it is necessary to take this factor of growth *explicitly* into account . . . the question has to be asked – what amount of saving will prove justified, *taking into account the factor of growth* which the saving necessarily entails? . . . Whenever saving is in question, the factor of growth must appear as an explicit term in the laws of supply and demand.

Harrod concluded that his linkage of saving to growth was 'a tentative approach to this new branch of economics. But it is merely a rough sketch of what ought ultimately to be so elaborated as to constitute the second main division of any treatise on economic principles. Fresh fields of thought await the pioneer'.[5]

Viewed in retrospect, Harrod's growth equation is also implicit in these passages. However, much more is involved here than simply stating that by equating saving and investment and the supply of and demand for saving, Harrod generated the equational component of his approach to growth and dynamics. In fact, the fundamental nature of Harrod's approach is intrinsically related to the 'mental revolution', as Harrod put it, needed to proceed from thinking in terms of the 'static analysis' involved 'in the formulation of the laws of demand and supply as applied to a particular commodity' to his form of 'dynamic analysis' which involved the notion of growth.[6]

Harrod expanded on these themes in his 1939 Essay when he dealt with them by reviving what Kaldor called 'the classical dichotomy' (Harrod, 1939a). In doing so, Harrod made the distinction between the labour-based and capital-based growth potential of an economy. In Kaldor's view, since Harrod treated them as given exogenously and characterised by mutual invariance, their reconciliation was, in effect, the problem Harrod tried to deal with in his approach to growth and dynamics. However, Harrod's approach also reflected his concern with the problem of maintaining a 'progressive state' or 'advancing community' and keeping it from moving into a 'stationary state'. In order to deal with the issues of growth and dynamics, therefore, Harrod proposed something much broader than a 'model'. In fact, he took issue with those who viewed his approach as simply a narrowly-based 'model' of growth. Rather, what he developed was a broad-based equational-definitional approach which, on his view, enabled him to take account of the complex nature of the processes he was trying to represent and interpret.[7]

Far from being a tautology, then, Harrod's approach, as will be shown, is a rich treatment of growth and dynamics involving variegated actual and notional growth rates, expectations, entrepreneurial behaviour, and saving-investment behaviour, with special emphasis being placed on the problematic role of the interest rate. In addition, as will be seen, Harrod's approach – in conjunction with Meade's early work in this area – formed the basis for the growth research programme in economics.[8]

Harrod and the Dynamisation of Keynes

In his 'Retrospect on Keynes' (Harrod, 1963a) Harrod made what is possibly one of the most insightful evaluations of Keynes's role in the development of modern economic thought. According to Harrod, it was Keynes who laid the foundation 'for the elaboration of . . . dynamic theory' by providing what could be called 'a macroeconomic theory of statics', something which was 'indispensable', as Harrod put it, since 'the traditional micro theory did not provide the necessary tools'. In Harrod's words, 'Thus Keynes may be truly regarded as the father of dynamic theory. And that, in the long run, will prove to have been his greatest contribution of all'. As is well known by all those who have studied economics over the past 50 years, it was Harrod who originated modern growth and dynamic theory in his seminal essay published in 1939. What was the reason, then, for Harrod citing Keynes's 'macroeconomic theory of statics' as being 'indispensable' to the development of his own dynamic approach? Moreover, which 'macroeconomic theory of statics' of Keynes was Harrod referring to here – the *General Theory* or the *Treatise*? And, if it *was* Keynes that set him off on his search for an economic dynamics, which of Keynes's works initially focused Harrod on the problem of analysing the trade cycle, growth, and dynamics – the *General Theory* (1936), the *Treatise* (1930); or, for that matter, the *Tract* (1923)?[9]

Now, in the same year as its publication, Harrod already took issue with Keynes's *General Theory* approach in his book the *Trade Cycle*; this was due, in Harrod's view, to the lack of a dynamic outlook in the *General Theory*. Additionally, in his IS–LM paper (Harrod, 1937a), Harrod criticised Keynes's *General Theory* system for being 'still static', and in a letter dated 7 April 1937, Harrod criticised Keynes for his reluctance, in Harrod's opinion, to 're-orient your mind to the dynamic point of view'. Furthermore, in a note added in 1952 to his reprint of 'The Expansion of Credit in an Advancing Community' – which originally appeared in 1934 – Harrod said that while his 1934 Essay

> bears marks of having been written before the appearance of Keynes's *General Theory* and suffers from that . . . for all the path-breaking importance of that great work, it is in one respect *retrograde* [my emphasis – WY] by comparison . . . for, in dealing with the subject . . . namely the balance between saving and

investment, which can only validly be tackled in dynamic terms, it uses static concepts.[10]

Thus, it is not surprising that Harrod explicitly stated that he had dynamised Keynes's *Treatise*, rather than *General Theory* approach in his 1939 Essay (Harrod, 1939a). What *is* surprising is that this has been overlooked by most observers even though Harrod repeated the theme in *Towards a Dynamic Economics* (1948), in his 'Retrospect on Keynes' (1963b), and in his books *Money* (1969) and *Economic Dynamics* (1973). The rationale for having dynamised Keynes's *Treatise* approach, which Harrod saw as Keynes's 'diagnosis of the trade cycle', was that it provided more fertile ground for underpinning his dynamics than the *General Theory* approach which, in Harrod's opinion, was constrained by a macrostatic world view. While Harrod's approach was based upon a specific equational-definitional framework, then, it was above all directed towards dynamising Keynes, albeit his *Treatise*, rather than *General Theory* approach, as will be shown. But what set Harrod off on his effort to dynamise Keynes?[11]

B. THE ORIGINS OF HARROD'S APPROACH – CURRENT MYTHS AND THE NEED FOR REASSESSMENT

Harrod's Approach and Keynes's *Tract*

What catalysed Harrod's approach remains somewhat of a mystery, unless Harrod's early unpublished work on the trade cycle and growth – written between 1924 and 1933 – is taken into account. Although over the past 50 years much has been written about Harrod's approach, there are still a number of questions regarding its origin and development as initially manifest in *The Trade Cycle* (Harrod, 1936a) and 'Essay' (Harrod, 1939a) and the subsequent refinement and extension of it into a general theory of economic dynamics in Harrod's 1948 volume, *Towards a Dynamic Economics*. These questions emanate first, due to the fact that up to now no detailed account based upon the primary source material, that is, Harrod's papers, has been provided as to the evolution of his overall approach to the trade cycle, growth and dynamics, and the discovery of his growth equation system. Secondly, as a result of the propagation of an anecdotal myth regarding the development of Harrod's

approach which, in turn, attained a degree of 'credibility' – irrespective of its historical accuracy – the origin of Harrod's growth equation
has been misrepresented by some observers. Thirdly, due to a number of myths resulting from the misinterpretation of Harrod's published work on the part of other observers and their failure to take
cognisance of Harrod's unpublished work on the trade cycle
(1924–33), what actually catalysed Harrod's approach has been completely overlooked. And this, in spite of the fact that information
regarding Harrod's early work has been in the public domain for
some time. These myths will be dealt with below. At this point suffice
it to say that there has been a considerable amount of misunderstanding surrounding Harrod's attempt to dynamise Keynes. But this
is not surprising since until now the appropriate questions had not
been posed regarding Harrod's approach.[12]

Interestingly enough, Harrod's biography of Keynes (Harrod,
1951a) provides some indication as to what actually set him off on his
quest for a dynamic economics. At the end of 1923 Keynes's *Tract*
was published. And, in Harrod's opinion 'a claim could be made on
behalf of the *Tract*' as having the 'most ultimate significance' amongst
Keynes's works. While this point is debatable, as Harrod duly noted,
the *Tract* had great significance for Harrod himself, as will be shown,
for it was the *Tract* and the problems it raised that catalysed Harrod's
interest in the trade cycle and thereby in growth and dynamics.[13]

In his biography of Keynes, Harrod showed how the *Tract* was
Keynes's first attempt at an analysis of 'the credit cycle' and the
problem of unemployment. But the lack of a theoretical foundation
for the practical policies Keynes advocated in the *Tract* and over the
next few years for controlling the credit cycle, and for 'curing'
unemployment, bothered Harrod considerably. Indeed, as Harrod
related, 'I felt that there was some missing clue, something unex-
plained' in Keynes's attempt to find remedies for both the credit cycle
and unemployment. The attempt to find a 'cure' for unemployment,
or in other words to discover, as Harrod put it, 'an explanation in
terms of fundamental economic theory of the causes of unemployment' received Keynes's attention for a considerable time afterwards.
But, as Hawtrey noted in his review of Harrod's biography of
Keynes, in the *Tract* Keynes had already 'accepted whole-heartedly
the doctrine that deflation causes unemployment . . . Nor had he
been at a loss to say what might be the causes of deflation'. In
Hawtrey's view, 'the problem' Keynes 'faced . . . from 1924 onwards
was rather to find in terms of fundamental economic theory the

justification for the policy which his practical judgement told him was the remedy'.[14]

In any event, the problem Harrod set for himself was to deal with specific issues that emerged from the *Tract* and the lack of theoretical foundations for Keynes's practical policies, such as the problems emanating from 'the trade cycle and the theory of distribution', 'the effect of falling prices on employment', and 'the trade cycle' itself – all subjects of essays with these titles Harrod wrote in 1924 and 1926 respectively. As early as 1924, then, Harrod had set off on his quest for a general theory of the trade cycle, growth, and dynamics.[15]

Furthermore, in his 1951 'Notes on Trade Cycle Theory' Harrod maintained that his idea regarding boom and slump 'as oscillations around a line of steady growth' rather than 'as deviations from static equilibrium' in his analysis of the trade cycle resulted not as a result of the problem emanating from 'the balance between Investment and Consumption but in relation to the problem of central banking credit policy', that is, to the issues raised by Keynes's *Tract*.[16]

Moreover, in his paper entitled 'Increasing returns' published in the *Festscrift* for Chamberlain (1967), Harrod noted that not only his essay on 'Doctrines of Imperfect Competition' (Harrod, 1934b) and its final section on the 'significance of . . . increasing costs for trade cycle theory' but his 'original interest in the whole subject [of imperfect competition and increasing returns and costs] had sprung from' his 'concern with the trade cycle and with Keynesian policy'. In other words, it was the outcome of theoretical problems emanating from the *Tract* and the practical policies advocated by Keynes in it, and in the period following its publication.[17]

Thus, the various interpretations put forward by some observers regarding what initiated Harrod's effort to develop a theory of growth and dynamics – such as it being 'initially based on his innovative work on imperfect competition', or due to Harrod's 'early dissatisfaction with the Austrian trade cycle theory put forward by Hayek' is not supported by the facts. For, as will be shown, it was the *Tract* that initially set Harrod off on his quest for a growth theory and a dynamic economics.[18]

Myths and Reassessment, Dynamics and Generality

While anecdotal myth has somewhat overtaken Harrod's own version of the origin of his growth equation system, Harrod himself was not absolutely consistent over the years in his account of the circumstances surrounding its discovery. The anecdotal myth is the contention that it was Tinbergen's review of Harrod's *Trade Cycle* that catalysed Harrod's ideas into his growth equation system. It will be shown, however, that this is not necessarily the case; rather, it may be that the meetings between Tinbergen and Harrod over the period 1936–8 in Oxford and Cambridge had much more of an effect upon Harrod than Tinbergen's review, which Harrod claimed he never saw.[19]

With regard to Harrod's own account of the development of his approach to growth and dynamics and the discovery of his growth equation system, two problems emerge. The first problem emerges from Harrod having maintained in a number of places that his paper 'The Expansion of Credit in an Advancing Community' (Harrod, 1934d) constituted his 'first contribution to growth theory' and attempt at dynamising the *Treatise*. And yet, elsewhere he said:

> Macro-statics has for a number of years loomed large, but its importance will, I feel sure, prove to have been only temporary. Its elaboration should be thought of as a bridge, but an absolutely necessary bridge, to the development of economic dynamics. I think that I may claim that since *1933* [my emphasis], I have recognized that quite different tools would be needed for the development of economic dynamics from those required for micro-statics and macro-statics.

It should be noted here that Harrod's papers on 'Doctrines of Imperfect Competition' (Harrod, 1934b) and 'The Expansion of Credit in an Advancing Community' (Harrod, 1934d) were published in May 1934 and August 1934 respectively. On the other hand, his book *International Economics* (Harrod, 1933a), in which he dealt with issues related to the trade cycle and a progressive economy, was published in 1933. In addition, Harrod also wrote an essay – albeit never published – 'On the political economy of the trade cycle' in 1933. As will be seen, out of these and his earlier unpublished essays, Harrod's book *The Trade Cycle* evolved, which he later described as attempting 'to give a dynamized version of Keynesian doctrine'.[20]

Thus, those observers who have utilized only Harrod's published work, without taking into account his unpublished work and papers, have been led not only into claiming that his interest in the trade cycle, growth, and dynamics was 'set off by the publication . . . of Hayek's *Prices and Production*' but into maintaining that his 1934 papers are those in which his interest in these areas are first evident.

Again, however, as will be shown, this simply does not fit the facts.[21]

The reason for Harrod's lifetime objective of dynamising Keynes is clear. It was expressed by Harrod in his 1938 'Scope and Method' paper in concise and lucid terms, when he stressed the importance of developing 'general laws', especially in the area of 'dynamic economics'. For Harrod, then, dynamics meant generality, and to dynamise Keynes was to generalise Keynes's approach, thereby extending its validity and applicability.

Over the years from the publication of his classic 'Essay' (Harrod, 1939a) to *Economic Dynamics* (1973) – which was, in effect, a revised and updated version of *Towards a Dynamic Economics* (1948) – Harrod continually stressed the essential difference between his 'macrodynamic approach' to Keynes, that is, the dynamisation of the *Treatise* in contrast to the 'macrostatic approach' of Keynes himself as expressed in the *General Theory*. In fact, Harrod went so far as to assert that Ricardo was more 'dynamic' than Keynes's *General Theory*. But more is involved here than Harrod simply dynamising and thereby generalising Keynes. Since the notion of dynamic implied generality for Harrod, by dynamising the *Treatise* approach, he was generalising it and thereby developing a more general approach than Keynes's *General Theory*.[22]

C. MISSING LINKS IN THE DEVELOPMENT OF HARROD'S APPROACH – RECONSTRUCTING THE INFLUENCES ON, AND EVOLUTION OF, HIS IDEAS

The problem here ostensibly relates to Harrod's own version of the process of discovery of his growth equation system which, as will be seen, was regrettably not consistent over the years. This may be due to the fact that – as Hicks has put it in another context – 'memory is treacherous'. Alternatively, Harrod's inconsistency may be due to the difficulties one faces in reconstructing just how and when one exactly makes a conceptual breakthrough. Strangely enough, Harrod was also inconsistent with regard to the importance he placed upon establishing priority in discovery in economics. However, the issues of exact dates and priority of discovery – while interesting in their own right – are not the key ones here. Rather, the exchange and cross-fertilisation of ideas and what can be called sequential conceptual synthesis will be the focus of our concern in this context. And, as will be shown, these processes took place to a considerable degree

during the course of evolution of the growth research programme.
But the question posed above regarding missing links in the development of Harrod's approach still remains, and as a result of material recently found in the Harrod and Meade papers, a number can be identified here:

(i) Harrod's early unpublished work on the trade cycle (1924–33) which was catalysed by the *Tract*.

(ii) Harrod's other activities over the period 1926–34, including his review of Robertson's *Banking Policy and the Price Level* (1927), his book *International Economics* (1933a), his critique of Pigou's *Theory of Unemployment* (1934a), and his *initial* effort at dynamising the *Treatise* in his 1934 *Economica* essay and the debate with Robertson, Haberler, and Bode that followed it.

(iii) The up-to-now unnoticed influence – both upon Harrod and the development of the growth research programme – of Meade's almost forgotten book *The Rate of Interest in a Progressive State* (1933); this, as manifest in the Harrod-Meade correspondence on the book and the role of interest rate and capital-labour substitution over the period 1933–6.

(iv) The previously unknown existence of what Harrod called his 'Trade Cycle Group', whose members assisted him in both the development of the *Trade Cycle* (1936a) and the transition from it to his 1939 'Essay', and the inputs they provided over the period 1936–9. Included among these are: the previously unknown and unpublished, but crucial comments of Meade on the draft manuscript of the *Trade Cycle* (Meade, 1936a), in which he proposed an alternative to Harrod's approach, and actually set out the framework of the neoclassical branch of the growth research programme; the comments of Allen and Henderson on the draft of Harrod's *Trade Cycle*; and Marschak's detailed 'line-by-line' commentary on Harrod's 1939 'Essay' and diagrammatic representation of the equational system Harrod proposed in it (Marschak, 1939).

(v) The Harrod-Keynes and Harrod-Robertson correspondence on the *Trade Cycle* and the draft manuscript of the 'Essay'.

(vi) The critiques of Harrod's *Trade Cycle* made by Hawtrey, both in his book *Capital and Employment* and in the correspondence between them on it.

(vii) The exchange of ideas between Harrod and Durbin over the period 1936–7, after Harrod's review of Durbin's book *The*

Problem of Credit Policy (1935).

(viii) The influence upon Harrod of reviews and critiques of the *Trade Cycle* made by Robertson, Robinson, Haberler, and Hansen over the period 1936–8.

(ix) The influence of Cassel's *Theory of Social Economy* (1923), of Kalecki's 1935 *Econometrica* paper, and of Lundberg's book, *Studies in the Theory of Economic Expansion* (1937) upon Harrod as manifest in his review of it, and in his subsequent 'Essay' (1939a).

(x) The influence of Tinbergen upon Harrod over the period 1936–8, during which they exchanged views on the trade cycle, growth, and dynamics, with Tinbergen reviewing Harrod's *Trade Cycle* (1937), and culminating in Harrod's reaction to Tinbergen's treatment of the acceleration principle (1938), and its impact upon Harrod's essay (1939a); where in this context Lange's work on optimum saving (1938a) and its influence upon Harrod must also be considered.

D. EVALUATING HARROD'S CONTRIBUTION TO THE GROWTH RESEARCH PROGRAMME: THE ROLE OF HIS EQUATIONAL APPROACH AND ANALYTICAL TOOL KIT

At first glance, the issues seem clear cut and relate both to Harrod's originality and the degree to which his work actually contributed to the development of growth theory. Now, since a number of observers have maintained that there are antecedents to Harrod's approach – such as manifest in the works of Cassel, Kalecki, and Lundberg – this must be dealt with in detail. In the same context, however, the relationship between Harrod's 1939 'Essay' and Domar's subsequent work must also be analysed, and the dissemination of Harrod's ideas focused upon accordingly.[23]

In order to fully understand and assess the role of Harrod's approach in, and contribution to, the growth research programme, however, a number of additional issues must be dealt with here, including:

(i) Harrod's overall view of statics and dynamics and the relationship between his approach and that of what has been called the 'classical' and 'magnificent' dynamic systems that antedated his.

(ii)   Harrod's view of the relationship between dynamic theory and
       growth theory or, as he put it, between the 'pure economics'
       and the 'political economy of growth'.
(iii) The nature and characteristics of the growth research pro-
       gramme as a whole encompassing both neo-Keynesian and
       neoclassical branches, and how Harrod's approach enabled it
       to develop.
(iv)   What Harrod's central message actually was, and how it related
       to the core concepts of the growth research programme.

   With regard to the first point, Harrod was in fact quite consistent in
his view of the matter. For him, dynamics was not simply an 'offshoot
of or appendix to static theory'. Indeed, he not only attacked Mill for
having 'killed dynamic theory for a century' by treating dynamics as
an appendix that could be 'tacked on to a treatise on statics' but, as
will be seen, also explicitly criticised Jevons, Menger, Walras, Marshall, and implicitly even Keynes, for the 'new lease of life given to
static theory' by their respective writings.[24]
   As for the second point, it will be shown how Harrod made a clear
distinction between what he called 'the theory of economic growth'
and 'dynamic theory', with the former, in his view, actually en-
compassing the latter. The importance of the third point will be dealt
with by showing how the growth research programme and its neo-
Keynesian and neoclassical branches actually emanated from the
work of both Harrod and Meade, and thus must be dealt with as a
whole. Finally, as will be seen, Harrod's central message, and his
retrospective contribution to the growth research programme, must
be dealt with in the context of his lifelong effort at bringing about a
'mental revolution' amongst his fellow economists and the degree to
which it, in fact, succeeded or failed.[25]

1 Harrod's Early Activities, 1924–34

In a letter to Robertson in May 1926, regarding his recently published book *Banking Policy and the Price Level* (BPPL), Harrod wrote:

> I have read your book. In one sense I might have said that some weeks ago. But I mean it now as defined by you, namely, I have read it twice thro! And I think I have understood a good deal of it. Tho' certainly not quite all. I enjoyed it very much; it opened out many new vistas to me; it was also slightly painful in that it made me see how jejune my own utterances in lectures on the trade cycle have been.[1]

Interestingly enough, Harrod had started thinking about the problem of the trade cycle at least two years before; set off, it would seem, by the lack of a theoretical underpinning to the issues raised by Keynes's *Tract* (1923). Over the years 1924–6 Harrod wrote a number of essays regarding the trade cycle – on his own initiative and for the British General Federation of Trade Unions – with both theoretical and policy orientations. In addition, between 1926 and 1932 Harrod focused on the international economic implications of the trade cycle – as manifest in his book *International Economics* (Harrod, 1933a) – and on the political economy of the trade cycle, as seen in his 1933 essay on this topic (Harrod, 1933b). Moreover, after the publication of Keynes's *Treatise* (1930), Harrod took up the Keynesian *Treatise* position.[2]

A number of issues emerge with regard to this crucial formative period in the development of Harrod's thought. First of all, to what extent did Harrod's early unpublished essays on the trade cycle (1924–33) foreshadow the approach he took in his later published works on the trade cycle and growth, and what influence did Keynes's work have on him at this stage of the development of his thought? Secondly, to what extent did Robertson's book *BPPL* – among other early works by him – influence Harrod? Thirdly, what was the role of Harrod's work on the international economic implications and the political economy of the trade cycle in the development of his thought? Fourthly, why did Harrod adopt and advocate Keynes's *Treatise* position?

A.   KEYNES'S TRACT AND HARROD'S ESSAYS: 1924–6
     'THE TRADE CYCLE AND THE THEORY OF
     DISTRIBUTION', 1924

In his 1931 Harris Lecture, Keynes cited the fundamental equations
he presented in his *Treatise* (1930) as 'the clue to the scientific
explanation of booms and slumps'. Now, Keynes's concern with the
'alternation of boom and depression', or as he called it 'the "credit
cycle"', was already manifest in his *Tract* (1923). However, Keynes
was quite explicit in pointing to the theoretical shortcomings of the
Tract when he wrote that 'it is beyond the scope of this volume
(*Tract*) to deal adequately with the diagnosis and analysis of the
credit cycle'. Harrod took up Keynes's call for deeper research into
the problems of the 'credit cycle', and over the next few years
produced a number of essays on the subject. In these Harrod focused
on the theoretical basis for – and policy options related to – issues
raised by Keynes in his *Tract*.[3]

Harrod's first effort consisted of an essay he called 'The Trade
Cycle and the Theory of Distribution' which he wrote in 1924.
Harrod started it with the caveat that it was, first and foremost 'an
essay in economic analysis and should be taken as a propaedeutic to
any study of the trade cycle rather than as a study of the trade cycle
itself'. He then went on to place the central question concerning him
in the context of the movements in trade. As Harrod put it:

> Before plunging into an investigation of all the many alleged causes
> of the alternating expansion and shrinkage in the volume of trade,
> ought we not to ask: What in any case are the circumstances which
> cause the volume of trade to be what it is, neither more nor less? It
> is absurd to express surprise at the oscillation of an object, while
> ignorant of what the forces are which determine its movement or
> its stabilization.
>
> The Classical economists were notoriously inadequate in their
> treatment of the trade cycle; this inadequacy was but part of a
> larger one, their failure to explain with precision why the volume
> of production is at any time what it is. They did not go much
> further than saying that the volume of production was proportion-
> ate to the labour and capital available; they held that general
> overproduction was impossible.[4]

Harrod then discussed the various theories of the cycle, including
that of Jevons ('harvest theory') and the psychological theory. At this

point, Harrod proceeded to 'suggest another possible cause' of the cycle in terms of 'fluctuation' and 'expansion' of 'industry as a whole'. In Harrod's words:

> The subject to be considered is fluctuation in industry as a whole in a given area. There is of course a vast distinction between fluctuation in a particular business or industry and fluctuation in industry in general. Let us assume for convenience that all particular industries are tied together in such a way that when an expansion occurs in one, an expansion occurs in all the others such that the value of a unit product of the one remains the same. If a single industry expands while the others remain stationary the value of its products must fall. But if they all expand together the value of each product in terms of the other will remain the same. I define all expanding together as each expanding by such an amount that the value of its unit product is held constant. This does not imply an equal percentage expansion in all, since the demand of the community for each commodity has not an equal degree of elasticity . . .
>
> Now, it may be objected that arguments about this kind of universal fluctuation are uninteresting, since in fact when a trade cycle occurs, tho' there is *some* expansion in all lines, there occurs fairly regularly a discrepancy between the expansion in different lines and that this discrepancy is of the essence of the cycle. For instance, it is the rule that during a depression the value of constructional goods in terms of other goods falls. These kinds of discrepancies are very important, but one problem must be tackled at one time. It is admitted that there is generally *some* fluctuation common to all and that is our problem.[5]

Harrod then went on to 'examine how' what he called the 'general principle of the economic maximum' governed 'the conduct of the entrepreneur, whose will', according to Harrod, 'controls the volume of production'. In the following pages Harrod discussed how the trade cycle was linked to distribution between workers and entrepreneurs and the bargaining strength of the unions.[6]

Harrod then turned his attention to the notion of 'stationary production' in a 'progressive society' and what he called the 'fundamental conditions' needed to maintain it. In his words:

> The propositions which we have so far established, then, are, that the volume of trade is a function of the system of distribution, and

changes in the one will be accompanied by changes in the other, that any change in the system of distribution favourable to the entrepreneur and unfavourable to the worker will cause production to expand in the short period, and vice versa. These, however, will have to be made a little more accurate. Since the conditions of fluctuation in production are to be investigated, the notion of stationary production should be defined.

It is convenient to define stationary production as that volume of production which keeps a constant fraction of the total population in employment a constant number of hours per year and with a constant intensity of effort. Thus if the population was expanding, stationary production would involve that the aggregate of produce expanded at the same rate; and if the average efficiency of the working hour was increasing, then likewise stationary production so defined would involve that the aggregate of produce increased correspondingly.

It is stated above that if production in this sense is to be stationary, the system of distribution must be stationary too. But this is not quite correct. The system of distribution required to keep a given volume of production stationary might have to change if what I shall call fundamental conditions changed.

What I mean by fundamental conditions is the ratio of the rate of increase of population to the rate of increase of capital and enterprise and the ratios of each to the rate of increase of labour saving inventions. Thus, if capital was increasing more quickly than the population the system of distribution required to keep the volume of production stationary would change in favour of the working man. But, if capital was increasing insufficiently quickly to keep pace with labour saving inventions the system of distribution required to keep the volume of production stationary would change against the working man.

Thus, a change in the volume of production, this meaning a movement away from the stationary state as above defined, might be brought about in one of two ways: 1. through a change taking place in the system of distribution when there was no change in fundamental conditions. 2. through a change in the system of distribution *not* taking place when there was a change in fundamental conditions. Now the system of distribution depends largely on the bargaining strength of the great unions; it remains, therefore, to ask how far changes in that bargaining strength are likely to correspond to changes in fundamental conditions.[7]

After further discussion of these points, Harrod focused on the relation between monetary and trade fluctuations and the 'fundamental principles' or 'conditions' he had proposed. According to him:

It has been the purpose of the foregoing argument to relate the well known connection between monetary and trade oscillations to fundamental principles. The monetary oscillation by automatically altering the bargaining strength of the parties brings about a change in the system of distribution and so in the volume of production and employment. No doubt there are many other . . . which might also bring a change in the bargaining relation of the parties, without there being any change in the 'fundamental conditions'.

If it were possible to prevent monetary oscillation, an important condition of trade oscillation would be removed. Failing monetary stabilization, it would be desirable to base wage bargains on an index number . . . A discussion of what particular type of index number is most suitable to obviate the effect of monetary oscillation is too elaborate to be undertaken in detail . . .

Secondly, a change in the terms of trade may occur through a change in fundamental conditions not accompanied by a change in bargaining strength. Something of this sort has happened since 1914. The fundamental conditions are probably such that stability of production compared with 1914 could only be secured by a change in distribution unfavourable to the wage earner. It might be objected that this is isolated and not connected with the trade cycle. But it is possible that this kind of discrepency might occur cyclically even in a monetary utopia.

It is to be expected in a progressive society, as Adam Smith long ago urged, that fundamental conditions will continually so change, as to allow the system of distribution to move in favour of the wage earner. Suppose that we have a monetary utopia. It might still happen that while the continuous change in fundamental conditions was going on, the wage earners secured their improvement in jerks. If this happened, there would naturally be a cycle in trade. While the wage earners were marking time, the entrepreneurs' share would be increasing and he would expand trade. Then when the wage earners began to force an advance it would no longer pay the entrepreneurs to do as much trade as they had been doing while they were appropriating the whole of the extra residue due to general progress.

And so the expansion would be followed by a depression until such time as the general progress once more went beyond the point which the wage earners had reached in their recent advance, and once more the entrepreneurs, receiving the extra residue, would want to expand. It might be objected here: Why should this cycle occur? If the so-called monetary cause was removed, why should there be a cycle? Why should the wage earners secure their advances in jerks? Why should not the curve of their advance be as regular as the change in fundamental conditions itself? This leads to some observations which seem to me to be very important.[8]

Harrod concluded his essay by proposing theoretically-based methods of maintaining price-wage stability to overcome the central problem raised by Keynes in his *Tract* (1923), that is, that of attaining 'maximum stability' and moderating 'the amplitude of the fluctuations' in an economy.[9] As Harrod wrote:

In all investigations of the cycle it is much easier to discover the interconnection of the movements of the different factors than to discover the fundamental causes of movement. Thus, it is easy to see that a movement in the volume of production is connected with a change in the system of distribution; it is easy to see that a change in the system of distribution is connected with a change in the value of money.

It is much more difficult to see what, deep down, is the cause of all these changes taken together. But it is clear that if we could somehow artificially secure stability in money, that would lessen the other movements. So much we can state, still leaving quite open the question whether in the past the other movements have caused the movement in money, or the movement in money the other movements. It is also clear that with stable money the other movements might still persist, though in a less violent form. And since we are no nearer to discovering what the cause of the cycle as a whole has been, we have no reason to suppose that the tendency to cyclical movement will not persist.

We do not profess to have struck at the root cause in striking at monetary oscillation. Suppose we have obtained either monetary stabilisation or the general use of suitable wages sliding scales. Cannot we proceed by this same method of obtaining stability one stage further?– of securing general stability by producing artificial stability in one of the interconnected factors. It is clear that the cycle might continue through wage changes not taking place with the same even continuity as the change in fundamental conditions.

He went on to say:

> Without knowing why there is this persistent tendency to cyclical movement, we might seek to prevent it by securing a more even continuity in wage changes. This might be done in a very rough and ready way by the use of a sliding scale connecting wages with national per caput output. By this means in a progressive community wages could be made to advance evenly and not in jerks. An advance in wages proportional to the increase in national per caput output would not necessarily be the advance required to keep production stable. But it would probably be as close an approximation to that ideal advance as is worth our thinking about for the time being . . . To attempt to secure the adoption of these kind of sliding scales would probably be the most sensible kind of interference in general industrial conditions which a government could undertake.

Harrod ended his 1924 Essay by saying:

> There is no time to discuss the terms of the bargain which the entrepreneur makes with the capitalist. If modern theories of banking are to be accepted, this question becomes indefinitely more intricate. If the banks create and destroy units of purchasing power, then they add to and subtract from the supply of capital. For the purchasing power which they create is handed over as capital to the entrepreneur. If a government creates money, it usually spends it as a consumer; if a bank creates money, it is usually spent as capital. Thus, in a short period considerable oscillations may occur in the quantity of capital available to the entrepreneur and in the terms on which he can obtain it and therefore in his residual earning and hence in the volume of production.
>
> The foregoing discussion is very rough and smudgy. I have tried to plead that these fundamental principles are relevant to the problem of the trade cycle.[10]

There are a number of interesting facets of Harrod's 1924 Essay that deserve mention here. These involve his definition of (a) 'stationary production' in a 'progressive' economic system and (b) the 'fundamental conditions' required to maintain 'stationary production'. With regard to (a), it should be emphasised that Harrod's notion of 'stationary production' here is not the same as the classical 'stationary state', which is the last stage in the development away from the 'progressive state'. Rather, Harrod's definition is characterised by a dynamic equilibrium which ensures what is, in effect, the 'steady state solution' of a progressive economic system – that is, the maintenance of 'a constant ratio' between its components. In this sense, Harrod's definition of 'stationary production' here foreshadows his later notion of the 'steady advance' of output, as seen in his books *International Economics* (Harrod, 1933a) and *The Trade Cycle* (Harrod, 1936a), and in his treatment of 'regular economic advance' in his *Economica* paper (Harrod, 1934d).[11]

As for (b), the 'fundamental conditions' which maintain 'stationary production' are related to the ratios of the 'rate of increase' – that is, growth rates – of labour and capital, in addition 'to the rate of increase of labour saving inventions', that is, technological progress. Again, Harrod's notion of 'fundamental conditions' for 'steady advance' here foreshadows his subsequent approach as seen in the *Trade Cycle*, and in his 'Essay in dynamic theory' (Harrod, 1939a).[12]

'The Trade Cycle', 1926

In contrast to his 1924 essay, which was written on his own initiative, Harrod's 1926 essays entitled 'The effect of falling prices on employment' (1926a) and 'The trade cycle' (1926b) were drafted as 'confidential' memoranda for the British General Federation of Trade Unions. In his 1926 essay on the trade cycle, Harrod reiterated the conclusion he reached in his earlier essay regarding 'falling prices' when he wrote:

> in another memorandum the effect of falling prices on employment has been discussed. It was there shown that falling prices had a depressing effect on employment, principally owing to the increase in prime costs which they involve (1) in respect of short credits and (2) in respect of wages. Rising prices, on the other hand, produce a precisely opposite effect.[13]

Harrod went on to emphasise the importance of price stability for employment and the detrimental effect of price fluctuation. He then turned to an examination of 'the contention of those who say that the eradication of the trade cycle would increase employment as a whole'. In Harrod's words:

> Consider the period when trade is recovering from a depression. At first, men get taken into work who are only out because of the depression. But hardly is that process complete when the artificial price stimulus takes new men into an employment which cannot be permanent and thus renders them unavailable for the normal demands of normally expanding trade. It probably takes them into employment too soon and at the wrong place. Once that has happened, we cannot have general progress without the painful process of the new depression.

After a detailed discussion of the causes of fluctuation in prices, Harrod went on to describe what he called 'the remedies for the trade cycle'. As he put it

> The alternating rise and fall of prices has been due to alternating expansion and contraction of trade. It is also the case that expansion and contraction of trade has been due to the change in prices for the reasons stated in the other memorandum. It has been thought that if only money could be genuinely stabilized in value, the trade cycle with all its attendant evils might be eliminated or at least largely reduced in dimensions.[14]

Harrod continued on to discuss technical 'remedies' such as a 'tabular standard for all goods' combined with 'comprehensive wages sliding scales', and that proposed by Irving Fisher for stabilising the monetary unit via a universally accepted inverse relationship between the value of gold and the value of money. He then focused on the methods used by the US Federal Reserve system to deal with the trade cycle, especially stabilisation and regulation of credit expansion, and contrasted it with the case in the UK. In answer to the question he posed ('how does the policy of the Federal Reserve stand with regard to the trade cycle?') Harrod wrote:

> The theory of the [Federal Reserve] system is always to allow an expansion of credit when the increase of employment consequent upon the expansion of credit is, so to say, *justifiable* . . . they do their utmost to provide credit facilities for the expansion of production so long as there are no signs that inflation is underway. The

mere policy of preventing inflation is not sufficient. It should be combined with the policy of encouraging production at all other times than those at which there is a danger of inflation.

Harrod concluded his memo by saying:

> The Federal Reserve banks use three chief guides for their issue of credit (1) the price of industrial securities – a study of the trade cycle has shown that the price of industrial securities tends to rise before the price of commodities. Thus these former prices may serve as a better guide for policy than the commodity prices on which the monetary theorists lay more stress; (2) commodity prices; (3) the state of stocks of commodities in the country. When stocks tend to accumulate – which means that production is growing ahead of consumption – the Federal Reserve authorities think it is time to restrict credit.
>
> The result of this policy so far has been apparently that the main cycle has been broken in two: we have instead short periods of alternating boom and depression. There have been minor booms in the Spring of 1923, the Autumn of 1924, the Autumn of 1925. It is not yet possible to judge the ultimate effects of this policy.
>
> Critics of the Bank of England think it ought to have been able to work on the same lines. Since it publishes no general statements and its balance sheets contain only very meagre information, it is difficult to know what the policy of the Bank is. At least there are no signs that it has been at work on the collection of those statistics, the possession of which the Federal Reserve authorities regard as the indispensible basis for intelligent action.[15]

As in his earlier essay on the trade cycle (1924), it is clear that in his 1926 memo, Harrod followed the line initiated by Keynes's *Tract* regarding the cardinal importance of price and monetary stabilisation. Moreover, in his 1926 memo (Harrod, 1926b), Harrod also focused – as Keynes did in his *Tract* – on the need for providing adequate statistical information upon which, as Keynes put it 'those in authority can base their judgements'. And this, Keynes continued, so that they may 'understand the right time and method for controlling credit expansion', given, according to Keynes 'that the *objective* of the authorities . . . should be the stability of prices'.[16]

Harrod's treatment of 'justifiable' credit expansion in his 1926 memo was a theme to which he was to return in his 1934 *Economica* article (Harrod, 1934d). But more important is Harrod's use of the term 'justifiable' here. For, as will be shown, the definition and use of the term was central in both his private and public comments on Robertson's treatment of 'justifiable output' in *Banking Policy and the Price Level*, while Harrod's own notion of a 'steady rate of advance' – that is, a growth rate – that is 'justified' appeared a decade later in his book *The Trade Cycle* (Harrod, 1936a), and evolved from there into his concept of 'warranted growth' as presented in his 1939 'Essay in dynamic theory' (Harrod, 1939a).[17]

B. ROBERTSON'S BANKING POLICY AND THE PRICE LEVEL (BPPL) AND HARROD'S REVIEW, 1926–7

Harrod's Initial Reaction to BPPL, 1926

Harrod's review essay on Robertson's *BPPL* appeared in the June 1927 issue of *Economica*. A year before, in his letter to Robertson dated 18 May 1926 regarding *BPPL* – the opening paragraph of which was cited above – Harrod also wrote:

> Would it bore you if I make a few observations about it? It stimulated such an intellectual effort that I am afraid I have overshot the mark of understanding it and become hyper-critical. One salient point. Much of your argument depends on the view that justifiable expansions as defined by you are desirable. Why are they desirable? You give the reasons . . . why you think *some* instability in output desirable. But the reasons mentioned there (and I can't find any others) don't seem particularly directed to show that the special form of instability constituted by the so-called 'justifiable' expansions and contractions is desirable. They seem to me to show that perhaps some instability, presumably, of less degree than we have been accustomed to in the past, is good, but no means precisely how much is good.[18]

Harrod now posed the question as to what the desired degree of instability in Robertson's notional system would be if workers, for example 'were able to govern output according to their own self interest'. On Harrod's interpretation 'there would still, according to the arguments of Ch. 2 be *some* instability'. Harrod then asked Robertson 'Would not that be enough? Or if you want more, why stop at the "justifiable"? Why not have some of that due to "second-ary" causes?'. Harrod then summed up his view of the first two chapters of *BPPL* as follows:

> It seems to me that you have been led away by purely aesthetic interests to identify the more moderate amount of instability we really need . . . with that which we would get 1. if secondary causes were removed and 2. if control of output stayed where it is now – in the hands of the entrepreneurs. I don't see how you can say to the banks more than 'damp down fluctuation a bit, but leave some fluctuation, as that is healthful for the body economic'.[19]

Harrod then turned to his initial impression of the third chapter of *BPPL*. In his words:

> With regard to the arguments of Ch. 3 concerning the various possible currency policies, I have made notes which seem to me to prove that you exaggerate the amount of additional currency needed to stimulate the employer immediately to make the re-quired addition to output ('required' that is, as defined by you). I am not sure that the amount needed would involve a rise in the general price level. If it would not weary you, I will write out my view.[20]

Harrod ended the first part of his letter to Robertson as follows:

> I was much excited by your Ch. 5 sec. 9. I have been arguing in my lectures that even to attain stability of output (assuming, as I did, stability to be desirable) the need to provide the right amounts of circulating capital might, at times, conflict with the stable price policy . . . Even with a second reading, I have not had time to absorb your views – for which consummation I am eager.[21]

In a long addendum to his letter, Harrod took up in detail a number of specific points of disagreement with Robertson, the first of which involved differences in their respective treatment of 'variations in output'. Harrod wrote:

> You say 'let us define as follow:– "capitalistic" variations are those which an enlightened self-interest of capitalists tends to bring about. "Ideal" variations are those which an enlightened self

interest of group members would tend to bring about'. The capitalistic variations in point, however, are not those which enlightened capitalistic self interest (i.e. the capitalists, psychological causes apart) tends to bring about under *our* banking policy.

With our existing banking policy, enlightened capitalists would accept the bribe of the banks to bring about greater variations than those meant in your definition. The degree of variation is, as you would agree, a function of among other things, banking policy.

Harrod continued:

We want more definition. Let us treat 'capitalistic' variation as a function of the banking policy (i.e. as nothing fixed but as those diverse variations which enlightened capitalist self interest would respectively dictate under different banking policies). And let us call 'justified capitalistic variation' that special case of capitalistic variation which would occur if our banking policy were changed in a given manner, which would occur, say, under an ideal banking policy. The ideal banking policy is not, according to you, a stable price policy, but a banking policy which immediately promotes those variations which would occur in an imaginary frictionless state of barter (as in your Ch. 2).

Harrod then posed a number of questions for Robertson's consideration. As he put it:

You agree, I take it, that under *our* banking policy 'capitalistic' variations are greater than they would be under the one which you envisage. Then might not one be devised which would cause capitalistic variations to be less? And might not such a policy be desirable? Could we not, by a suitable banking policy, reduce capitalistic variations to the dimensions of what we might by analogy call 'justified ideal' variations?

Harrod continued:

You might object that ideal variation would differ from your capitalistic in quality as well as in quantity. Let us confine ourselves to quantitative differences. I propose that under a capitalist system we might have a banking policy which would bring about variation equal in magnitude to what we define as 'justified ideal' variation.

Harrod concluded his addendum as follows:

> Against this view of the matter, the only argument I know of are those of your p. 22. But they only show that *some* variation is desirable, not how much. Therefore, I don't see why you should identify 'good' variations (those 'which in all circumstances we ought to acquiesce in and promote') with 'justified capitalistic' variations. 'Good' might be more or less.[22]

Finally, Harrod drew a diagram for Robertson to illustrate what was meant by the categories of 'capitalistic fluctuation', 'justified capitalistic variation', and what Harrod called 'justified ideal variation' brought about by what, in his view, was 'suitable banking policy'.

Harrod's Review Essay on Robertson's BPPL, 1927

Harrod started his 1927 review essay of *BPPL* by outlining what he took to be Robertson's 'principal propositions', which, on his view, were that in the 'frictionless state of barter' proposed by Robertson, 'output would be liable to alternating expansion and contraction'; where 'such a fluctuation, but neither more nor less, is desirable', so that in the case of a money economy 'output would be made identical with the output of frictionless barter, not by price stability, but by an alternating rise and fall of general prices'.[23]

In his review essay, Harrod also returned to some of the issues he raised in his 1926 letter to Robertson. In some of the passages in his review essay, Harrod stressed his disagreement with Robertson's position, paraphrasing or simply repeating arguments he made in his 1926 letter. For example, in his review essay Harrod wrote that 'Banks, according to Mr. Robertson, ought so to determine their policy that the resultant scale of output is that defined as "justifiable"'. But, in Harrod's view, 'this will show some variability'. Harrod also posed questions similar to those he put to Robertson in his 1926 letter regarding why variation was desirable, and went on to cite the 'arguments in favour of variation in general' that could be 'found on p. 22' of *BPPL*. Harrod continued on to say 'their general effect is that with our existing capitalist system, complete stability might involve stagnation. Hence some variation is a good thing. But the variations of our unregenerate money economy are excessive . . .'. Harrod proposed that one could conclude from this that 'Banks should reduce industrial fluctuation, but not extinguish it'; a conclusion he also reached in his 1926 letter.[24]

Harrod then made the important point that 'it should be clearly understood that we have so far two separate sets of arguments. One shows that there would in fact be fluctuation in frictionless barter, the other that we ought to retain some fluctuation in our capitalist system'. He continued:

> But there is nowhere to be found any reasoning to the effect that the particular degree of fluctuation which would occur in frictionless barter is identical with the degree which it is desirable for us to retain, which is the right one, that is, for promoting progress.

Again, this argument closely parallels that in his 1926 letter to Robertson. Harrod went on to say 'and yet this identification is illicitly assumed throughout. It must be that some latent aesthetic interest led Mr. Robertson to make this identification'. Here, Harrod even used a similar phrase to that in his 1926 letter for critical effect. Harrod then presented his own views in the following words:

> As it is, there is a missing link in the explicit chain of reasoning. For if we grant that he has shown that stable prices would not allow of the full industrial fluctuation of frictionless barter, yet it is still tenable that stable prices would allow of some industrial fluctuation, sufficient for promoting progress in a capitalist system.[25]

Harrod summed up his review essay on *BPPL* by saying 'there is no doubt that Mr. Robertson has given a masterly analysis of the detailed processes of monetary fluctuation, and that he has made important contributions to the theory of the subject'. However, Harrod claimed that the review essay had 'only touched the "bare bones"' of Robertson's 'argument'. Thus, Harrod concluded 'it is submitted that the skeleton is incomplete, and that the practical conclusion that banks ought to promote a fluctuation of prices is not established'.[26]

Robertson, for his part, did not reply to Harrod's 1927 *Economica* critique. Rather, in the March 1928 issue of *Economica*, Tappan replied to the points made by Harrod in his review essay. After presenting her interpretation of Robertson's views, Tappan took issue with Harrod's conclusion cited above. Briefly put, Tappan's defence of Robertson's position relied upon her acceptance of the proposition – attacked by Harrod in his review essay – 'that monetary stabilisation would by no means eliminate the trade cycle'. Since Harrod's object, as that of Keynes in his *Tract*, was the greatest possible moderation of 'the amplitude of fluctuations' in the economy, it is not surprising that he was reluctant to accept Robertson's argument in *BPPL* regarding 'justified capitalistic variation'. Rather, Harrod proposed the notion of 'justified ideal variation' which, in his view, as noted, could be attained via 'a suitable banking policy', that is, 'justifiable' credit expansion and monetary stabilisation.[27]

It is evident from both Harrod's May 1926 letter to Robertson, and his review essay, that *BPPL* greatly influenced him during this crucial formative period in his thought. The impact of *BPPL* upon Harrod, however, was not to convert him to the Robertsonian world view, but to strengthen his resolve in his search for general concepts that could assist him in understanding and analysing the trade cycle. To this end, Harrod's line of investigation led him, as has been shown, quite early in his career, to consider the notions of 'justified', 'desired', and 'ideal' phenomena. And these notions, as will be seen, evolved into the central message and core concepts that appeared in his later works on the trade cycle, growth, and dynamics.

C. HARROD ON THE POLITICAL ECONOMY OF THE TRADE CYCLE AND INTERNATIONAL ECONOMICS, 1933

The Political Economy of the Trade Cycle

In his 1971 Chichele Lectures, when reflecting on the development of his approach to economic growth and dynamics, Harrod maintained that as early as 1933 he had come to recognise that he would require 'quite different tools' than those of what he called 'micro' and 'macrostatic' analysis if he desired to develop what, on his view, was a 'truly' dynamic economics. It would seem then that 1933 marked a turning point in his thought and, for that matter, in his career. For, in that year he published his first book, *International Economics* (Harrod, 1933a), a work which brought him to the notice of the economics profession. In the same year he wrote an insightful essay on the political economy of the trade cycle which was never published. And it was this essay (Harrod, 1933b) – in conjunction with his earlier work on the trade cycle and his treatment of it in *International Economics*, as will be seen – which formed the basis for his definitive book on the subject, *The Trade Cycle*, published three years later (Harrod, 1936a).[28]

Harrod's 1933 essay will, then, be dealt with first here. The significance of *International Economics* will then be discussed and placed in the perspective of Harrod's correspondence with Robertson and Meade on it. Finally, the direct influence of Keynes's *Treatise* (1930) upon Harrod's treatment of the trade cycle in both his 1933 essay and in *International Economics* will be dealt with, while consideration of the overall influence of Keynes's *Treatise* approach upon Harrod will be left to the next section.

Harrod opened his essay – written in mid-1933 (Harrod, 1933b) – by stating that the 'economic crisis' had precipitated a 'political crisis' of 'a peculiar nature' due to the fact that the 'economic problem' faced was a 'new' one. In Harrod's view, a distinction had to be made between what he called 'the old economic problem and the new'. According to him, the 'old problem' was – as Marshall had also defined it – that of 'poverty', the scarcity of goods, and their maldistribution. The 'new economic problem', on the other hand, was, in Harrod's view, not one of abundance, as the conventional wisdom of the day held. Rather, he asserted that the specifically 'new' or 'modern' economic problem:

> is that of unemployment. Unemployment is normally thought of in terms of labour, but in this context it may well be used in the broader sense of the failure of productive resources in general to be fully utilized. Factories lay idle. New capital cannot find channels of investment . . . The classical economist's doctrine lays down the condition for the best distribution of productive resources among different occupations. It might be better to put it negatively and say that it lays down the condition for productive resources not being distributed wrongly . . . The condition does not preclude the possibility that some of the productive resources will not be distributed among occupations at all. That is, that they will just not be utilized. This is a grave lacuna in economic theory which has not always been frankly admitted. There has perhaps been an implicit suggestion that the lacuna does not exist and that laissez faire would ensure full employment. It is not possible to find cogent arguments in favour of this suggestion.

Harrod then considered the argument that unemployed productive factors could 'offer their services at a lower price and thus secure employment in accordance with the law of demand which prescribes that any service when offered more cheaply will be bought in greater quantity'. But Harrod noted that 'the law of demand is limited in its application' when the commodity considered was only 'one among a number on the market', and the 'transfer' of demand in the aggregate 'cannot be generalized' since, for example, 'if all classes of labour reduce their offer price there will be no transfer' of demand between commodities due to lower labour costs. As Harrod put it 'the gain in employment at the cheaper price is due to the transfer. If there is no transfer, no class of labour gains additional employment'.

However, Harrod went on to say that:

> If labour comes to be offered at a lower price, while the offer prices of other factors of production . . . remain the same, factors will come to be used in different proportions in the productive process; labour more freely, and the other factors more sparingly. Labour will be substituted for the other agents of production. Thus, reduction in the offer price of labour, the offer prices of other factors remaining the same, may lead to some increased employment of labour at the expense of some of the other factors.

'But', Harrod continued:

> if all the factors of production are partly unemployed, and all seek greater employment, a reduced offer price by all of them cannot be shown to increase employment.

This, in Harrod's view, was because:

> Factors of production constitute the consumers. Their incomes shrink as the price they offer for their services is reduced. The market for goods shrinks in proportion to the cost of making them and is therefore incapable of absorbing more goods in the aggregate when they are offered at a lower price.

Harrod went on to say:

> The law of demand only applies to the market for one commodity or group of commodities and cannot be applied without fallacy to the market for goods in general. In the model of the economic

system constructed by the classical school, there is no mechanism for ensuring that full employment shall occur.

However, Harrod admitted that:

Fairly full employment did occur in the days when the model was constructed and the absence of a problem was no doubt the cause of the absence of scientific enquiry into the matter. Looking back we may ask why fairly full employment did occur and be left wondering.

Harrod then attempted to explain why this had, in fact, occurred. According to him:

The modern economic system had its origins in a system in which each man worked in order to consume his own product or to sell it on his own account. If his market deteriorated he did not abandon work; often on the contrary – he worked harder to make good his diminished receipts per unit of output by increasing output.

In Harrod's view, however:

The capitalist system works differently. Faced by a recession of demand, the capitalist may find it best to meet the situation by laying off hands who then have to fend for themselves and draw relief of some kind from another source.

Harrod continued:

The transition from one system to another proceeded slowly . . . But as capitalism grew the trade cycle became steadily more marked.

According to Harrod, in the period between the end of the First World War and the early 1930s 'the amount of output compared with total world output' produced by what he called 'men working on their own account' fell greatly. 'But', Harrod asserted, 'it was the pro-ducers of this type that gave stability to the old system', and in his view 'whose decline' could have been the cause of 'the growing instability of output as a whole' which faced the economy in 1933.

With regard to the trade cycle aspect of the 'new economic problem', as he called it, Harrod maintained that:

> The perplexities of this subject are directly connected with the lacuna in the old economic theory . . . just because they were ignorant what the forces were which would keep the economic system in a full employment position in a regime of laissez faire and whether there were any such forces, economists were at a loss where to look for explanations of the movements to and from such a position.

Harrod continued:

> Indeed, the old economics not only fails to explain *if* there are forces tending *towards* a full employment position, but gives no clue as to *what kind* of forces are required to fulfil this function. If these things *had* been known, trade cycle analysis would have been greatly facilitated.

Harrod then cited what he called Keynes's 'great work – that is, the *Treatise* (1930) – as a prime example of a trade cycle study, as he put it, that 'has been productive with positive results'; albeit one, in his view 'whose theoretical construction is incomplete and imperfect', although 'it goes far towards providing a coherent account of the matter'.

Harrod summed up this part of his essay by maintaining that:

> The immediate position with which we are faced is that of great unemployment of productive resources with consequent misery and political tension which is threatening civilisation itself. Immediate action is required. An important lacuna has been revealed in the theoretical construction on which the advocacy of laissez faire was based. It is not known to contain a mechanism for securing full employment.

In the second part of his essay Harrod went on to describe the specific measures he advocated for reviving the economy and overcoming the political problems involved in implementing them. As he put it:

> It remains to say something of the mechanism for securing full

utilization of productive resources. To some extent the problem is solved by being thus simply formulated. The appropriate party should say: We are determined to secure full employment with the assistance of whatever state intervention may be necessary without on the one hand degrading the standard of living which has been achieved for labour and has been shown in the near past to be consistent with fairly full employment and on the other without aiming at any drastic redistribution of wealth.

Harrod continued:

A study of the trade cycle seems to have yielded this much of a result: that recessions in production are associated with fluctuations in the value of money and that a stable money is required. Monetary stability can only be secured with the cooperation of the banking system.

But, in Harrod's opinion:

It is not likely that banking action would be sufficient by itself. The state may have to intervene directly in controlling the volume of monetary demand. This control might take two forms: (1) it might consist of regulating the volume of capital output in the country; (2) it might consist of deliberate variations in the balance between the money received in taxation and the money distributed as incomes by the government (and by local authorities) to its servants and debt-holders.

A very important point was then made by Harrod regarding the relation between output and stabilisation policy. According to him 'regulation of the volume of capital output' was 'intimately connected with monetary stabilisation and control over the forces generating the trade cycle'. In Harrod's view, state intervention could be implemented in a number of ways. These were, as he put it:

(1) by a suitable policy of timing public works.
(2) by the control over new issues through a national investments board.
(3) by subsidies to improve capital construction combined with an appropriate degree of control over the subsidized enterprises.
(4) by the guarantee of interest on approved undertakings.

In order to implement policies such as those listed above, Harrod claimed that:

> it would be necessary for the authorities to establish rules not only for testing schemes on their own merits but also for regulating the total volume of such schemes with the view to stabilizing the level of activity in the country as a whole.

Additional policy measures advocated by Harrod in his essay involved industrial reorganisation aimed at deliberate expansion of industries and cartels. This on his view could be achieved when industrial expansion rather than contraction would become, as he put it 'remunerative' by means of 'a system of fines and bounties'. In addition, Harrod advocated the provision of employment subsidies to stimulate industrial expansion.

Harrod then went on to examine what he called the 'political corollaries' of 'the new economic problem'. In his words:

> The problem of poverty and particularly the problem of maldistribution has come more and more to the front in recent years and has largely determined political alignments. That we are now [1933] confronted with a problem of a wholly different nature has not yet been assimilated by the political mind. That it cannot be solved without intervention by the central government seems clear. Conservatives are reluctant to recognize this because the introduction of appropriate controls would make the old order recede farther into the background. Socialists rightly perceive that their old line of advance is blocked for the time. This perception leads the very timid into conservatism and reaction. Hence the political atrophy. Yet, the need for action has never been more urgent.

Harrod continued on to say:

> The new problem differs from the old in this respect, that it is a problem of prices. Failure to solve the old problem was compatible with political stability. There was room for trial and error. Time was of comparatively little account. The continuance of poverty was lamentable but did not necessarily entail worse things. Sleeping dogs could lie. But economic recession and deterioration, the sharp pain of new adversity, stimulate the sufferer into action. And if a program of suitable action is not offered by political leaders,

man will seek relief in his old bad habits – political reaction and war. The immediate future of civilization will be jeopardized.

Finally, Harrod turned to summarise the arguments he made in his 1933 essay. As he wrote:

It has never been shown that there is any mechanism in the system of private enterprise for securing full employment. But is has *not* been shown that there is *no* such mechanism. Still less, that full employment is incompatible with private enterprise. In the past there has been some confidence that while unfettered private enterprise is wasteful in allowing lapses away from full employment to occur, it does provide a mechanism of recovery: that expansion follows depression by some sort of inner law. The nature and even the existence of this law is unknown, but it may nonetheless be at work.

Harrod went on:

The present depression [1933] is far more severe than any of the past, but it may be of the same nature. And forces *may* be at work within the system generating revival. If this is so, drastic state intervention may, after a further lapse of time, prove unnecessary in the present emergency. Things *may* get well of their own. The obstacle which the depression opposes to social advance will then disappear . . . These considerations do not take the force out of my argument. Rather, they add to it. In the first place, since we do *not* know that the recovery will come of its own and hardly have greater grounds for believing that full recovery will come than that it will not and since if it does not, prognostications of disaster are likely to be fulfilled, it is essential to act as if recovery would not come of its own. Secondly, this doctrine of the ineluctable advance of the trade cycle and a system of uncontrolled private enterprise suggests not only release from our present distress but another relapse into it of something worse. The evils which we may escape on this occasion will threaten again and perhaps descend. In the intervening phase of prosperity, people will be lulled into a false sense of security. There will be less inducement to hammer out a policy of appropriate state intervention then, than now. But it will not be less important that this should be done. This consideration *increases*, therefore, rather than diminishes the force of my argument

that politicians should take cognisance of the new economic problem and devise a suitable plan of action. The problem of securing
full employment then becomes merged into the more general one
of preventing industrial recession and eliminating the trade cycle.

Harrod concluded his 1933 essay by reiterating the programme he
proposed so as to ensure 'advance' towards what he called 'the new
social order'. In his words:

> The broader problem will require measures of the same general
> nature as the immediate one. The program outlined is one of state
> intervention to control the level of industrial output as a whole,
> through currency policy and banking policy – state control of the
> whole banking system would only be required in the unlikely event
> of its inability to secure loyal cooperation – public finance, invest-
> ment control, and perhaps through a system of fines and bounties
> operating evenhandedly with different industries. This policy is
> prior to and independent of the reorganization and possible nation-
> alization of particular industries which can be considered on its
> own merits in each case. It is independent of – though its success
> would immensely facilitate – the policy of further advance towards
> the new social order.[29]

Two major points emerge from Harrod's 1933 essay. First of all, it
is clear that in it, Harrod had outlined the policy measures and
programmes he proposed to stimulate a stagnating economy which
were later to appear in his 1936 book, *The Trade Cycle* (Harrod,
1936a). Secondly, it is also evident from his essay that in mid-1933
Harrod was still at a loss to account for the trade cycle itself, that is,
the 'unknown law', as he put it, that brought about the fluctuation in
economic activity that concerned him so much. And it was his search
for such a law, and its discovery and refinement by him, that was to
occupy the rest of his working life.[30]

International Economics, 1933

Harrod's book, *International Economics*, for its part, also marked a
turning point, not only in his career, as noted, but also in the
development of his thought. This is because it was there that he
started to elaborate the theoretical 'tools' he required for under-

standing the 'advancing' or 'growing' economy, and maintaining its growth. For example, in the book he not only outlined the 'monetary conditions that would be the prerequisite of a steady advance' and the means by which to avoid deflation, but also presented what can be called a threefold 'classification' or 'taxonomy' of 'advance'. In this context, he distinguished between 'rapid', 'steady', and 'stationary' advance. According to Harrod, the first case, that of 'rapid' advance, would be characterised by inflation, while the third case, that of 'stationary' advance, would be the outcome of a 'deflationary monetary system', that is, deflation. The intermediate case, that of 'steady' advance on the other hand, would be characterised as Harrod put it, by both 'stability' and 'output per head' that is 'rising', that is, growth.[31]

The most important professional reaction to Harrod's 1933 book came in the form of the comments of Robertson and Meade on the draft manuscript prior to its publication, and Haberler's review of the book and his subsequent choice of Harrod as one of the experts on the trade cycle to whom he sent the draft manuscript of his League of Nations memorandum, which later became *Prosperity and Depression* (1936).[32]

Robertson, for his part, commented both as the book's editor, and, in his view, as a 'reviewer' of the book would. This is clear from his letter to Harrod of 6 April 1932, in which he provided detailed criticism for Harrod's consideration, but also called into question the level at which the book was written, since he thought it would be too advanced for students.[33]

The specific points of Robertson's critique of Harrod's *International Economics* will not be gone into detail here. Suffice it to say, however, that Harrod was somewhat upset by them, especially Robertson's critical comments as editor, and even went so far as to consider giving up the book entirely. Robertson reacted to Harrod's suggestion of turning his proposed book into a long paper or series of articles, as seen in his letter to Harrod of 26 April 1932, when he wrote:

> I have talked over your letter with Maynard. We are both definitely of the opinion that you should finish writing your book *as* a book, i.e. shouldn't boil it down into an article or couple of articles and that you should make it the sort of book you would want to make it.[34]

On this basis, it would seem, Harrod went on to publish *International Economics* in book form after revising the draft manuscript on the basis of Robertson's detailed comments. This is evident, for example, in Harrod's letter to Robertson 13 October 1932, in which he mentions that he both added and deleted text and notes according to Robertson's 'points' of criticism and 'objections'. The impact of Keynes's *Treatise* on Harrod's approach as manifest in *International Economics* can also be seen, for instance, in a letter from Harrod to Robertson dated 29 April 1933, in which Harrod outlined his own 'doctrine' regarding the role of the 'foreign balance' as compared with that of the *Treatise*.[35]

In this long and important letter to Robertson, Harrod tried, as he put it, 'to ease the pain caused by our failure to decide what the doctrine of the *Treatise* in its crude form implied. The truth is another matter'. Harrod continued:

> May I return to the balance. My doctrine is that improvement in the foreign current credit account has the same potentiality of giving employment as public works. But if that potentiality becomes an actuality (i.e. is not countered by hoarding or some such process) the increased employment will wipe out the balance. The extra credit will be offset by an extra debit. What JMK ought therefore to have looked at was not the doctrine of the balance but the decline of the credit account.

He went on to say:

> Where I think Maynard has got muddled is in his attempt to include in one formula the stimulation that may be given (i) by an improvement in the credit account and (ii) by an improvement in the balance due to a tariff or change of taste.
>
> In both cases the good thing takes the form in the first instance in an improved balance. But in so far as the improved balance does stimulate employment in full measure it disappears. And in fact its improvement and its annihilation may well go pari passu. So it is very deceptive to attempt to measure the gain to the country in a period of time by the net outstanding improvement in the balance at the end of the period.

Harrod concluded his letter by saying:

Taking the balance as the criterion has another danger. It may be due to internal deflation. In that case it has no stimulating effect. The most one can say is that the balance enables you to reflate and undo the bad effects of the previous deflation which secured you the balance.[36]

Harrod's concern with the relationship between the balance of payments, deflation, and the trade cycle, here followed from his detailed treatment of the problem in his book. For example, in his chapter on the balance of trade he devoted a long section to the issue in which he wrote:

> To examine the interaction between changes in the monetary requirements of a community . . . and changes in the equilibrium rate of output of capital goods would take us to the heart of the problem of the trade cycle. This is largely an unsolved one.[37]

Harrod also sent the draft manuscript of his book to Meade for comment, and in correspondence debated with him the importance of the relative velocities of circulation as a factor in determining the spread of unemployment on the one hand, and increasing employment on the other. As Harrod put it in a letter to Meade dated 25 November 1932: 'Your note (of 18 Nov.) is most valuable and throws a flood of light on the matter. But I don't think it is velocity on which the beam should be concentrated'. Harrod then went on to describe how, in his view 'differing velocities of circulation in the different spheres could be treated as a special case'.[38]
Meade replied to this on 30 November 1932, and said:

> I am returning the typescript of your book. I am afraid I have not had time to study it as I should like to have done. I fear I have only raised this one small point . . . Clearly the rate at which unemployment is decreased in the one country by the . . . rise in its incomes and decreased in the other depends upon the proportion of income spent on imports and similarly the rate at which unemployment increases in the other country . . . But these rates at which employment and unemployment spread will also depend upon the relative velocities of circulation in the two countries.[39]

It should be noted here that, at the time, Meade was himself engaged in the writing of a book entitled *The Rate of Interest in a*

Progressive State (1933), and told Harrod about the work in his letter to him of 18 November 1932 mentioned above. The importance of this book in the development of both Harrod's ideas and for the growth research programme will be dealt with below. Suffice it to say at this point, however, that the Harrod-Meade-Robertson connection and the creative interchange and cross-fertilisation of ideas between them lasted – fortunately for economics – far beyond their early exchanges on Harrod's *International Economics*.[40]

Harrod's 1933 book (Harrod, 1933a) was reviewed by Haberler in the February 1934 issue of *Economica*. His critique was, on the whole, positive, although he did point out what, in his view, were technical and stylistic shortcomings in Harrod's book. Interestingly enough, Haberler cited the chapters in which Harrod elaborated his approach to the trade cycle (chapters 6–8) as 'the most original and, for the expert, most interesting part of the book'. It is not surprising, therefore, that Haberler turned to Harrod for comments on the draft manuscript of the League of Nations memorandum he had just completed, which was later to become the basis for his famous book *Prosperity and Depression*, published in 1936. And the significance of this memorandum, the correspondence between Harrod and Haberler on it, and Haberler's reaction to Harrod's subsequent work on the trade cycle for the development of Harrod's thought will be seen below.[41]

D.   HARROD'S REVIEW OF PIGOU'S THEORY OF UNEMPLOYMENT AND KEYNES'S TREATISE INFLUENCE

Harrod's Review of Pigou, 1934

One of the most interesting – albeit previously unnoticed – examples of Harrod's economic *weltanschauung* is his review article on Pigou's book *The Theory of Unemployment* (1933) which appeared in the March 1934 issue of *Economic Journal* (*EJ*) (Harrod, 1934a). Indeed, when placed in the perspective of his later work, Harrod's review of Pigou can be seen as the first indication of the position he was to take over the next four decades *vis-à-vis* Keynes – of both the *Treatise* and *General Theory* – and what he called 'the traditional theory'. Moreover, in this review essay Harrod gives us some insight as to his views of the nature of the development of economic thought and how it should develop.[42]

Now, Harrod was not originally asked by Keynes, as editor of *EJ*, to review Pigou's book. Although Harrod had sent a long comment on the book to Keynes for possible publication in *EJ*, Keynes initially replied to Harrod regarding it in a letter dated 10 October 1933, in which he said that while he found Harrod's submission interesting, he did not know what to do with it. And this, since Keynes, on his own account, was not very clear as to how to deal with Pigou's book in the *EJ*. The book had actually been sent by Keynes's co-editor, Macgregor, to Beveridge for review. But, as Keynes told Harrod, he thought that this wasn't suitable and, moreover, that Beveridge had been making no progress and would probably abandon the review. If that happened, Keynes was prepared to review the book himself or, alternatively, to publish the comments he would have made in his review in a note in the *EJ*.

In Keynes's view, his comments would complement those of Harrod, although he thought Harrod was concentrating on a different aspect of the same question, and also had some misgivings as to the correctness of Harrod's argument and the appropriateness of his analytical technique. Keynes ended his letter by telling Harrod he would let him know in due course about the book review, but in the meantime he was returning the manuscript of Harrod's comment on Pigou's book, so that Harrod could consider and reply to his criticisms.[43]

Keynes next wrote to Harrod regarding Pigou's book on 27 October 1933. In this letter Keynes suggested that both he and Harrod should comment on the book in the issue of *EJ* in which it was to be reviewed by Beveridge. Keynes told Harrod that his own argument would differ from both that of Harrod and from the position he took earlier. He went on to tell Harrod that his critique of Pigou would be based upon his current work on whether or not the classical assumptions were applicable to what could be called a monetary entrepreneur economy. Keynes admitted, however, that he did not expect Harrod to necessarily agree with his views until Harrod had read about a hundred pages of his unpublished work, and suggested that they get together to talk about Pigou's book in order, as Keynes put it, 'to determine what Pigou is doing and in what particular hypothetical world he is moving'.[44]

Two months passed before Keynes wrote to Harrod again on the subject of Pigou's book. In a letter dated 30 December 1933, Keynes advised Harrod that Beveridge had given up his attempt at reviewing the book and that Harrod would be approached by Macgregor to review it. Keynes then suggested to Harrod that he put together his review of Pigou in the form of a review essay so that he could include the points he made in the comments he had previously sent to Keynes for publication in the *EJ*. Keynes went on to say that upon reflection he had decided not to publish his own critique of Pigou. This was because he found himself unable to present his argument in what, in his view, was a successful way, without including a considerable amount of his own unpublished material for which there would not be room and would be inappropriate in a short note. He had, at that point, therefore, abandoned the idea. However, Keynes was to put his criticism of Pigou's book into print in a much more 'effective' way when he included them in his *General Theory* two years later.[45]

Harrod, for his part, was not as critical of Pigou's book in his review as Keynes proved to be in his later treatment of the book in the *General Theory*. In fact, Harrod called the work 'a supreme intellectual achievement, a masterpiece of close and coherent reasoning', and praised 'the great beauty, the exquisite workmanship, the painstaking lucidity' of the book. Moreover, he concluded that it was 'a rich storehouse containing many and various treasures . . . anyone who devotes patience and effort to exploring it will reap abundant profit'. In the *General Theory*, on the other, Keynes cited Pigou's analytical approach as the best illustration of 'the pitfalls of a pseudo-mathematical method', after maintaining that even Pigou's title was 'something of a misnomer', since on Keynes's view 'his book is not really concerned with this subject'. Keynes went on to call Pigou's approach simply 'bad theory'.[46]

Why, then, was Harrod 'easier' on Pigou's book than Keynes?, and what did he consider to be its redeeming aspects? The answers to these questions are evident in the body of Harrod's review, but in order to spot them we must know what we are looking for. Now, in his review Harrod is actually critical of Pigou on one point only, that is, Pigou's treatment of 'employment as a whole', in other words, his position regarding 'whether a . . . wage reduction' – money and/or real – 'is likely to cause an increase of employment'. Moreover, Harrod said:

> It must not be supposed that I have attempted to replace Professor Pigou's affirmations by contrary negations. I only claim that the case for wage-reduction is not established by his reasoning. Nor must it be supposed that I have attempted to impugn the value of Professor Pigou's general analysis; for I have singled out one

strand in the great texture of his reasoning for consideration from one point of view.[47]

With regard to Pigou's analytical toolkit, it is clear that Harrod was quite willing to accept its applicability to the issue with which Pigou was dealing, that is, when it was concerned, as Keynes put it, with 'how much employment there will be, given the supply function of labour, when the conditions for full employment are satisfied' or, in other words, again, as Keynes put it, when it explained 'the functional relationship which determines what level of real wages will correspond to any given level of employment'. Harrod justified his position by pointing to the positive aspects in Pigou's approach such as, in his view, the 'revival' of older theories and the 'close family relationship', as he put it, between Pigou's 'general monetary analysis' and that of Keynes.[48]

In Harrod's words:

> The principal weapons which Professor Pigou uses for his attack on the problem of unemployment are the theory of marginal productivity and a theory which bears close kinship with the old Wages Fund theory, and which we may christen the Wage-Goods Fund theory. This revival is a welcome one. 'Popular writers' have been in the habit of stating that the old classical theories of this type have been long since disproved and superseded by the marginal productivity theory. Such statements are both erroneous and harmful. These old theories are firmly founded on tautology, and may well prove, as is evidenced by Professor Pigou's book, to be most useful analytical tools. Nor is there any incompatibility between them and the modern theory of marginal productivity. Professor Pigou is able to use both the old and the new in the utmost harmony . . . he fits them neatly together with great artistry. His use of the Wage-Goods Funds theory does not imply a rejection of the Wages Fund theory in its strict classical form, for these two may also be fitted together.

As for Harrod's view of the relationship between the positions of Pigou and Keynes of the *Treatise*, he wrote:

> The general monetary analysis of Professor Pigou has a close family relationship to that of Mr. Keynes. This may be explained as

follows. Professor Pigou's analysis bears to the Wage-Goods Fund theory the same relation that Mr. Keynes' equations [of the *Treatise*] bear to the Wages Fund theory proper . . . Just as the Wage-Goods Fund theory is complementary to and not contradictory of the Wage Fund theory proper, so the analysis of Professor Pigou may prove to be complementary to that of Mr. Keynes, and the standard system desired by the former to be identical with that desired by the latter . . . Which tool of thought is most helpful in application to practical problems can only be solved by experience.[49]

With regard to Pigou's hypothetical representation of the wage regulation process, Harrod cited an example of the problem involved in reconciling Pigou's notional approach with real-world problems of wage determination. Interestingly enough, Harrod cited the same example over a year earlier in a letter to Meade dated 4 January 1933, which dealt with, among other things, Meade's concept of 'neutral money'; the example being the question of what actually would happen if a 'Trade Board' raised wages in a specific industry and its effects upon relative wages and the average of real wages. Suffice it to say at this point, however, that despite Pigou's criticism of 'neutral' money in his book, Harrod favoured Meade's concept as against the 'standard monetary system' that Pigou proposed, as is evident both in his review and his earlier letter to Meade on the subject.[50]

Finally, as for Pigou's policy prescriptions – besides wage cuts – to increase employment, Harrod agreed with them in principle, if not in practice. For, as Harrod showed, in certain circumstances Pigou advocated both public works expenditure and an employment subsidy to overcome the unemployment problem. Interestingly enough, Patinkin commented that in his 1933 book, Pigou presented his proposed 'public works expenditure policy' in a manner similar to that of Keynes in the *Treatise*, that is, advocating discriminatory interest rate reduction with domestic borrowers subsidised, and foreign borrowers paying the market rate of interest. However, as Harrod noted, Pigou also advocated direct public loan expenditure 'in times of deep depression', a policy with which Harrod, as Keynes, could readily agree.[51]

We are now able to deal with the points raised above regarding the role and significance of Harrod's review of Pigou in the development of his thought. In his review Harrod took the first step towards his position that Keynes's work – both the *Treatise* and later on the *General Theory* – was reconcilable and should be reconciled with the classical theory. To this end, in his review Harrod even went so far as to use the newly-devised notions of conceptual complementarity and relativity as the basis for his argument that the Keynesian and Pigovian systems of thought could be reconciled. Furthermore, as manifest in his review, Harrod saw the development of economic analysis in general, and Keynes's work in particular, as characteristic of an evolutionary process; a point on which he was consistent throughout his working life.[52]

Now, I have previously dealt with this aspect of Harrod's economic *weltanschauung* and view of Keynes's work in the context of Harrod's IS–LM approach – as manifest in his paper 'Mr. Keynes and Traditional Theory' (1937) – in which he played down the 'revolutionary' nature of Keynes's *General Theory*. There, as elsewhere, Harrod emphasised the linkages and continuity between Keynes's *General Theory* system and the orthodox theory, rather than the discontinuity and break with accepted doctrine some others stressed so much. Harrod again returned to this theme in his retrospective treatment of the 'Keynesian revolution' in his book *Money* (1969), where he maintained that certain aspects of Keynes's approach could be 'accommodated' to the classical theory.[53]

Perhaps the best – albeit least known – illustration of Harrod's position regarding the nature of the development of economics as a 'discipline' appeared in the chapter he wrote for *The New Outline of Modern Knowledge* (1956). In this essay (Harrod, 1956b), entitled 'Economics, 1900–1950', Harrod surveyed, for a general audience, the development of economic thought over the half-century of its transformation from a loosely-organised collection of doctrines of 'political economy' to what could be called a scientifically-oriented 'discipline'. In this, Harrod, in effect, agreed with Marshall as to 'the continuity of economics', and also reiterated themes he had introduced almost two decades earlier in his 1938 'Scope and method' paper regarding the limitations of economics as a science.[54] In Harrod's words:

> Economics was (and is) a young discipline; as a science its main success so far has been conceptual and classificatory; it had not and – despite the development of statistics – still has not to its credit many laws that can be expressed quantitatively; it can do little experiment.

Harrod continued:

> A subject of study in this phase can all too easily become a field of fierce terminological controversies; the inexpert can mistake these conflicts for disagreements about matters of substance, and the controversialists may in their egoistic zeal themselves lose their firm grasp of the slender body of doctrine which is all that their science can vouchsafe. By such strife gains previously won may be dissipated and lost. In such a phase, skill in the choice of terms and modes of enunciating principles may require a wise sense of expediency; this does not imply any compromise with truth, for the same laws can be formulated in alternative ways.

Finally, Harrod wrote:

> It may be wise expediency to instil and even if you can to impose . . . what may be called a linguistic conservatism, for this will tend to curb the natural tendency of each new generation of students to mistake linguistic novelties for real contributions to the subject. And this in turn will canalize their energies into making real contributions.[55]

Keynes's *Treatise* Influence on Harrod, 1930–39

It is clear that Keynes's *Treatise* influenced Harrod during the formative period of his approach to the problems of the trade cycle, growth, and dynamics much more than the *General Theory*. The reasons for this, however, must be understood before we go on to describe the sequential conceptual synthesis and cross-fertilisation of ideas that characterised the evolution of his published work on these problems. Moreover, Harrod's attitude towards the *Treatise* was significantly different from other members of the 'General Theory group' – such as Kahn and Joan Robinson – and even from that of Keynes himself. For example, Keynes saw the *Treatise* as 'static' and the *General Theory* as 'dynamic' in terms of their respective treatment of 'output and employment as a whole'. Harrod, on the other hand, asserted that the *Treatise* was, in fact, the more dynamic of the two, albeit still limited, in his view, as regards the degree of its dynamic outlook, and thus his effort at dynamising it accordingly.[56]

The *Treatise* served as the basis, then, for Harrod's early efforts at developing a theory of the trade cycle (1930–39), and later on, for his formal treatment of the issues of growth and dynamics (1936–9). Even before the *General Theory* was published – and, as he put it, without 'having seen it', as will be shown – Harrod had, in his view, almost completed his task. What was lacking, however, was the operational formalisation of his approach; something which he only achieved in his 1939 'Essay' (Harrod, 1939a). What then, were the elements in Keynes's *Treatise* that caught Harrod's imagination and stimulated him into utilising it as the theoretical foundation for his enquiry into the trade cycle, growth, and dynamics?

First of all, Harrod considered the *Treatise* to be Keynes's definitive work on, and analysis of, the trade cycle. In Harrod's view, the *Treatise* emanated from the need manifest in the *Tract* for a theoretical basis for dealing with the 'credit cycle'. Indeed, as Patinkin noted, 'the basic problem that Keynes set out to analyze in the *Treatise* was that of the "credit cycle" and the fluctuations in employment and output which characterize it'. It is not surprising, therefore, that Harrod based his approach to the trade cycle, growth, and dynamics on the *Treatise*, since it was published at the time that his energies were becoming directed towards these problems. Harrod had recognised the need for a theory of the trade cycle which emanated from the *Tract*, and had made some effort towards this, as shown above. With the publication of the *Treatise*, Harrod could proceed, on its basis, to develop a 'dynamic' theory of the trade cycle and extend it to the problems of growth and dynamics in general.[57]

Secondly, the *Treatise* stimulated Harrod into a search for a system of even more 'fundamental' equations to explain the trade cycle, growth, and dynamics than those provided by Keynes's *Treatise* approach. This is because, as will be shown, Harrod realised the shortcomings in the *Treatise* that limited its applicability in the dynamic sense, necessitating both its dynamisation and the formulation of a 'truly' dynamic equation system.[58]

Finally, Harrod was also influenced by the very nature of Keynes's 'fundamental equations'; and this, in contrast to the position taken by some contemporary critics of Keynes's *Treatise* approach, that it was ineffective since its equational system was based upon identity, truism, and tautology. For Harrod intuitively knew that in economics identities, truisms, and tautologies had analytical efficacy, and their correct utilisation and application could be just as beneficial for the progress of economic inquiry as that of, say, advanced mathematical techniques. Indeed, in Harrod's view, they could prove to be very useful tools for economists, not only for formulating self-evident truthful propositions, but also for checking the consistency of their analytical framework.[59]

To sum up, then, Harrod's activities over the formative period of his thought initially focused (1924–30) upon providing a theoretical basis for Keynes's *Tract* approach to the 'credit cycle' – parallel to Keynes's own initial efforts over the period 1924–7. As Patinkin noted, 'in the course of his subsequent work on the *Treatise*, however, Keynes greatly expanded its scope'. Once Keynes's *Treatise* was published, Harrod also extended his efforts to developing a general theory of the trade cycle (1930–36), and subsequently, by dynamising the *Treatise* approach, to develop what, in his view, was a 'dynamic' treatment of the problem of economic growth (1936–9). Now, during these years, 1930–39, cross-fertilisation of ideas occurred between economists in Oxford and Cambridge with whom Harrod was in contact. And it was this exhange of ideas that both expanded the scope and extended the frontiers of economic inquiry far beyond that set by Keynes's *Treatise* and *General Theory* approaches, as will be seen in the chapters following.[60]

2 Individuals and Groups in Oxbridge, 1930–39

Shackle observed in a letter to Harrod written some years before the publication of his book *The Years of High Theory* (1967), that 'there really is a need for a thorough, accurate, and rather "personal" history of the economic thought of Cambridge and Oxford since the 20's . . . and written before it is too late'. In his book Shackle outlined the evolution of economics from the perspective of a participant-observer who played an active and significant role in the development of economic theory during the crucial formative period of the inter-war years. While his personal perspective dealt with the interaction between Oxford and Cambridge based economists, it did not focus upon the cross-fertilisation and interchange of ideas evident in their papers and correspondence, since Shackle's stated objective was to give his own personalised account of the period.[1]

Up to now, the best known example of the interaction between economists over the years 1930–39 was that of Keynes and the members of the 'Cambridge Circus'. But perhaps the most striking example of conceptual cross-fertilisation in the sphere of economic inquiry during this period was that of Harrod and those Oxbridge economists with whom he was in contact in the 1930s, some of whom also became members of what he called his 'trade cycle group'.

One of the most important of Harrod's intellectual relationships over the period – besides that with Keynes, and as will be shown, with Robertson as well – was the ongoing exchange of ideas he had with Meade. This focused, initially, upon Harrod's *International Economics* (Harrod, 1933a) as seen above, extended to Meade's work regarding the 'progressive state', and culminated in the Harrod-Meade correspondence on Harrod's *Trade Cycle* (Harrod, 1936a) and the issues that emanated from it. And, as will be seen, the cross-fertilisation and exchange of their ideas on the trade cycle, growth, and dynamics was to bring about the growth research programme in economics. At this point, then, let us turn to Meade's early work and the significance of it and his contact with Harrod for the development of Harrod's ideas.

A. FROM THE 'CIRCUS' TO THE RATE OF INTEREST IN A PROGRESSIVE STATE: HARROD, MEADE, AND THE INTERCHANGE OF IDEAS, 1930–34

During the year he spent visiting Cambridge, Meade was – on all accounts – an 'active' member of the 'Cambridge Circus' and took part in all its discussions. Moreover, Meade consistently maintained that he left Cambridge with a clear outline of what was for him the essential elements of Keynes's *General Theory* system (Keynes, 1936). This being so, upon his return to Oxford in the Michaelmas term (autumn) of 1931, Meade's attention focused upon the problems of what he called 'the progressive state', and the development of a theoretical approach for understanding and analysing its economic characteristics.[2]

In his review of Akerman's book, *Economic Progress and Economic Crises*, in the September 1932 issue of the *EJ* (Meade, 1932), Meade gave some indication of the direction he had taken in the work he was then completing on the problems of the 'progressive state'. In the context of this review, Meade criticised Akerman's division of the 'methods of economic study into three groups', namely, 'the economics of equilibrium, the historical school', and what Akerman called 'the economico-statistic conception'. As Meade put it:

> There is a fourth type of economic study, which is quite independent of statistical enquiry, in which certain assumptions are made and from these assumptions the process of change due to important inventions or the continual accumulation of capital is deduced. Such a dynamic theory supplemented by statistical enquiry is likely to be the source of future progress in economic science, but it will be very closely allied to the 'economics of equilibrium'.[3]

Meade's book, *The Rate of Interest in a Progressive State*, appeared in 1933 and, as Solow recently noted, it represented Meade's first important attempt to go beyond the conventional economic wisdom of the time. In his preface, dated January 1933, Meade wrote that is was:

> justifiable, and indeed desirable, that economists should publish their thoughts on a problem on which a great number of other economists are working, even if their work is . . . incomplete; for

advance can most efficiently and quickly be made by such sharing of ideas and by co-operative work.

In fact, Meade related in the preface that not only did Robertson influence his work, but both Kahn and Maurice Allen also 'contributed ideas' to the book. As Meade frankly put it in his preface:

I always find it impossible to remember where I first came across any particular idea. I hope, therefore, that they – [Kahn and Allen] and indeed anyone else whom I have treated in a similar way – will forgive me if they see ideas of their own expressed in this book without acknowledgement. This is, I think, an inevitable consequence of working with other persons on a particular problem.[4]

Joan Robinson reviewed Meade's book in the June 1934 issue of *EJ* (Robinson, J., 1934). In her review, she made a number of important observations regarding the nature of Meade's approach. First, she recognised that Meade's work related to the 'dynamic equilibrium of the economic system'. In this context, she cited Meade's remarks in his preface to the effect that his object was to analyse 'the conditions of dynamic equilibrium as a necessary preliminary to a study of disequilibrium' since, in his view, 'economists must make a much more intensive study of the monetary conditions of dynamic equilibrium before the theory of trade fluctuations and disequilibrium can be much further advanced'. She also went on to take issue with the analytical efficacy of Meade's notion of 'neutral money' and a neutral monetary system, which she saw as 'monetary mysticism'. Finally, although critical of many points in what she called his 'original contribution', Robinson concluded that Meade had in his work 'reached a point from which the next step will not be difficult to take'.[5]

Harrod, for his part, also noticed difficulties in Meade's notion of 'neutral money'. For example, as early as his letter to Meade of 4 January 1933 mentioned in chapter 1, Harrod indicated that he was not completely at ease with Meade's concept of neutral money, since he believed 'that there may be a number of different definitions of neutrality which vary with the interpretations given to individual decisions'. However, Harrod still saw the concepts of neutral money and a neutral monetary system as useful and significant in certain cases such as that of 'a monetary system which allows real forces to operate in the way that they would if not disturbed by monetary factors'.[6]

But far more important was Harrod's initial reaction to Meade's book. In a letter to Meade on 13 November 1933, Harrod expressed his admiration for the book, in addition to some constructive 'criticism'. In Harrod's words:

I need hardly say how greatly I admired and enjoyed your book. I sincerely think that it is a brilliant work and contains a number of points that one will need to remember.

Harrod then said 'I have a few little criticisms of varying degrees of importance – none of them very serious'. In order to deal with Harrod's 'criticisms' of the book and with its influence upon him, it would be beneficial to recall the main points of Meade's book here. Briefly put, Meade dealt with 'the effects of changes in the economic situation in a progressive society upon the equilibrium rate of interest', where he defined a 'progressive society' as 'one in which output per head is increasing'. Meade then outlined his concept of a 'neutral money system' which, as noted, was somewhat problematic. However, in fact, this notion only played a minor role in his analytical scheme. Indeed, as Robinson noted in her 1934 review 'the main part of his book is completely free from it, and his analysis is conducted throughout in a rigour and thoroughness which inspire great confidence in the reader'.[7]

The major innovative elements in Meade's book were: (i) his adaptation of modified *Treatise*-type definitions to the analysis of dynamic equilibrium; (ii) his treatment of the effect of expectations upon investment; and (iii) his stress on the role of interest rate in maintaining dynamic equilibrium.[8]

With regard to the first point, Meade focused upon what he called 'the difficulties' in using Keynes's (1930) *Treatise* 'definition of the terms profits, earnings, and savings'. The problem, in his view, was that Keynes's *Treatise* definitions caused 'difficulties' in 'defining a position of dynamic equilibrium'. Thus, Meade decided 'not to employ them in his [Keynes's] sense'. Meade's definitions will not be gone into here. Suffice it to say that he developed and used definitions of profits, income, and savings which enabled him, in his view, to deal with 'dynamic equilibrium' and its 'maintenance', something which, as will be shown, was also done by Harrod.[9]

As for the second point, Meade not only introduced the effect of 'expected profits', but of expectations regarding prices, wages, and the rate of interest as they influence business outlook and especially investment. Meade's treatment of 'expected price movements and investment' here is quite unique. Indeed, it foreshadowed the later Keynesian development of the importance of expectations in the determination of investment and, as will be seen, influenced Harrod as well.[10]

Regarding the third point, here Meade was also breaking new ground. According to him, in periods of rapid price movement the power of the interest rate to act as an economic 'regulator' may be lost. In these periods, in Meade's view, interest rate variations may need 'to be very violent in either direction to maintain equilibrium'. In a note to this statement, Meade asserted that it expressed his 'main argument for a controlled policy of public expenditure with a co-ordinated monetary policy'. In Meade's opinion, in a period of falling prices, the state should intervene, undertaking investment 'at the given rate of interest to stop the fall . . . so that the market rate of interest may again control the situation'. When prices undergo a rapid rise, state-backed investment 'should be cut to a minimum . . . so that the rate of interest may gain be used as a control'.[11]

Harrod's view of the importance and role of the rate of interest in attaining and maintaining 'dynamic equilibrium', however, varied from that of Meade. In fact, this became a source of prolonged discussion between them, as will be seen in Meade's detailed notes and comments on Harrod's draft manuscript of the *Trade Cycle* (Harrod, 1936a), and Harrod's replies to them. Harrod's criticism of the book as evident in his letter of 13 November 1933 focused initially upon the definition of neutrality in it – a theme he first raised in his letter to Meade of 4 January 1933 – and then went on to bring up some minor points regarding Meade's graphical representations. The most important of Harrod's 'little criticisms' related to his interpretation of the passage in the book where Meade wrote that 'the advantage of substituting capital for the other factors would be diminished by the fall in the price of these other factors'. Harrod did not fully agree, for, as he put it in his letter:

I don't think that this will do . . . for it would be a good point against wage reducers if it would! I think there are cost schedules of which it would be true. But it is not universal, I think, e.g. with cheaper labour the amount of labour which it would be proper to use with the *old* amount of capital might be greater, and the rate at which capital could profitably be substituted for labour in response to a *fall* in the rate of interest might be the *same*. Your sentence takes cognisance of the effect of the diminished price of labour on possible increments of labour and capital employed, but seems to omit reference to the increased amount of labour that would be co-operating with capital at the starting point of capital expansion.[12]

For Harrod, then, there were indeed a 'number of points' in Meade's book he thought it worthwhile 'to remember'. But regrettably, Meade's 'brilliant work', as Harrod called it, was almost completely forgotten by the economics profession and its historians of thought.[13]

B. CONCEPTUAL 'CLEARING-HOUSES' – HARROD, ROBERTSON, MEADE, AND ALLEN

Over the decade of the 1930s, a number of Oxbridge economists played the role of intellectual 'sounding boards' for their colleagues and functioned, in effect, as 'clearing-houses' for the critical evaluation of new ideas and their dissemination. That this type of intellectual relationship existed between Harrod and Keynes is both well known and documented. The fact that Harrod also turned to others – such as Robertson, Meade, and Maurice Allen – for their critical evaluation of his ideas, is much less known. Furthermore, the extent of intellectual contact between Harrod, Robertson, Meade, and Allen, and its significance for the development of economics in the 1930s, has also not received the attention it deserves.

Robertson's contacts with Maurice Allen and James Meade is evident in the early 1930s, and their contributions to his work is mentioned both in his published articles and correspondence during this period. For example, in his September 1933 *EJ* paper 'Saving and Hoarding', in which he criticised Keynes's *Treatise* approach to savings, and attempted to develop his own concept, Robertson cited his indebtedness to Allen for contributing to his argument. More important, however, is the fact that in his 'extended reply' of 19 May 1933 to Keynes's criticisms of 4 May on his article, Robertson asked Keynes for a proof copy of it to send to Allen, for, as he put it 'I should like to try it on the Prof. [Pigou] before publication and on my one faithful disciple Maurice Allen'. Interestingly enough, in his initial reply to Keynes on 4 May, Robertson told Keynes that he was 'off to Oxford [to stay with Meade] for the week-end, so I shan't settle down to study your comments till next week'. Whether or not Robertson discussed Keynes's critique with Meade at the time is a moot point. Suffice it to say, however, that Meade did make a contribution to the sequel to Robertson's September 1933 *EJ* article. In this paper, entitled 'Industrial Fluctuations and the Natural Rate of Interest', which appeared in the December 1934 issue of *EJ* (Robertson, 1934b), Robertson thanked Meade for pointing out some 'limitations' of his approach.[14]

It is also interesting to point out here that Robertson's 1934 *EJ* paper was described by Kaldor as being representative of the transition from the pre-Keynesian to the Keynesian approach. As he put in a review of Hicks's book on the trade cycle (Kaldor, 1951) 'Since the mid 1930s (and more particularly since the publication of Keynes' *General Theory*) . . . most of the theories [of the trade cycle] are built around the essentially Keynesian concept of an equilibrium level of output or employment'. In a note to this statement, Kaldor wrote:

> this remains true, even though some of the path-breaking work in this field-such as Frisch's paper in the Cassel *Essays* or Kalecki's paper in *Econometrica*, 1935, preceded the publication of the *General Theory*. In the early 1930's, Keynesian ideas were in the air, long before the publication of the *General Theory* gave them a systematic expression. Professor Robertson's paper in the December, 1934 issue of the *Economic Journal* ('Industrial Fluctuation and the Natural Rate of Interest') is illuminating, for it clearly marks the transition from the old to the new methods of thought.[15]

Harrod and Robertson

Now, as has been shown in chapter 1, the intellectual contact between Harrod and Robertson had started in the mid-1920s, and strengthened over the 1930s. The private correspondence and public exchanges between them on Harrod's 1934 *Economica* paper (Harrod, 1934d), Harrod's 1936 book *The Trade Cycle* (Harrod, 1936a) and Robertson's review of it, and on Harrod's 1939 'Essay' (Harrod, 1939a) will be dealt with in chapters 3 to 5. What is important to point out here, however, is that according to the private correspondence between them found in the Harrod papers, Harrod relied upon Robertson's critical judgement and evaluation of his ideas to almost the same extent as he relied on that of Keynes's.

One of the most outstanding – albeit up to now unknown – examples of this relates to Harrod's paper 'Mr. Keynes and Traditional Theory' which he presented at the September 1936 Oxford meeting of the Econometric Society, and which appeared in *Econometrica* in January 1937 (Harrod, 1937a). I have, elsewhere, dealt with the relationship between Harrod's paper and what later became known as the IS–LM approach to Keynes's *General Theory*, and also reconstructed what I call the Harrod-Hicks-Meade IS–LM approach on the basis of correspondence between these individuals, and between them and Keynes, found in the Meade papers. Recently, however, in the course of studying the Harrod papers, his correspondence with Robertson on this has also come to light.[16]

Harrod's correspondence with Robertson on what was to become 'Mr. Keynes and Traditional Theory' actually started in November 1935, only a few months after Harrod had outlined his initial interpretation of the *General Theory* approach for Keynes in late August, and Keynes, in turn, reacted to it in early September 1935. In a letter to Robertson dated 11 November 1935, Harrod said:

> I am hoping to write a posh article on JMK's book when it appears and part of my ambition – though God knows whether I shall achieve it – was to trace the development of his thought from certain origins in you. For that purpose, I intended to re-read *Banking Policy and the Price Level* and 'Theories of Banking Policy' in your joint volume with Pigou.
>
>   It would be a great kindness if you would tell me of any other sources for discovering Robertsonian doctrine. I also thought of the last chapters of the last edition of *Money* which you think would be relevant to that particular task.[17]

Some six months later, in a letter dated 18 May 1936 – three months after the publication of Keynes's *General Theory* – Harrod again discussed his proposed article on it with Robertson. As Harrod wrote:

> To refer to Maynard, there was some idea of my doing for *EJ*, after the official review appears, an account of how the theories of the *GTE* seem to me to stand in relation to orthodox theory. I gave an address on these lines to our own political economy club here which they seemed to think helpful.

It would not indulge in polemics, either pro or con. Its burden would be that Maynard has not made more than a small modification in the general theory of value, but that even a small modification in a body of doctrine consolidated out of the minds of Marshall, Wicksell, Pareto, and the rest of them is a great thing. You see, on reading Prof. Pigou's review, I could not help feeling that whether his admonitions were salutory or not, he simply has not tackled the main point.

Harrod went on to say:

It may sound rather conceited to suppose that I can accomplish what Maynard, with his famous lucidity, has failed to get across, namely explain what he is *really saying*. But perhaps a new line with a new angle might be able to clarify. Do you think that would be a good idea?[18]

It would seem that Harrod sent Robertson a copy of his paper only after having presented it at the symposium on Keynes held on 26 September 1936 which opened the Econometric Society's Oxford Conference. A month later, in a letter dated 28 October 1936, Robertson wrote to Harrod:

I have this evening at last read your paper. I do not return it because I want to ask if I may hand it on to Pigou. May I?

It is very clear and should be very useful even to those who can't accept your appraisal (for in spite of disclaimer you do very definitely appraise!). My chief difficulty with it, of course, is with the book itself, in that the generally recognized traditional . . . doctrines with which the *General Theory* is contrasted often seem to me a kind of bogey man, created out of straw, bearing little relation even to what I was taught in 1911–12; still less to what I have learnt, read, and taught in post-war years.

Robertson continued:

We seem to agree on certain things, viz. that (in spite I should say, of persistent suggestions to the contrary in the book itself) the *GT*: (1) doesn't introduce any new pieces but only rearranges the old ones in a way which you find to be illuminating and I find to be muddling; (2) isn't really doing dynamics at all. I should add, *is* doing an exceedingly uncomfortable compromise between comparative statics and dynamics which may be very misleading in practice.

He then went on to say:

> But I don't think it is much good arguing. It has become a problem of what Frank Ramsey called comparing notes or testifying to personal experiences which are obviously different, though I have tried to learn from the book what I can. We have certainly suffered a strong stimulus to thought from it and the discussion to which it has given rise. In any case, my notes in the *QJE* for November will be published before many critics, though they only deal with part of the piece . . . so I won't waste your time by anticipating them.

Robertson concluded:

> Meanwhile, I hope you feel as charitably as you can towards our irritation. It *is* irritating to be misrepresented, as Pigou was misrepresented, or to be regarded, as I am, as a victim of premature arterial sclerosis. But I think you must credit us also with some deeper feelings of more or less disinterested regret and anxiety about the effect of all this (at all events temporarily) on economic education; on the reputation of economics with the outside world; on public policy. No doubt you will say all this is worthwhile if a real advance has been achieved in theory and the ground laid for a real advance in practice. You are fortunate to believe it has, and I unlucky enough to be sceptical.[19]

Harrod, it seems, agreed that Robertson could hand his paper on to Pigou, and a fortnight later, on 9 November 1936, Robertson again wrote Harrod regarding it; this time attaching Pigou's comments on Harrod's paper to his letter. In Robertson's words:

> At last I return your paper with apologies for keeping it so long. Pigou's notes attached were for my information, but he says I may transcribe and transmit them.
>   On re-reading the paper, I find that the things which surprise me most are the claims made for illuminating change in respect of
>   (1) the importance of expectations . . .
>   (2) the pursuit of the concept of liquidity preference (proper) and

its relation with the marginal principle and the rate of interest . . .
(3) the manner in which changes in the quantity of money operate
through the rate of interest . . .
(4) the influence of rigidity of wage rates in terms of money.

Robertson then provided detailed references to his own works and
those of Marshall, Lavington, and Pigou in which these points appeared. He went on to say:

> The (neo-Keynesian) formulation seems to me definitely retro-
> grade in various respects. In particular, it divorces money held for
> precautionary motives from direct connection with the rate of
> interest, which is supposed to be relevant only to money held for
> speculative motives, i.e. because it is thought that the rate of
> interest may change. Thus interest is paid because interest is
> expected to change.[20]

Robertson then gave Pigou's comments on Harrod's paper. According to Robertson's transcription, Pigou's notes were as reproduced below (because of their importance for the history of economic
thought, they are cited here in their entirety):

Pigou's Notes

1. Down to page 7, the symbols seem to refer to real income, real
rates of interest, and so on. I don't follow how or why Roy jumps
to refer to money.
2. It seems to me quite wrong to make Marshall's supply equation
$x = \Phi(y)$. Marshall laid stress on ability to save. His second equation is $x = \Phi(y, i)$. This gives two equations and three unknowns.
3. If we assume that the real rate of wages is plastic in such ways
that everybody is employed and write r for the quantity of productive resources in existence, the required third equation is
$i = \Psi(r)$, r being for short-run purposes a constant. This, it is
plausible to say, is the classical school's solution for some purposes.
4. If we assume, per contra, that workpeople insist on a certain
money wage, w, and i is the money income, the third equation
becomes $i = \Psi(I/w)$.
5. The great discovery seems to be that in these circumstances the
system is indeterminate until account has been taken of the influences that govern i!

6. These can be set out in a variety of different ways showing the part played by banking policy and Marshall's k (liquidity preference) in two equations that contain only one additional unknown apart from constants. The circle is then completed.

7. I should have thought that everybody who had ever written about industrial fluctuations knows all this perfectly well . . . Indeed, if he didn't acknowledge it, he would have to deny that monetary policy . . . had anything to do with industrial fluctuations.

In Pigou's notes as reproduced above, x stood for, as Harrod put it 'the amount which individuals choose to save, which is equal to the amount of investment'; y signified 'the rate of interest which is equal to the marginal productivity of capital'.[21]

A month later, in a letter dated 9 December 1936, Harrod sent Robertson his reaction to the comments on Keynes's *General Theory* that Robertson had made in the November 1936 issue of *QJE*. In this letter, Harrod wrote:

May I say just how greatly I admire your article in *QJE*? I admire the great erudition and the masterly way in which you have brought together strands of thought from all over the place. I admire the consumate restraint of its tone and temper. You asked me if I agree. I can only say that it is all so much a matter of emphasis and the convenience of concepts that I find it hard to say precisely how much I do agree with.

However, Harrod concluded:

It obviously would be a waste of time for me to take up detailed points since I expect Maynard is bombarding you.[22]

C. ECONOMIC SCOPE AND METHOD, THOUGHT AND LANGUAGE, AND ANALYSIS AND POLICY

Harrod, Fraser, Robertson, Meade, and Hitch, 1932–8

Harrod and Fraser

The 1930s were not only 'years of high theory' for economics. Advances were also made along a broad front, ranging from what could be called economic 'method and taxonomy' through 'semantics and rhetoric' to 'education and pedagogy'. There were, in fact, a large number of Oxbridge and London based economists engaged in these activities over the decade. Indeed, it may be said that they constituted at least as large a proportion – if not a greater one – of 'practising' economists, than those involved in either the development and dissemination of the 'new' ('Keynesian') economics in its various forms, or those defending the 'old' ('classical') world view.

In his 'Scope and Method' paper (1938), Harrod surveyed what, for him, were the major developments in economics. According to Harrod, his survey of the scope of economics was 'confined to what may be called its scientific aspect – namely, the formulation of general laws and maxims'. So as to 'make the course' of his 'argument more easy to follow', Harrod divided the field of what he called 'economics as a whole' into three areas. These were, in his view, (i) 'the general theory of value and distribution', that is, 'causal laws' which could be deduced 'from the law of demand' which, in his opinion, was 'static theory'; (ii) 'dynamic economics', that is, 'the simple laws of growth'; and (iii) 'the search for causal laws outside the realm of deductions from the law of demand or simple laws of growth'. He then went on to economic 'method'. With regard to the method of economics, Harrod cited Robbins's *Nature and Significance of Economic Science* (1932) as the main contribution to the subject, but also noted that 'Fraser has contributed some important articles and his book on *Economic Thought and Language* [1937] lies on the borderline of methodology'. In Harrod's view, Robbins's book was 'brilliant', although he went on to say 'my differences from him will become manifest'.[23]

Fraser, for his part, also took issue with Robbins, both in his articles and 1937 book. Now, this is not the place for a detailed analysis of the differences between their respective approaches to economic 'method'. We would, however, achieve a better understanding of Harrod's economic world view and view of 'economics as a whole' if their respective positions were briefly reviewed here.

It was Fraser, in fact, who took the initiative in his important – albeit almost entirely forgotten – critique of Robbins entitled 'How do we want economists to behave?'. In this paper, which was published in the December 1932 issue of *EJ*, Fraser questioned Robbins's fundamental premises regarding the nature and purpose of economic method and enquiry. According to Fraser, Robbins implicitly took 'for granted that economics is a science' and deduced 'that its subject matter must be confined to what is capable of yielding *a priori* certain results'. Fraser attempted to undermine Robbins's position by proposing equally valid counterarguments. For example, on his view, obtaining '*a priori* certain results' was 'not in the least part of the concept of science'. Rather, he asserted 'the certainty of the best attested laws of physics', for their part, were, in his view, more 'a matter of high inductive probability than of necessity'. Moreover, he continued 'nor can the phenomena of life and evolution be effectively studied by *a priori* methods. Yet physics and biology are recognized as sciences not less than geometry or mechanics'. Fraser then posed the question: 'Why not also acknowledge an *a posteriori* economics?', and also asked 'if by means of speculation, observation, or experiment it is found possible to make generalities about economic phenomena which have a measure of inductive certainty, why should they not be added to the corpus of scientific knowledge?'[24]

Fraser then focused on Robbins's view that induction and empirical studies were subordinate to deductive analysis in all problems of economic enquiry. As Fraser put it:

> In some problems they may play but little part; the task of collecting facts may be subordinate to, and come wholly before (or wholly after) analysis. But in others they are closely interwoven. A deductive argument will suggest a question of fact, the answer to which may require further deductive analysis, leading to still further inductive investigations, and so on. In cases of the latter type, theory and empiry represent not different *fields* of research, but different *tools* of research.

On this basis, Fraser asserted that 'deduction without induction is empty; induction without deduction is blind'.[25]

Fraser then turned to the issue of the distinction between 'theoretical' and 'applied' economics. In his view, this demarcation was tenuous at best. This resulted from what he saw as the cardinal factor differentiating the natural from the social sciences. In the former case, the area of inquiry open to the scientist is set by nature itself. Pure science, in his view, is concerned only with truth, and not the practicality or usefulness of the outcome of scientific inquiry. This is left to the applied scientist or technologist.

In Fraser's view:

> Economists, on the other hand, are faced continually with practical

questions. Their theoretical work is important not so much because it yields truth as because it provides a technique whereby practical and social problems may be solved. Knowledge in economics is valuable as being 'fruit-bearing' rather than 'light-bringing' – as assisting human well-being rather than as providing knowledge of ultimate reality.[26]

Fraser continued on to say:

> If by a science is meant the building up of a system of knowledge for its own sake, then economics is *not* a pure science. Its investigations are bound up with practice, and it is by its practical usefulness that it must be judged.[27]

Fraser ended his critique of Robbins's doctrine by maintaining that the main objection he had to it did not relate to either Robbins's reasoning or even his conclusions as such, but to the fundamental assumption from which he started out. According to Fraser, 'Economists cannot remain in the secluded contemplation of pure truth', since, in his view, their role was to 'help the community to solve its problems'. As Fraser saw it, while it seemed necessary that economists were equipped with sophisticated analytical techniques in order to adequately fulfil this task, it would be a great error to also think that, since they should 'reason scientifically', they should not do any more than that. For, in Fraser's view, this would be 'to mistake the means for the end'. As he put it, if this occurred, the economist would become, in effect, a 'psychological monstrosity', or in other words, 'an intellectual miser – a man who desires an infinite accumulation of theoretical dodo-bones'. Fraser concluded by saying 'let us hope that economists in general will not forget that in the social studies the end of knowledge is action'.[28]

Fraser returned to these themes in his 1937 book *Economic Thought and Language*. In this almost totally overlooked but none the less important work, Fraser set out key issues in both the methodology and semantics of economic analysis; and this some two decades before Machlup's treatment of the problem, and almost 50 years prior to McCloskey's study of 'economic rhetoric'. Again, this is not the place to evaluate Fraser's contribution to economic thought. What may be said here is that it deserves detailed assessment and recognition. In any case, while Fraser toned down somewhat his critique of Robbins's own view in his 1937 book on the basis of discussion between them regarding what Robbins's 'really meant', he still reiterated his criticism of Robbins's followers and students who advocated axiomatic theory to the exclusion of all other methods of economic inquiry and analysis.[29] As Fraser put it:

> I am still disquieted by the perspective with which some of his friends and disciples continue to exalt value theory at the expense of other areas of economic study, on the ground that being deductive it is uncontroversial. To refuse to study things because one cannot be sure of finding a precise answer seems to me to be cowardice; to suppose that only deductive studies are 'scientific' seems to me to be a misunderstanding of what science is.[30]

Fraser concluded by directing the reader to what, in his opinion, were 'the admirable remarks' regarding these issues in Harrod's *Trade Cycle* (Harrod, 1936a). What, then, were the remarks Harrod made in his book that Fraser found so 'admirable'? In Harrod's words:

> It is the hall-mark of science – of science, that is, actual and realized, not the science of Aristotelian dreams – that its conclusions do not have demonstrable certainty. Those theorists who seek to make economics more scientific by eschewing the uncertainties, which are necessarily attached to empirical methods, are in fact taking the path which leads away from science to pure scholastic.[31]

In his 'Scope and Method' paper (1938), however, Harrod expanded on this and went even farther. First of all, Harrod maintained that the economics of his time was neither a 'mature' nor an 'exact science'. According to him 'in fact its achievements outside a limited field are so beset on every side by matters which only admit of conjecture that it is possibly rather ridiculous for an economist to take such a high line'.[32]

Secondly, in dealing with 'empirical studies', and adherents of this approach, Harrod recognised that there existed a basic distinction 'between the outlook of the more and the less empirically minded'. One group, according to him, consisted of those like Wesley Mitchell, who took the view that 'the facts will' eventually 'speak for themselves' that is, 'by patient and continuous observation, the investigator will find the appropriate generalisation borne in upon him'.

Another group, according to Harrod, believed that the close inspection of 'the existing body of theory . . . will reveal gaps', and in these 'may be found clues suggesting new generalisations which will render the theory more coherent, or even wider generalisations leading to a revolution of the kind which occurs from time to time in physics'. This group may, alternatively, place stress upon 'observation, but urge that this should be done very much in the light of existing theory, to test hypotheses directly suggested by that theory'.[33]

Finally, Harrod held that a number of characteristics of economics constrain the 'scientific' nature of economic method. Among these is the inability to conduct a 'crucial experiment' in economics. On Harrod's view, this is a cardinal element in 'mature sciences' such as physics. Moreover, according to him:

> It is extremely difficult to test hypotheses by the collected data of observation. The operation of the plurality of causes is too widely pervasive. Thus, numerous hypotheses are formed, and never submitted to decisive test, so that each man retains his own opinion still.

Harrod's rationale here was, as he put it 'to upset the complacency of dogmatic upholders of one exclusive method'.[34]

Briefly put, then, Harrod saw the development of economics in evolutionary terms, and took the philosophic viewpoint of the necessity of complementarity in economic methodology.

Robertson, Meade, and Hitch

Now, one of the most important, albeit lesser known, aspects of the period, involves how and in what form the 'new' (Keynesian) economics reached the sphere of what was called above 'education and pedagogy'. In my view, perhaps the most interesting example of this relates to Meade's textbook *An Introduction to Economic Analysis and Policy*, originally published in the UK in 1936. A second edition appeared there in 1937, while the US version – with an introduction by Alvin Hansen and published in 1938 – was adapted and edited by Hitch. Between the initial UK edition of the book and its American version, Meade expanded a number of key sections. These alterations, however, were neither the result of Americanising it, nor were they the outcome of contemporary events – like the publication of the *General Theory* in the meantime, and any comments Keynes may have made on Meade's book. Rather, as Meade put it in his preface to the American edition of the book, his arguments were 'recast . . in the light' of the 'criticisms' of Robertson and Hitch, and their rewriting was 'helped by suggestions' made by Robertson and Harrod.[35]

Robertson's criticism focused upon Meade's treatment of a money wage cut and its effect upon employment. Since I have dealt with their 1937 correspondence on this issue and cited from it at length elsewhere, it will not be presented here. Suffice it to say, however, that according to Robertson, his attention was first drawn to the problem by one of his students in 1937. Moreover, as a result of his repeated questioning and Hitch's constructive criticism, Meade eventually revised the text in the American edition of his book. In fact, Meade actually expanded on and altered the focus of his original text, while not actually changing its substance in the least.[36]

For example, in his 1937 edition, Meade considered the question of whether a cut in the money wage rate would 'cause an increase in employment'. According to him, this depended 'upon whether it will cause the real wage-rate to fall'. Meade went on to analyse the question in detail and reached what he called 'important' conclusions and a 'precise' answer. In his 1938 American edition, on the other hand, Meade wrote 'unfortunately no precise answer is possible. The effects of a reduction in money wages are complex and diverse, and it is almost impossible to assess the relative importance of different effects'. Meade then went on to provide both reasons 'why a reduction in money wage-rates might be expected to reduce real wage-rates', and thus positively effect employment, and explanations of why the opposite could occur, that is, why they 'might have adverse effects upon employment'.[37]

Meade reached the same conclusion, however, in both editions of his book, namely, that since the outcome of a money wage cut is problematic, it is better 'to rely' upon other 'methods' that Meade suggested for 'stimulating' and 'increasing' employment, and 'reducing' or 'curing' unemployment. Finally, Meade held that raising money wages would not necessarily generate employment by 'increasing "purchasing power"'. Rather, in his view, there were other, more effective ways to increase employment.[38]

Now, if Meade's book had appeared only in the UK, its influence would have been quite limited. That it was also adapted by Hitch for use in American universities and colleges greatly increased its influence at the time. Moreover, as Hansen noted in his introduction, 'the publication of an American edition of Mr. Meade's book should help to hasten the coming of the day when we shall no longer be a nation of economic illiterates'.[39]

Finally, as I have shown elsewhere, the book was based upon Meade's IS–LM type interpretation and representation of the Keynesian system. Thus, while almost totally forgotten by historians of economic thought – and even by those, such as Solow, who recently surveyed Meade's many contributions to economics over the past half-century – the book did influence many economists and students at the time. Indeed, as Meade himself put it in an interview, if not for the war, his book could very well have become the 'Samuelson' of its day.[40]

D. GROUPS AND GROUPMEN

It should be clear by now that the accelerated development of economics in the 1930s was not only the product of brilliant and original individual minds. In fact, there were a number of 'magnetic' personalities in Oxbridge and London around whom small groups 'naturally' formed, or who 'positively' interacted with their colleagues. Other 'forceful' personalities consciously brought together economists of a similar economic world view to their own. The best known example of the former case is that of Keynes and the earlier 'Circus' and later 'General Theory group' that crystallised around him. The collection of academics that Robbins gathered together at the London School of Economics (LSE) best exemplifies the latter case.[41]

In developing the ideas for his book, *The Trade Cycle*, when writing it, and in what followed, Harrod adopted Keynes's *General Theory* pattern. This involved using a group of colleagues as an informal sounding-board for ideas and discussion ('oral tradition'). Some of these colleagues – and others sympathetic to the ideas – also participated in an 'in-house' but still formal critical evaluation of the draft manuscript, both as it was being written and afterwards. This was accompanied by an ongoing revision of the manuscript, incorporating ideas developed during the course of its 'in-house' evaluation ('written tradition'). The draft manuscript was also sent for the formal critical scrutiny of 'outside' colleagues who did not share similar views.

The process operated, therefore, on two levels. The first was notional and informal, that is, the level of initial conception of ideas.

The second involved the actual and formal presentation of the ideas, that is, the level of their critical evaluation, two types of which were actually sought. The first was that of critical but sympathetic evaluation. The second was that of critical but not necessarily sympathetic evaluation as such.

In the *General Theory* case, the 'Circus' functioned at the conceptual level, while the 'General Theory group' provided 'in-house' critical evaluation. The 'outsiders' to whom Keynes also turned for constructive – albeit not necessarily sympathetic – critical evaluation were Robertson and Hawtrey, among others.[42]

In the case of *The Trade Cycle*, as will be seen below, what I define as Harrod's 'Trade Cycle group' provided the essential sounding-board for his ideas and also the sympathetic 'in-house' critical evaluation of his written work. In other words, it functioned both at the conceptual level – in an informal manner, which resembled the activities of the 'Circus' – and at the level of 'in-house' critical but sympathetic formal evaluation of the draft manuscript as it was being written. This was actually undertaken by Maurice Allen and James Meade, who also participated in the ongoing discussions of what Harrod himself called his 'trade cycle group'. Harrod turned for 'outside' formal critical evaluation to Robertson and Henderson, among others. Robertson also reviewed the book – a critique which upset Harrod somewhat, as will be seen – and Harrod also engaged in correspondence with Keynes on the *Trade Cycle*, albeit only after its publication.[43]

To sum up, the function of Harrod's 'Trade Cycle group' in my definition was broader than simply any discussions on the problem of the trade cycle which took place, for it also included the ongoing 'in-house' evaluation of the draft manuscript of his book. And this evaluation may have even been more important for the development of the growth research programme, as will be seen below.[44]

But perhaps the most striking example of the attempt to bring about the 'sharing of ideas' and 'co-operative work' amongst Oxbridge- and London-based economists in the early 1930s is evident in a letter from Harrod to Meade dated 4 October 1934. In this letter, Harrod replied to a memorandum drafted by Meade setting an agenda for co-operation between Oxbridge economists. This involved the setting of research needs and priorities, co-ordination of research work in progress, and the collection of national economic statistics seen by Meade as pre-requisites for theory building and assessment. Harrod completely agreed with the aims of the document, and added his own ideas as to how to implement them in his reply to Meade. In Harrod's words:

> I think your memo would form an excellent basis for discussing pertinent matters for investigation. Most of the matters you want to know about are of general interest to all theorists. Some of them, e.g. national income, have already been much worked on and it is important that we should know all that has already been done.

Harrod continued:

> I feel that we *must* form a committee to develop this. Its object would be to enumerate and classify the quantitative enquiries the results of which would be of interest to theorists. I suspect that many of us would want to know much the same things. It should be emphasized that our object is not to discover some subject for investigation that would be appropriately undertaken by a university, but to discover what subjects of investigation would yield results actually required by working theorists.

He went on to say, however:

> I feel that the weakness of the committee would be – I hope I am not doing an injustice to my colleagues – ignorance about sources and work already achieved . . . Your document presupposes an immense amount of work and is therefore *good* if we are figuring out a big scheme. I hope you will preserve it for future reference.

Harrod then said:

> The two subjects in theory which are interesting me particularly at the moment and on which statistic[al] theory could throw light are:
> (i) the question of increasing returns in imperfect competition, which is first cousin to your short period elasticity of the demand for labour, and
> (ii) to put it dramatically, whether the equilibrium rate of interest is at present zero, or, more generally, the actual relation of the rate of saving to the rate of investment in a society which has reached our stage of development.

'But', he went on to say:

I confess that my ideas of how to enquire into this are at present amorphous in the extreme.

Harrod then wrote:

Do you think the time has come when we can get down to business, pooling our ideas and our needs? If so, we must boldly organise the committee, notifying the professors and inviting them to meetings, but proceeding about our business in our own way.

He continued on to say:

I have the feeling that it ought to be organized on the basis that we as theorists, are seeking to organize our needs and our *existing* resources, and *not* as a committee to formulate plans for the R. [Rockefeller] foundation. I think the question of an impending benefactor might be a distracting thought. The *result* of our proceedings is bound to indicate a need of money. But I don't think that should be its *purpose*.

Harrod concluded his letter by saying:

I am perfectly willing to do any donkey work required of the secretary, unless you can think of someone else. The only disadvantage of that arrangement that occurs to me is the danger that it might be thought that I was trying to set the pace or forcing people's hands or becoming a sort of dictator of research! If there is any danger of that, quite frankly, it had better be someone else. It isn't a matter on which I can form a judgement myself.[45]

Meade's memorandum, in fact, may have catalysed – for Harrod and others, such as Henderson – the idea of setting up what eventually became the Oxford Economists Research Group (OERG), which was led by Henderson, and in which Harrod was an active member. Now, the history of this group will not be recalled here, for it has been admirably dealt with by Lee. Suffice it to say, however, that a number of participants in Harrod's 'Trade Cycle group' – such as Marschak and Hitch – were also active members of the OERG, while Harrod himself, as noted, was one of the leading figures in its research and publication activities.[46]

Now, in his letter to Meade of 4 October 1934, Harrod also apologised for not having replied earlier, since Meade had, in fact, sent his memo and a covering letter to him on 30 July, asking for an 'immediate answer'. In the letter Harrod said 'I can't tell you how guilty I feel in not having replied . . . before. It came to me at a time when I was very busy and also rather worried . . .'. What Harrod was 'busy' with and 'worried about' at the time were the private and public exchanges and debates with Robertson, Haberler, and others, surrounding his August 1934 *Economica* article; but more about this in chapter 3.[47]

3 Towards the Trade Cycle, 1934–35

In 1934, Harrod published two papers which dealt, in part or in full, with the trade cycle and the growing dynamic economy. The first paper, entitled 'Doctrines of Imperfect Competition', was published in the *QJE* in May 1934 (Harrod, 1934b). In this article Harrod surveyed the then newly-developed notion of imperfect competition as it related, among other issues, to the trade cycle. However, the paper aroused no serious critical response. The second paper was entitled 'The Expansion of Credit in an Advancing Community' and appeared in *Economica* in August 1934 (Harrod, 1934d). This paper, which dealt with the problems inherent in such a 'community' and the means of maintaining its progress, elicited, on the other hand, considerable comment and criticism.[1]

Now, it is not my intention to simply summarise or analyse either of these papers here. Rather, the main thrust of Harrod's arguments in his *Economica* paper – which can be seen as the last significant stepping stone towards his 1936 book *The Trade Cycle*, and which Harrod himself considered to be his first attempt at dynamic analysis – will be dealt with in the context of the public debate and private correspondence he engaged in regarding it. These exchanges on his 1934 *Economica* paper took place with Robertson, Haberler and Bode, and Kahn, among others. The Harrod-Robertson exchange will be dealt with in the first section of this chapter; that between Harrod and Haberler and Bode will be dealt with in the second section; while the exchange between Harrod and Kahn will be surveyed in the third section respectively. Moreover, in August 1934 Harrod received a League of Nations memorandum drafted by Haberler. The memo, which formed the basis for Haberler's subsequent book *Prosperity and Depression* (1936) was also the focus of correspondence between them. This will be dealt with in the final section of this chapter. And, in fact, as will be seen in chapter 4, Harrod's initial positive reaction to Haberler's memo, but his subsequent lack of reference, both to it, and the material it contained, was one of the reasons for Haberler's critical review of *The Trade Cycle*.[2]

Before going on to deal with the exchanges resulting from Harrod's 1934 *Economica* paper, however, an important point regarding these arguments must be taken into account. Amongst the generation of economists active in the 1930s, arguments of substance were conducted on two levels – public and private. Thus, in the case of Robertson's critique of Harrod's 1934 *Economica* paper and Harrod's published reply, for example, their correspondence reveals that not only did Robertson inform Harrod of his intention to publicly comment on the paper, but there was, in fact, a pre-publication exchange of draft material between them. Thus, Harrod saw Robertson's critique, and Robertson both saw Harrod's rejoinder and replied to it in correspondence before they even appeared in print. A similar process also took place in the case of the critical comments made on the paper by Haberler and Bode which appeared in *Economica* in February 1935, along with Harrod's reply to them.[3]

Furthermore, what is interesting to note here is that despite Harrod's 'horror of public debate', as Robertson put it, he was none the less more than willing to attack what he took to be 'unsound views'; even going outside the sphere of academic journals to do so. Indeed, Harrod's letter to the editor of *The Economist* on 'Banking policy and stable prices', published on 6 October 1934, elicited responses from, among others, Haberler and Kaldor, which were published on 10 November 1934, and answered by Harrod in the same issue. Moreover, as will be seen in the second section of this chapter, Harrod actually rewrote his *Economist* reply to Haberler on the basis of Haberler's comments on the first draft of it, which Harrod sent to Haberler for his reponse before its publication.[4]

Thus, in order to comprehend the development of Harrod's ideas and their reception, discussion and analysis of his published academic work has to be supplemented by reference both to the public and private exchanges and correspondence between Harrod and his critics. It is with this perspective in mind that we now turn to examine Harrod's 1934 *Economica* paper and the exchanges surrounding it.

A. CREDIT EXPANSION AND ECONOMIC ADVANCE: THE HARROD-ROBERTSON EXCHANGE, 1934–5

Harrod's 1934 *Economica* paper consisted of two parts. The first part dealt with the criteria which allowed the 'equilibrium of regular advance' of the economic system. The second part, the conclusions of which emanated directly from the first part, focused on the ostensible cause of 'fluctuation' over the trade cycle as seen by a number of contemporary observers, such as Hayek, among others. In this part, as Harrod put it, he dealt with:

> the troubles which have been supposed to be due to the infusion by producer's credits of such new money as is required for the maintenance of the desired price policy. This infusion has been supposed to necessitate the depression of the market below the natural rate of interest with a consequent disturbance of sectional price levels.

This 'infusion of new money' would, in the opinion of Hayek and others, upset 'sectional price levels'; a view which Harrod believed 'to be illusory'.[5]

In contrast, Harrod asserted that 'a rising aggregate income and a stable price level' required that 'the rate at which credit must be expanded in order to maintain the system' be 'equal to the rate at which aggregate income is rising'. He then defined 'the savings of the community' over any period 'as the difference between the value of its total income and the value of the consumable goods purchased therewith', and called this the 'amount of saving . . . S'. Harrod then went on to say that:

> if the banking system keeps its [interest] rates at such a level that the business community borrows X units from it, it will enable the business community to increase its real capital by S units, which is precisely equal to the difference between the income receiver's income and their expenditure on consumable goods.[6]

In other words, 'when a regular advance is under way', as Harrod put it, 'the addition to the real capital of the community' is equal 'to savings', and 'the whole system is perfectly self consistent', thus enabling 'the equilibrium of regular advance to be maintained'.[7]

Robertson initially reacted to Harrod's paper, which, as noted, appeared in the August 1934 issue of *Economica*, in a letter to Harrod dated 27 September 1934. In this, Robertson thanked Harrod for sending him an offprint of the article, but went on to say that:

> Part II seemed to me so misguided that I have written a brief assault which I propose to offer to the editors in the hope of

drawing from you a riposte. I *had* to do this, for if *your* line of reasoning is right, it makes nonsense of everything which I (as well as Hayek and company) have been trying to say for the last eight years. I want to think over the thing again quietly before sending it off . . . but when I do so will suggest to the editor to send it straight to you for reply.[8]

Harrod was seemingly upset by Robertson's intention to publish a critique of his article, but Robertson reassured him in a letter the next week that accompanied the draft of his critique. In this letter, dated 4 October 1934, Robertson said that he was awaiting Harrod's 'riposte with what calmness' he could 'master'. He then went on to say:

I expect to be slaughtered, for you have a much clearer and firmer head than mine. Yet I feel sure that you are missing something of fundamental importance which has been revealed to me, and I think to Meade, Hicks, and Durbin, as well as the stricter Hayekians.[9]

In his letter of 4 October, Robertson also answered Harrod regarding the problem of 'public debate', and how to avoid the unnecessary friction that it could generate. As he put it:

I don't really share your horror of public debate, though I think that in certain hands, that should be nameless, it has tended to become quite unnecessarily rude. So I suggest that when I have seen your draft, we should consider whether there are any phrases in either product which might be toned down as an example to our elders and betters.[10]

It would seem that Harrod sent Robertson the draft of his rejoinder by return of post, and Robertson immediately replied in a letter on 6 October, thanking Harrod for it. With regard to what he called Harrod's 'riposte', he wrote:

It seems to me perfect in tone and temper and I have no emendment to suggest . . . If you have any suggestions, please let me know before we send in the proofs.

In reaction to Harrod's comparing the state of economics to that of the natural sciences, Robertson said:

I think you idealize the state of the other sciences. Surely physics, above all, is in much the same state as we are, i.e. different people trying to build workable pictures which don't always fit in together because the real world is too complicated to be studied directly . . .

Robertson then turned to what he saw as the fundamental difference between his approach and that of Harrod and the reason for it. In his words:

But I admit I am surprised at the size of the gap which . . . yawns between us. It appears to me that your new scheme resembles Maynard's *Treatise* one . . . in that setting out to be an analysis of causes, it ends by being a recognition of results. You are really . . . dealing with a succession of static positions and not as you set out to be, with a process of change. That is a very crude and perhaps erroneous way of putting what I take to be the cause of the gap. At any rate, I feel sure there is a gap, and that it is best, therefore, that it should be brought to light.[11]

Both Robertson's critique and Harrod's rejoinder appeared in the November 1934 issue of *Economica*. As mentioned above, Robertson's criticism focused on the second part of Harrod's article. According to him, Harrod had 'succumbed to the charms' of what Robertson called 'the Grand Monetary Tautology'. On his view, besides being 'long found useful by bankers as a cloak for their misdeeds', it was 'now being rediscovered with alarming frequency by theoretical economists'. As he said:

The bank's balance-sheet always balances: *alias* Savings always equal Investment: *alias* all money which is anywhere must be somewhere . . . Mr. Harrod makes use of this principle to argue that, if real income is increasing, equilibrium is consistent with a policy of expanding bank money at the same rate, so as to maintain stability of the price level.

Robertson then went on to say:

But surely his argument proves too much. The principle can be used equally well to justify the expansion of bank money at any rate whatever, since the newly-created money will always be 'saved' by someone, i.e. will find its way into *somebody's* deposit account. The bank 'has only lent what has been deposited with it': not only is there an asset to be set against every liability, but, what is even more gratifying and disarming, there is a liability to be set against every asset![12]

Robertson then distinguished three possible reasons for the increase in real income in order to 'discover what banking action will maintain equilibrium'. According to him, the increase in income would result from (i) improvement in technology, where the factors of production, in quantity terms would not change; (ii) population growth; and (iii) capital increasing at a higher rate than population growth, viz. capital growth with a constant population.[13]

In order to ensure equilibrium in case (i), in his view 'money' must be 'held constant', so that 'the real value of balances will increase in proportion to the increase in real income, but automatically, and without abstinence on the part of anybody'. In case (ii), Robertson asserted that 'the maintenance of equilibrium would rely' on 'the speed with which balances' of 'each new worker and entrepreneur' would be 'built up', in addition to 'the preferences of the bank with regard to the character of its assets'. Robertson seemed to accept the validity of case (iii). He agreed, as regards this case, with Meade and Hicks, since they also took the view, as he put it 'that population being constant, equilibrium requires constancy of aggregate money income'; this being the 'revelation' he mentioned in his letter to Harrod of 4 October 1934 cited above.

Robertson concluded that:

not every departure from equilibrium has fatal consequences . . . as I have tried to show, there seems to be a long road to travel before we can be quite clear what, under all the various possible conditions of the several kinds of progress, it entails. But I feel pretty sure that we shall get nowhere at all if all kinds of progress are to be smothered up together in the blanket of the Grand Tautology![14]

In his rejoinder, Harrod replied:

Mr. Robertson accuses me of succumbing to the charms of tautology. But I would point out that tautology has played a notable and useful part in economic theory, especially in checking up on fallacies.

Harrod went on to say:

> I feel that Mr. Robertson's difficulties arise from his method of approaching the problem. I suspect that he illicitly assumes that the period prior to that considered was one of complete stationariness. Now, no doubt it is interesting to consider what happens in the transition from a stationary period to one of advance.

However, he continued:

> The problem is complex, since in the general uncertainty about what the banks and other people will do, there is a great deal of indeterminateness with regard to what the representative person will do with his money. Arbitrary assumptions have to be made. And on certain quite reasonable assumptions curious and untoward repercussions may occur, even if a stable money policy is maintained.

Harrod then said:

> But these problems throw little light on a period of regular advance. The difference between the two sets of problems is analogous to the difference between the dynamics of getting a train to move and the dynamics of a train in motion at a constant velocity.

Harrod went on to specify what he identified as the 'dynamic approach' in his 1934 *Economica* paper:

> I was concerned to investigate the latter problem, and for that purpose it is proper to take a cross-sectional view, assuming that the immediately preceding and succeeding periods yield similar developments, and to find out what assumptions with regard to the increase and mutual relations of the factors concerned are self-consistent and consistent with normal economic motives.

Harrod concluded his rejoinder to Robertson by saying:

> One result of this investigation was to show that the assumption of a steady infusion of new credit by the banks is consistent with regular advance and normal monetary behaviour by the general public. This kind of investigation is not likely to provide a ready-made explanation of the trade cycle. But it may well expose the

weakness of erroneous explanations.[15]

A year later, in a letter to Robertson dated 3 October 1935, Harrod returned to the theme, after being again criticised by Robertson for his view on credit expansion and price stability. In this letter, Harrod wrote:

> With regard to the point on which you take me up, I enclose my review of Durbin, of which the second paragraph deals with it. I don't think there can be any disagreement on it between us. The disagreement, if any, must surely be not about the correct solution but about what condition it is least misleading to take for granted when making passing references to the subject.

Harrod continued:

> Perhaps there is this point also. I agree that stable prices may be inflationary if costs are falling. But my criterion is the effect on profit. I do not accept the Hayek analysis of adding new bank advances to saving in order to find investment on the view that new money tends to depress the natural below the market rate. In general, I like to think of saving as equal to investment. Of course, your definition of saving by reference to the preceding period is a possible one, but I have not so far been able to use it in any way in my own thinking. I think I can bring the matter to a head and ask a question which shall be a sort of *experimentium crucius*.

Harrod then said:

> Take it that we are agreed about what is inflation by reference to the result, i.e. the behaviour of prices relatively to money costs. If prices rise relatively to money costs, there is inflation, and not otherwise. Now, when *you* define saving in *your* way, you want, I presume, to be able to say that when investment is greater than saving, there is inflation. In order, therefore, to justify your definition of saving, you have got to show that whenever investment is greater than saving in that sense, prices will be above costs.

He then asked

> But have you ever shown that? Can it, in fact, be shown? But if it is not the case, we have two different kinds of inflation: (1) about

which we agree, of which the criterion is the cost to price relation and (2) depending on your definition of saving, when investment is greater than saving.

Harrod concluded this part of his letter by asking:

What is the relation of these two? Is it undesirable to have inflation of type (2) if inflation of type (1) is not present? If so, why?

In the final part of his letter, Harrod went on to say:

I also suspect that Economics will sink deeper and deeper into some sort of scholastic morass until we all become Wesley Mitchells, and that is rather gloomy. I just can't become a Wesley Mitchell, so what am I to do? My only ray of sunshine is Maynard's book (*GTE*). I think I agree with him (as against you) that his book, *if true*, is pathbreaking.

Harrod ended his letter by making a suggestion in line with his 'committee' outlook for evaluating new economic ideas, as expressed in his earlier letter to Meade, cited in chapter 2. As he put it:

I hold that a strong committee of economists ought at once to be formed to decide whether or not it *is* true, or at least to draw up an agreed list of propositions, embodying, in their own language, what the book is intending. Only if that is done as a preliminary, will there be any possibility of assessing it.[16]

Now, with regard to Harrod's review of Durbin's (1935) book, *The Problem of Credit Policy*, mentioned in his letter to Robertson, it actually appeared two months later, in the December 1935 issue of *EJ*. Suffice it to say, at this point, that in it Harrod criticised Durbin's view that 'the maintenance of a constant level of money income per head' is the most desirable 'choice of policy'; a view similar to that also 'revealed' to Robertson, Hicks, and Meade, as Robertson himself had mentioned in his letter to Harrod a year before.[17]

To sum up, then, Harrod's specification in his rejoinder of the dynamic nature of his approach – as distinct from that of Robertson – does show that his 1934 *Economica* paper can indeed be considered as his first attempt at dynamic analysis, as he later maintained. But, there were other 'attacks' on his publicly expressed views, and on the paper itself, and it is to these critiques that we now turn.[18]

B. HARROD, HABERLER, BODE, AND KALDOR: PUBLIC AND PRIVATE DEBATE ON THE 'PROGRESSIVE' ECONOMY

Over the period August 1934 to March 1935, Harrod corresponded with Haberler, among others, on a number of areas of mutual interest. This correspondence ranged from discussions on Harrod's 1934 *QJE* and *Economica* papers and *Economist* letter, to Haberler's League of Nations memorandum and his critique of Harrod's views in *The Economist* and *Economica* respectively. Since these letters occasionally dealt with a number of issues, for the sake of clarity in presentation I will focus upon the parts of the correspondence dealing with Harrod's *Economica* paper and *Economist* letter in this section, while those parts of the Harrod-Haberler correspondence dealing with Haberler's League of Nations memorandum will be presented in section D below.

Interestingly enough, Harrod actually sent an offprint of his August 1934 *Economica* article with an initial positive response to the request for comments from Haberler on his own League of Nations memorandum. This is attested to by a letter from Haberler to Harrod dated 3 September 1934, in which he thanked Harrod for sending a copy of his *Economica* paper, which Haberler promised to read with care and to let Harrod know what he thought of it. In his letter Haberler went on to say that he did not blindly admire Hayek's theory, and that he had concluded that a degree of price stability by means of stabilisation policy was not as bad an idea as he originally thought. Haberler also mentioned that he had disagreed with Hayek's argument against price stability when the economy stopped progressing; and this, in a paper he had written for a festschrift for Speithoff.[19]

Haberler then told Harrod that he had read his May 1934 *QJE* article (Harrod, 1934b) and enjoyed it greatly, especially the first two parts, with which he agreed. Haberler disagreed, however, with Harrod's views in the third part of that paper, which dealt with the implications of the doctrines of imperfect competition for trade cycle theory. According to Haberler, while Harrod's treatment of the cycle given in the paper was possibly correct logically, it did not, in his view, have any link with the business cycle in actuality.[20]

Later that month Haberler sent Harrod detailed comments on his *Economica* paper. Haberler stated that while he liked the first part and agreed with what Harrod said there, he could not understand – in the literal sense – the second part of the paper. Haberler went on to take issue with both the fundamental assumptions of Harrod's theory and their meaning, and with Harrod's definitions, especially that of saving. Harrod informed Haberler in a letter dated 19 October that Robertson had 'written a reply' to his *Economica* paper, and that he had 'written a rejoinder' which, in his opinion, made his 'position much clearer than the original part II of the *Economica* article', and promised to send him an offprint.[21]

About a month before, however, on 23 September 1934, Harrod had sent a letter to the editor of *The Economist* on banking policy and price stability. This was published in *The Economist* issue of 6 October. On 18 October Haberler sent a letter to the editor of *The Economist* replying to the points Harrod had made. This, along with additional replies from Kaldor, Stafford (who later reviewed Harrod's *Trade Cycle* for the *Manchester School*, as will be seen), among others, and Harrod's reply to them, appeared in *The Economist* issue of 10 November 1934.[22]

In the meantime, in a letter on 21 October, Harrod had sent a copy of the draft of his proposed reply to Haberler for comment. Haberler replied in a letter on 25 October, in which he said that he would not alter the text of his own *Economist* letter, a copy of which was sent to Harrod, it would seem, by the editor of *The Economist* himself, in order that Harrod could reply. According to Haberler, he was not convinced by Harrod's reply. Moreover, Haberler asserted that it was written in a language he could not even comprehend, and claimed that others to whom he showed it also could not understand the points Harrod was trying to make. Haberler then suggested that Harrod turn to Marschak so as to obtain both his assessment of the disagreement between them and of Harrod's *Economist* reply. Haberler, in turn, focused on two aspects of Harrod's draft reply. The first of these was, in his view, Harrod's 'unconventional' definitions of savings and income. The second was Harrod's notion of the 'equality' of savings and investment in light of credit creation and contraction by banks.[23]

As it turned out, Harrod did alter, somewhat, the text of his reply to Haberler, dated 31 October, that appeared a fortnight later in *The Economist* issue of 10 November 1934. He made it much clearer, albeit admitting his rather unconventional – for the time – treatment of the notion of savings. For, as Harrod put it, the definition of savings he was 'implying' was indeed 'somewhat curious' in comparison to Haberler's definition. However, this was the core of the disagreement between them. Harrod, for his part, was willing to recognise several possible definitions of savings, while Haberler was only willing to accept the 'Robertsonian' definition, as will be seen below.[24]

In fact, Harrod wrote Haberler on 29 October, two days before sending the finalised text of his reply to *The Economist*. A few days later, on 2 November, Haberler replied to Harrod. On 5 November, Harrod responded, and Haberler answered him a week later, on 12 November 1934. These letters are crucial in understanding the story so far, and thus deserve detailed consideration here.

In his letter of 2 November, Haberler agreed with Harrod that the definitional problem regarding the term 'saving' was crucial, and blamed Keynes for the confusion surrounding it. This, on Haberler's view, emanated from what Haberler called Keynes's 'unusual' redefinition of the term. According to Haberler, this caused the disagreement between himself and Harrod, which was more one of exposition than substance.[25]

Haberler went on to say that Keynes neither discovered nor presented anything new in his *Treatise* explanation of the business cycle. He admitted, however, that the *Treatise* did contain a number of fruitful lines of approach to the problem, albeit being occasionally contradictory to their theoretical bases. Haberler then presented a number of cases to try to convince Harrod of the correctness and clarity of his view on the issue of newly-created money being paid out as income as a question of 'periods'.

Haberler concluded his letter of 2 November by suggesting to Harrod that he show their correspondence to Marschak and Opie, who, in Haberler's view, could both make things, in his view, clearer for Harrod and, in effect, adjudicate between their respective views. Haberler also sent Harrod a copy of a letter he had written to Lindahl on a similar point of disagreement between them, in which Haberler asked Lindahl to send Harrod a copy of a paper giving Lindahl's approach to the problem, which later appeared as a note on the 'dynamic pricing problem'.[26]

Harrod replied to Haberler in a letter dated 5 November 1934, in which he said:

I am very interested in your idea of arbitration. I have myself often advocated that something of this sort should be done in cases of disputes among economists. I think perhaps 'conciliation', to use the language of industrial disputes, would be more appropriate in the case of academic disagreements since 'a man convinced against his will is of the same opinion still'.

Harrod went on to say:

> I will certainly raise this question with Marschak and Opie when I
> get an opportunity, *but*, though open to conviction on any point, I
> still feel very far indeed from the threshold of conviction on this. I
> tried to bring my state of mind before you when I said in an earlier
> letter that I feel on this as I think you would feel if asked to deny
> the truth of a properly stated quantity theory.

Harrod then took issue with Haberler's treatment of newly-created
money and income as a question of 'periods'. As he put it:

> I do not think the period in which the newly created money is paid
> out as someone's income is the following period but a simultaneous
> period, and I do not think what happens then is another question
> but *the* question.

Harrod went on:

> This brings me back to my point that unless you define savings or
> investment in a 'funny' way the . . . assumption that savings equals
> investment, which is nothing more than the assumption that the
> amount of commodity sold must be equal to the amount bought, is
> true.

He then said:

> I quite agree that it is not possible to find out something about the
> real world by redefining terms, but it may be possible to *explain* a
> discovery already made by using terms defined in a somewhat
> different way. This, I think is what Keynes did. But such a method
> of exposition is attended with danger because the unusual defini-
> tions may bewilder the mind of the reader.

Harrod continued on to say:

> This has happened with the *Treatise*. Very few (even of the dis-
> tinguished economists) have followed what Keynes has said there.
> In particular, Keynes has given popularity to the notion that
> investment and saving need not be equal; many of those taking up
> this idea forgetting that it presumed an *unusual* definition of

saving, and would be quite invalid on an ordinary definition of saving. But Keynes' doctrines may be explained in other terms without using his 'curious' definitions.

Harrod then said:

> I do not want, at this moment, to play the part of defender of Keynes. All I said in my earlier letter was that his views ought to be recorded as an interesting contribution to trade cycle theory *not yet refuted*.

Harrod concluded his letter to Haberler of 5 November 1934 by summarising what he took to be the central message of Keynes's *Treatise*, counterpointing it to that of Hayek. In Harrod's words:

> the essence of his [Keynes'] view is this I think. If a market rate of interest gets established, which is not consistent with regular advance, or which, I think we may therefore say, is not equal to the equilibrium rate, no forces are at once brought into being to bring it *back* to the equilibrium rate. This is contrary to what usually happens in a market. If he is right in this, he has got onto the track of the kind of phenomenon which is required to explain the cycle. I quite agree with the point well expressed by Hayek in his *Monetary Theory [and the Trade Cycle]* that general equilibrium analysis leads us to *expect* that if there is a departure from equilibrium at some point in the system, forces come into play leading to a restoration. Yet the cycle phenomenon suggests a wider and wider departure. Now, Hayek's *own* explanation I regard as totally fallacious for reasons already given. Keynes gives a *kind* of explanation, but Hayek *desiderates* and I am not yet convinced. I know of no published refutation, except on some points of detail, that Keynes' explanation is wrong.[27]

Haberler answered Harrod on 12 November 1934. In this letter he rejected Harrod's points regarding the way income was spent over or during the period, and accused him of misusing the language to invent what, on his view, were artificial explanations and an unconventional terminology which generated, in Haberler's opinion, 'absurd' results. Haberler then went on to attack Harrod's advocacy of the equality of savings and investment which could, according to him, only be attained by the substitution of a set of 'absurd' definitions for those acceptable to him and to Robertson.[28]

Haberler and Bode's comment on Harrod's views appeared in the February 1935 issue of *Economica*, accompanied by Harrod's rejoinder. Their comment was a comprehensive critique of the position Harrod took in his August 1934 paper, in his public exchanges with Robertson in *Economica*, and with Haberler in *The Economist*, besides being based, on their own account, on correspondence with Harrod, in which he ostensibly confirmed some of their arguments, at least according to them.[29]

But it seems Harrod had, in fact, been sent a copy of their comment by the editor of *Economica* in order to prepare a rejoinder, and as a result, had complained to Haberler and Bode that his views had been misrepresented by them. This is evident from Bode's letters to Harrod during January 1935 – while Haberler, it seems, was away from the League of Nations office in Geneva. In these letters Bode told Harrod that the text of their comment would be altered according to his wishes, and that his comments on it would be taken into account in the finalised version. Moreover, Bode told Harrod that he and Haberler had previously talked over their comment with Kaldor, who had been in Geneva, and who agreed with their views on the matter.[30]

Upon his return to Geneva, Haberler wrote Harrod to express regret that he had taken their comment as misrepresenting him. Haberler hoped that all the text to which Harrod objected had, in the meantime, been removed by Bode, and sent, for Harrod's scrutiny, the final form of their comment. Haberler went on to say that, on his view, it was Harrod who had misrepresented Kaldor's view, and that this had been confirmed by Kaldor himself while in Geneva, and thus there was a mutual misunderstanding of their respective positions. Haberler ended his letter by stating that while he still disagreed with Harrod's definitional approach to savings and the conclusions reached on its basis, he hoped their comment was now in a form that neither misrepresented nor offended him.[31]

Interestingly enough, Haberler had also seen Harrod's rejoinder before its publication, and privately responded to the points made there, as is evident from the exchange of letters between them in February 1935. For example, in a letter to Harrod dated 7 February, Haberler stressed the importance of period analysis and the length of the period chosen for the argument, but also acknowledged the fact that Harrod, for his part, did not accept period analysis. In his response to Harrod's reply of 9 February, he said that in the *Economica* rejoinder, Harrod either evaded or left unanswered the arguments made in the comment. Rather than deal with their substance, in Haberler's opinion, in his rejoinder Harrod had spoken about 'absurdity' and 'inconsistency' in the arguments they had presented in the comment. Finally, Haberler asked Harrod, as an aside, whether he had seen Hicks's article on 'simplifying' the theory of money. According to Haberler, the economists with whom he was in contact in London liked it very much and thought that it opened new horizons in monetary theory, although he himself was somewhat disappointed by it.[32]

Harrod answered Haberler on 28 February 1935. In this letter Harrod replied to Haberler's accusation that he had sidestepped the arguments offered by Haberler in support of his Robertsonian-type definition of saving, Harrod preferring in Haberler's view, to call it 'absurd'. As Harrod put it:

> With regard to definition (4) of my rejoinder [Haberler's definition of savings], you speak as if my saying it absurd amounted to the same thing as saying that it was inconsistent. But there is a radical difference between the two allegations, any confusion about which might lead to hopeless troubles in economic analysis. A definition may be self-consistent and yet absurd because it violently offends against reasonable use of language. I suggested that definition (4) did this because, according to it, if A and B get an equal increment of income coming on top of an equal income, and if A spends the whole income of his previous period, while B spends the whole income of his present period, they are said to save the same amount. This appears to me to do violence to ordinary usage.

Harrod ended his letter to Haberler of 28 February by saying:

> Alas, Hicks' article is waiting to be read by me, but it is not yet read. I will let you know what I think of it.[33]

In their comment, Haberler and Bode advocated the sole usage of the Robertsonian concept of savings for the purpose of economic analysis and determination of banking policy, since it was, in their view 'much more in harmony with current usage, than the concept advocated by Harrod. In contrast to this, as Harrod asserted in his rejoinder, 'what banking policy will serve to prevent crisis and depression is a question of fact and cannot be decided by terminological wrangling'. Harrod continued on to say that he hoped that those who read his rejoinder would conclude that the Robertson-Haberler-Bode approach was inadequate to serve as a criterion for determining banking policy since, as he said 'there are many possible definitions of saving. The fundamental problem cannot be solved by enquiring which is most conformable to ordinary usage, but which, if embodied in the criterion, will lead to the right result'. Harrod concluded, therefore, that the argument he put forward in his article, that is, 'that stable prices are in certain circumstances quite consistent with regular progress' was still valid and, as he put it, remained 'unimpaired'.[34]

C. HARROD, KAHN, AND THE 'ADVANCING COMMUNITY'

Over the same period that he was engaged in correspondence with Robertson and Haberler regarding his 1934 *Economica* paper, Harrod was also corresponding with Richard Kahn on issues arising from it. In fact, between October 1934 and January 1935 Kahn became involved in the exchange between Harrod and Robertson, and even more so in the ongoing debate between Harrod and Haberler. In the latter case, Kahn's involvement extended to correspondence with Haberler on his controversy with Harrod and reading Harrod's rejoinder to Haberler and Bode in draft and providing him with detailed comments on it.[35]

For example, in a letter dated 22 October 1934, Kahn told Harrod that he had more sympathy with the second part than with the first part of Harrod's *Economica* article. This was in direct contrast to the positions of Robertson and Haberler, who agreed with the first part of the paper, but were in complete disagreement with the second part. In another letter to Harrod dated 28 October, Kahn told Harrod that he was 'giving away points' to the 'Hayekians' by agreeing with certain points made by Robertson and Haberler. However, in a letter to Harrod a few days later, on 1 November, Kahn had to admit that while Keynes's *Treatise* definition of savings was, in his view, badly chosen, the new definition of saving, as Saving equals Investment was, in Kahn's opinion, a superior one, since investment was always 'self-financing' and there was thus never any question where the money came from. According to Kahn, the new definition was also very helpful for trade cycle analysis since, in his view, given the propensity to save, the problem was reduced to a study of the causes of change in the rate of investment. In this letter, Kahn also mentioned the letter he had also received from Haberler regarding Harrod's views.[36]

Some two weeks later, on 13 November, Kahn wrote Harrod on issues involving the treatment of the rate of interest in his *Economica* paper, while on 24 November, he again wrote Harrod regarding what were, in his view, problems in that paper and also mentioned correspondence he had received from Haberler on it.[37]

Harrod realised, at this point, that he could rely upon Kahn for support in his debate with Haberler, and thus decided to send a copy of his rejoinder to the comment of Haberler and Bode on to Kahn for his assessment. Kahn sent his detailed comments to Harrod in a letter dated 8 January 1935, in which he expressed support for Harrod's position as against that of Robertson, on the one hand, and Haberler, on the other.[38]

Interestingly enough, Kahn and Haberler engaged in a similar controversy that emanated out of Kahn's review of Haberler's 'enquiry into the trade cycle' conducted for the League of Nations and entitled *Prosperity and Depression* (Kahn, 1937). In his comments on the review, published in the *EJ* in June 1938, Haberler took issue with Kahn on the same points on which he had disagreed with Harrod over three years earlier. Haberler also took the opportunity to again reprimand Harrod for making 'exactly the same mistake as Mr. Kahn' – this in Harrod's review of Lundberg's book (1937); a review which will be dealt with in detail below. Suffice it to say here that, in contrast to Kahn's later critique of Haberler's *Prosperity and Depression*, Harrod's reaction to Haberler's earlier League of Nations memorandum, on which it was based, was an important – albeit up to now unknown – element in the relationship between Harrod and Haberler. And this, as manifest in Haberler's reaction to, and review of, Harrod's *Trade Cycle*, as will be seen below. It is to the Harrod-Haberler correspondence on this memorandum, therefore, that we now turn our attention.[39]

D.   HARROD AND HABERLER: PRIVATE CORRESPONDENCE ON PROSPERITY, DEPRESSION, AND THE TRADE CYCLE

In a letter dated 20 August 1934, Haberler asked Harrod whether he would be willing to comment on or criticise the memorandum he had written for the League of Nations which dealt with the possible causes of recurrent periods of depression. Haberler said in his letter that he had sent a copy of the memo to Harrod, in addition to other well-known economists in the field. Haberler added that the memo being circulated was in draft form, and thus would be expanded and worked out in much more detail after the reactions of the experts to whom it had been sent, and on the basis of additional empirical work (Tinbergen's studies) conducted by the economic intelligence service of the League which was being supported by the Rockefeller Foundation at the time.[40]

Harrod's initial positive reply was responded to by Haberler on 3 September, who said that he would gladly receive any comments Harrod would care to make. Haberler went on to say in this letter that he would especially appreciate it if Harrod could advise him if he had correctly represented the various trade and business cycle theories in his memo.[41]

Harrod commented in greater detail on Haberler's memo in a letter dated 19 October 1934, to which Haberler replied a week later, on 25 October 1934. Because these letters are crucial for an understanding of the relationship between them, and may also reflect Haberler's influence upon the development of Harrod's thought during this important period, they are dealt with here at length. In his letter of 19 October, Harrod wrote:

> I was very greatly impressed with the masterly ability of your League of Nations memorandum . . . May I first make this suggestion? I do not know how you intend to proceed, but I feel that your powerful analysis has cleared up so much in regard to these theories that it could take us much further.

Harrod continued:

> I suggest a second, theoretical part, in which, as a preliminary to verification you probe still further into their logical relation. By doing so you might reach a further stage of simplification with regard to the logical schema of actual or possible theories. This would, of course, be inappropriate in your first part, in which you are still trying to show us the theories conceived by the authors. In part II, as I think of it, the theories would no longer be recognizable as Hawtrey's, Speithoff's etc., but would contain all the logically valid elements of those theories rearranged by you.

Harrod then commented in detail on a number of specific points with which he both agreed and disagreed in Haberler's draft memo, but went on to criticise him for not giving enough attention to Keynes's work. In his words:

I don't think you have attached, in spite of two interesting references, sufficient importance to the view of Keynes. You may be sceptical of this, thinking that I have come under his 'spell'. To this I can honestly plead that I don't think that is so. If his main view is right – of course it may be proved wrong, but I don't think it has been so yet, and it can't be dismissed as obviously so like those of Douglas and co. – I think it must be of importance.

Harrod then outlined for Haberler what he took to be the 'orthodoxy' Keynes was trying to disprove. As he put it:

The orthodox view is that if a market price diverges from a natural, forces are set up to bring the market price towards the natural. The case of interest is a special application. Ah, but in the case of credit, it may be objected, this tendency is obstructed if the banks artificially increase or decrease supply by their credit policy.

He continued:

But Keynes claims to show that the rates do not tend to converge, even if the banks *do not* artificially alter their supply. Surely, if that is right, it is very interesting and important.

Harrod then made a point which foreshadowed his later concern with the problems surrounding the 'centrifugal tendency' of an economy which departs from its 'warranted growth' path. In Harrod's words:

The puzzle of the cycle is that, when a departure from equilibrium occurs, the system tends to move further from, and not back to the equilibrium position. This movement seems contrary to the principles of supply and demand.

Harrod went on to say:

Now, if Keynes shows that these principles don't operate in the case of interest which clearly lies at the heart of the system, it would seem that he is supplying just the very kind of explanation that is required. Why don't the principles of supply and demand operate? Well, that simply takes one to the heart of the theory, where I can't go in this letter. Suffice it to say here that I do feel a lacunae in your summary in that you do not note that here is someone professing to give, by reasoning not obviously and palapably absurd, just the very kind of explanation which a rational account of the trade cycle requires. Mentioning one or two side points, you pass entirely over the central point. I do feel you need an extra section calling attention to this notable claim somewhere. Otherwise, you are treating him like Douglas, which is harsh.

Harrod then mentioned to Haberler the 'revised' version of the *Treatise* that Keynes was in the process of completing and said:

Unfortunately, it is no good urging you to a more intensive study of the *Treatise* when a revised draft of the theory is about to appear. Perhaps you would like to have an advance copy?

Harrod concluded his letter to Haberler by saying:

I hope I haven't bored you about Keynes. You may feel that at this point you don't see a way to a final critical estimate of these theories. But I think that is an additional reason for a paragraph giving a faithful, if you like, a photographic rendering.[42]

Haberler replied to Harrod on 25 October 1934. In this letter, Haberler told Harrod that the changes he suggested accorded with his own intentions, and that he was glad that Harrod had confirmed his intended approach. More important, however, were the references made in this letter to what Haberler called the 'principle of accelerated demand' and 'the acceleration principle'; a point to which I will return in chapter 4. With regard to his treatment of Keynes, Haberler reassured Harrod that he believed the *Treatise* to contain a considerable number of what he called 'fruitful' ideas. However, Haberler said that he still found difficulty in accepting the theoretical explanation of the trade cycle manifest in the 'fundamental equations' as they appeared in Keynes's *Treatise*, since he could not accept them at all as a convincing explanation of business cycle phenomena.[43]

Haberler took up Harrod's suggestion regarding an addition to his memorandum in the form of a second part which would synthesise the various theories of the trade cycle he analysed. In fact, as is evident from the published version of the memorandum which appeared in book form as *Prosperity and Depression*, Haberler added a second part, which he called a 'synthetic exposition relating to the nature and causes of business cycles'. On the basis of Harrod's suggestion, Haberler also expanded somewhat his analysis of Keynes's *Treatise* in the first edition of his book. Moreover, he widened his treatment of Keynes's theories to an even greater extent later, when he dealt with the *General Theory*.[44]

Haberler's review of Harrod's book *The Trade Cycle* appeared three years later, in the October 1937 issue of *JPE*. However, this critique – which will be dealt with in detail in chapter 4 – was not Haberler's initial reaction to Harrod's book. For, in fact, Haberler had written a letter to Harrod on 8 January 1937, in which he expressed his feelings upon having completed his first reading of Harrod's book.[45]

Haberler opened his letter by telling Harrod that he liked his book very much, and that there were many things in it which reminded him of his own treatment of similar problems in his own book which was then in press, and was based on his earlier League of Nations memorandum. Haberler went on to focus upon the many specific similarities of emphasis and explanation between the material presented in his book and that of Harrod. Haberler then pointed out that, both in his memorandum and his book, he had also dealt with the interaction of what Harrod called 'the Relation' and the 'Multiplier', albeit using slightly different terms. For, as Haberler saw it, this interaction was nothing more that what he called the 'Wicksellian process', although he did not suggest that Harrod had not broadened its scope in his presentation. Haberler concluded the letter by saying that most of the points on which he disagreed with Harrod emanated from differences in terminology between them, such as Harrod's insistence on S (Saving) being defined as I (Investment).[46]

Now, whether Harrod was actually either influenced by Haberler's views or the material he presented in his 1934 League of Nations memorandum is a moot point. Suffice it to say here that, in my view, it is more likely that the opposite is the case. This can be seen by referring to Harrod's detailed comments on specific points of agreement and disagreement with Haberler – as manifest in his letter to Haberler of 19 October 1934. Moreover, in the process of putting together *The Trade Cycle*, Harrod relied heavily upon the comments and suggestions of Meade especially, in addition to Allen, Robertson, Kahn, and even Henderson. Thus, any input he may have received from Haberler's 1934 memo – including the 'Wicksellian process', that is, the interaction between Harrod's 'relation' (accelerator) and multiplier – would have undergone a concentrated process of conceptual distillation and filtration, so that by the time Harrod's ideas reached fruition in the published version of *The Trade Cycle*, anything that appeared there would have had only tenuous links with Haberler's memo.[47]

4 The Trade Cycle: Group, Critics and Critiques

During 1936 and 1937, Harrod was, for the most part, occupied with the preparation, presentation, defence, and further development of the ideas and approach he outlined in his book *The Trade Cycle* (Harrod, 1936a). To this end he was in contact with a number of colleagues over the period. This was not only for the purpose of explaining his ideas in general and obtaining the reactions of his colleagues to them, but also for the more formal task of providing him with critical feedback to their specific written form, that is, their reactions to, and comments on, the draft manuscript of his book. Furthermore, after its publication he corresponded with colleagues on the further development of the approach he outlined there and its implications.

In order to give a clear and comprehensive account of the process, the primary source material – which consists of previously unpublished correspondence and documents found in the Harrod papers and in the papers of James Meade – and the secondary supplementary published material is arranged and presented in this chapter as follows. In the first section Harrod's correspondence with Robertson and Henderson over the period 1936–7 regarding his ideas and the book itself will be outlined, and the main issues raised in these letters summarised. In the second section the extensive correspondence between Harrod and Meade on the draft chapters of the *Trade Cycle* will be surveyed, and the comments of both Meade and Allen on the manuscript will be summarised. The most important of Meade's 'Notes' on the draft manuscript of the book, however, will be cited almost in its entirety (Meade, 1936a). This previously unknown and unpublished document found in Harrod's papers is, as will be seen, not only one of the keys to understanding the evolution of Harrod's ideas, but possibly one of the most important missing links in the overall development of the growth research programme in economics.

In the third section the effects on Harrod of the September 1936 Oxford Conference – to which he went expecting to receive professional approval of his *Trade Cycle* approach to dynamising Keynes, but which, instead, was overshadowed by Hicks's IS–LM diagram – are dealt with. In addition, evidence of 'trade cycle group' activity and discussion between Harrod and Meade months after the publication of the book is also presented. In the final section of this chapter the critiques and reviews of Harrod's *Trade Cycle* will be surveyed and summarised. These range from Keynes's post-publication critique and Hawtrey's treatment of it in his book *Capital and Employment* (1937), and the correspondence between Harrod and them surrounding their critiques, to Hansen's *QJE* review (Hansen, 1937) and its subsequent revised version in his book *Full Recovery or Stagnation?* (Hansen, 1938), to the reviews of the *Trade Cycle* by Robertson, Robinson, Tinbergen, and Haberler, among others, such as Stafford, Wynne, and even Hugh Gaitskell.

A. ROBERTSON AND HENDERSON: CORRESPONDENCE ON THE TRADE CYCLE AND ITS IMPLICATIONS

Harrod and Robertson

By early May 1936, Harrod had not only completed the first draft of his book, but most or all of its chapters had also been read and commented upon by Meade, Allen, and Hubert Henderson, as will be seen below. In a series of letters between May 1936 and October 1937, Harrod wrote to Robertson about *The Trade Cycle* and discussed with him the implications of the ideas he had presented there. In his opening letter dated 18 May 1936, Harrod told Robertson how he dealt with his views in the book. Harrod did this, as he put it, in order not to offend Robertson or to be charged with either misinterpretation, misrepresentation, or not doing justice to his views. In Harrod's words:

> The new book is to be called *The Trade Cycle: an essay*. Perhaps one ought not to publish in such a form. Many parts are incompletely worked out but I do feel a strong urge to see it out now. I feel that I have succeeded in making a new synthesis in trade cycle theory and also that there are beginnings of rudiments of what might be called a theory of economic dynamics.

He continued:

> I do not discuss Maynard much, except on certain points of difference between the *Treatise* and the *General Theory*. But I do

assume certain points of his, especially the doctrine of the multiplier. To do this has been a natural and inevitable part of my progress of thought. Certain things, though by no means all, in his theory have already become a sort of second nature. Am I damned?

Harrod went on to say:

What I greatly fear is that this use I have made, which has been almost half-conscious, may stick out when you read it and give offence and even distract your attention from what is essential to my argument. I do hope that it won't.

Harrod continued:

I have a section in which your name is repeated often. I even use the word Robertsonian; is this offensive? The section is not a criticism of you, or even, I fear, a summary and appraisment. I have merely used a view of yours as a theme for an exercise. May I quote the passage in which I introduce it?

Harrod then cited a long excerpt from the draft manuscript of his book which dealt with Robertson's definition of saving. In it he gave the reasons why, although he didn't reject Robertson's definition outright, he still could not use it in his book. The reasons for this, according to Harrod, emanated from the fact that it was more convenient for him to use a single definition of saving in the book, and that Robertson's period-based analysis would have made the task of specifying his 'fundamental principles' more complex and difficult to understand. Harrod thereby reassured Robertson that the treatment of his period-based view of saving in the book was not 'an introduction to an onslaught'. Harrod then told Robertson that he would 'be very glad to know' whether he thought his treatment 'fair'. Finally, Harrod maintained that 'if there is no injustice in the quoted passages, there is, I think, no injustice anywhere, since the rest is an analysis of consequences of this for my own theory'. It would seem that Robertson did not, in fact, object to Harrod's treatment of his view of saving, for the same passage appeared, with only very slight modification, in the published version of the book.[1]

Three days later, on 21 May 1936, Harrod again wrote to Robertson to say that he wanted to send him a copy of the draft manuscript too. However, as he put it:

The worst of it is that I want to get it off [to the publisher] fairly soon. One copy I am working on, one is held by Maurice Allen . . . [and] one by Hubert Henderson, to whom it is a red rag. He may have rent it into a thousand pieces for all I know . . . His reaction to it, when first manifested last term did, I confess, rather put me out. His great objection was that I made the wholly 'unrealistic' assumption that the entrepreneur tries to maximise profit. I dare say it is unrealistic, but what can the poor theorist do?[2]

Harrod wrote the next substantial letter to Robertson regarding his book on 25 December 1936. It would seem that while most Englishmen were preoccupied with either the abdication or Christmas festivities, Harrod was more concerned – and justifiably so – with the more serious problems of the trade cycle, economic growth, and related issues. In his letter, Harrod wrote that:

any analysis of the rate of interest is nonsense in which the rate of acceleration of income does not appear as a term in the equation by which the rate of interest is determined.

He then turned to the implication of this as manifest in one of the reviews of his book, that of Joan Robinson. As he said:

This absolute necessity for a dynamic analysis of interest and the consequent invalidity of all static (including classical) theories is a point which Joan Robinson doesn't seem to have cottoned on to in her review of my book which I have just read (a very decent review on the whole!).

Harrod continued:

Now, in certain circumstances, full employment requires a steady fall in the rate of interest, but the long term rate is of such a nature that we cannot contemplate a steadily falling rate as a normal feature in the equilibrium of the steady advance. One requirement of equilibrium is that anticipation should be justified. If the fall in the rate is *not* foreseen, the position will not be an equilibrium one. If it *is* foreseen, it will be anticipated in present values, and hence it will not occur. I believe this to be the fundamental flaw in the system. Maynard has made an important contribution to the elucidation of this.

He then went on to say, however:

> Greatly as I admire Maynard, Joan R. emphasizes my indebted-
> ness to him a little too much for my taste. Much of my book was
> thought out before I saw the proofs of his, and even apart from
> that, there seems to be more independent matter than she is
> inclined to allow. But this is the sort of thing one is bound to feel
> about oneself. Her mind readily accepts what is Maynard's and
> tends not to notice what is not.

He continued:

> What I feel about people broadly in your position is that you cling a
> little too tenaciously to the view that the classical analysis shows
> that the system must be self-adjusting in the end. You are inclined,
> therefore, to emphasize prices . . . and miscalculations. I believe
> the flaw to be more deeply seated on the lines suggested above and
> therefore feel that Maynard's bother is to some extent justified,
> though as I think I have repeatedly said, I sympathize with you in
> deflating his manner of emphasizing that and the needless polemics.

Harrod then turned to his IS–LM paper (Harrod, 1937a) and
Pigou's notes on it to illustrate the problematic treatment of growth
in what he called 'the classical system'. As he put it:

> When I thought of the classical system in that article, it was not
> Marshall whom I have principally in mind (I was amused to
> observe in Pigou's notes that he assumes as a matter of course that
> when I speak of traditional economists, I mean Marshall, though I
> took the trouble to insert a list of names in that article to show that
> my case is more catholic); but, this will seem strange, Bowley's
> *Mathematical Framework of Economics* (not that I like mathemat-
> ical foundations particularly, and I am unable to understand a lot
> of the detail in Bowley, so ill-educated am I).

He went on to say:

> But it seems to me to crystallize what is essential in the somewhat
> amorphous traditional confines of doctrine (I remember Frank
> Ramsey saying that he thought it a clumsy work, and he could do

much better. I told him he ought to, and he *did* toy with the idea.
Alas; but I expect he would have made it much too difficult.
Incidentally, Sisson of the OUP once told me that Bowley's book
was the only one of their post-war publications which Soviet Russia
had ordered in bulk).

Harrod continued:

Well now, in that book there is no reference to rates of growth, and
that being so, according to me, there ought to have been no
reference to the volume of saving. He should have made his
analysis, assuming certain quantities in capital goods, and left it at
that. He should have made it plain that the analysis was incomplete, since saving does in fact occur, but that since economics has
evolved no recognized techniques for dealing with acceleration,
the theory of saving could not, for the time being, be included in
this work.

Harrod then went on to outline his views on (a) what he saw as the
state of economics in his day and the distinct areas of possible
economic inquiry – static and dynamic; (b) what he took to be the
continuous nature of the development of economic thought; (c) what
constituted, in his opinion, the difference between his approach and
that of Keynes as regards the limits of the 'traditional theory', that is,
where the classical theory 'broke down'; and (d) the place of Keynes's *General Theory* approach in the scheme of economic theory.
Harrod was also giving Robertson here a 'taste' of what he would
later express in more depth in his 1938 'Scope and method' paper.
This is clear from the text of the letter, in which he went on to say:

Now may I put my idea about the position of Economics? I hope
you don't mind my going on so long. We have a body of static
doctrine which is a considerable intellectual achievement which we
can respect; and all honour to those minds who have successively
built it up. We have also in traditional economics certain dynamic
elements. For instance, Ricardo said that profits tend to fall and
rents to rise, and Marshall has certain things in Book VI. But these
types of propositions are all either very vague or very unsatisfactory.

Harrod then said:

I take it that the moment has come, and such moments are apt to come in the development of the science – this implies no discredit to those who have gone before – when a certain specialization and reordering of concepts is called for. In this case, it seems to me all to depend on the division into statics and dynamics. So far as the dynamics is concerned, all, or almost all the constructive work still lies before us. Nothing very systematic has been achieved. Writers like yourself have thrown out valuable hints. Maynard has thrown out a big hint. I have tried to make a tiny little nibble in my last book.

However, Harrod continued:

These hints and strivings cannot be divided into the orthodox and unorthodox, the traditional and the rebellious, *since there is no tradition against which to rebel*. The only rebellion consists of saying, or rather recognizing, that this reorientation is now necess-ary. The difference is perhaps between those who imply it and those who explicitly recognize it.

Harrod then added – as an aside – what he took to be the fundamen-tal difference between his approach to the 'classics' and that of Keynes. As he put it:

You will perceive that I don't quite like Maynard's distinction between his *General Theory* and the classical theory as covering the *special* case of full employment. The classical theory provides the mechanism for full employment, or is prepared to specify why the mechanism doesn't work – wages too high; *whereas I think the classical theory breaks down in not analyzing growth*. It is when you come to that, that you see that there *cannot* be full employment, however high or low wages in certain circumstances.

Harrod then turned to the pedagogical problem and the issue of demarcation that emerged from, as he put it, Keynes's macrostatic approach, as against that of his own macrodynamic views. In Har-rod's words:

Now the thing, I respectfully suggest to you as Chairman of the Board of [the] Faculty [of Economics and Politics in the University of Cambridge] is this. You say that there is a well recognized and solidly founded body of doctrine which the young may learn like Euclid – static economics. There is another very imperfectly explored field about which various modern writers – Robertson, Keynes etc., have thrown out hints – dynamic economics. All this is very much in the melting pot. We don't know how it will develop. Some think one set of concepts more valuable; others, another. But we don't know how it will all work out, and it is impossible to dogmatise at this stage. The undergraduates may be encouraged to read certain representative works and taught to think for themselves. Here I should observe that Maynard's book does *not* imply an orthodoxy of the static system, and in this he differs from the mere scallywags like Maj. Douglas. The static system retains its place *as a foundation*.

Harrod went on to say:

By recognizing this distinction between the developed and the underdeveloped departments of theory, it seems to me, you put Maynard in his right place. The only modification in the static theory is that the doctrine of what governs the volume of saving and the rate of interest must be thrown out bag and baggage.

However, Harrod continued:

By taking the line which I think you are inclined to take, that Maynard is a naughty boy who is upsetting the ordered development of economics, you only make confusion worse confounded. What are the poor undergraduates to think? Because, after all, Maynard *is* a clever fellow, and so are his followers.

Harrod then said:

What you want, in order to put the house in order, is to be able to draw a sharp line of distinction between the well established and the new terrain, and I believe you will only get a satisfactory line, *if you distinguish between the theory of value and distribution in a non-growing community and the laws of growth*.

Harrod then turned to his reference to and treatment of Pigou's works in *The Trade Cycle* – or, more correctly, the lack of it. In his words:

Of course there are many good men whom I have praised in my book. I have given very high praise elsewhere to Pigou in my review of his book on unemployment. In *this* work, *it was only appropriate to praise those who had stimulated the particular genesis of ideas therein contained.*

Harrod then dealt with the problematic aspect of his treatment of the 'acceleration principle', and placed it, interestingly enough, in the context of a complaint against Pigou's treatment of it and the influence of this on his early views. Harrod wrote:

So far as the 'acceleration principle' is concerned (I have only learnt since publication that this is a well established term of art) I am not prepared to present a bouquet [to Pigou] . . . In the last part of the early *Economics of Welfare* he discusses it, and while explaining that it accounts for the greater fluctuation of capital goods output, denies that it can be regarded as a true cause of the cycle.

Harrod continued on to say, however:

In the days when I first read it, I was very much overawed by Pigou's authority, and tended to accept what he said uncritically. I remember accepting and even expounding that view of his and, for a number of years, it put me off the scent.

Finally, and almost as an aside, Harrod ended his letter by asking Robertson for the name of the journal in which his review of *The Trade Cycle* would appear.[3]

Harrod's next letter to Robertson regarding *The Trade Cycle* was dated 3 April 1937. In this Harrod took the opportunity to retrace the problem involved in the way Keynes's definition of saving was interpreted, and also to deal with Robertson's review of *The Trade Cycle* and Hawtrey's treatment of it in his book *Capital and Employment* (1937). Harrod opened his letter by saying:

My impression about the course of events is this. JMK introduced into our minds, with much flourish of trumpets, the notion that *I* need *not* be equal to *S*. Am I wrong in supposing this an innovation. There was, of course, much before that about forced saving; a different matter. Then, as soon as his book [*Treatise*] appeared, we began to hear a lot, in the general literature, about the difference between saving and investment, but in a sense quite different from his. That is to say *his* definition of saving *excluding profit* was disregarded, and *I* was said to be greater than *S* if banks expanded credit.

Harrod continued:

Now, I suggest that to say this, *regardless of the state of profit*, and without giving the special definition to make sure of it, *is* a fallacy. I do not mean to include in my condemnation of fallacious those who provided such a definition.

He went on to say:

My contention is, in fact, that JMK's distinction of *I* and *S* was exploited in a way which disregarded his definition, which made the distinction possible, and without alternative definition.

Harrod then briefly dealt with Robertson's review of his book, and said:

I don't think I wish to write to the *Canadian Journal* [of Economics and Political Science]. On re-reading, I don't think I have much to complain of. Perhaps one ought not to reply to reviews unless one has a very definite grievance.

After this, Harrod turned to Hawtrey's detailed treatment of his views in *Capital and Employment*. As Harrod put it:

I was very amused to find that Hawtrey, in his account, makes me attribute an important role to 'absorption of cash'. Of course, I *do* mean an absorption of cash, but Hawtrey regards it as *cause*, and I *effect*. Perhaps I ought to rejoice that each writer attributes his own views to me.

Harrod then said of Hawtrey's book and his views on the role of the short-term interest rate:

I think the general . . . style . . . excellent, but its *central* intention seems to me hopeless. We may consider his theory in terms of the practical question: how to prevent a slump. So far as the effect of the short term rate is concerned, he is reduced to talking about variations in the stocks of manufactured goods held by legitimate producers. Now, this is pure mythology. I am sure that no producer varies his holding of processed materials, spare parts, etc. in response to changes in the rate of interest. He agrees with me about the ineffectiveness of the long term rate. What is left? The state of the capital market.

He continued:

When the slump comes, capital outlay may be maintained because the market will be able to satisfy people in the queue. But surely it will melt away.[4]

Some six months later, Harrod again wrote to Robertson on issues emanating from the *Trade Cycle*, linking them with his views on the efficacy of banking policy, which had, in fact, changed since his earlier *Economica* article. In this letter, dated 4 October 1937, Harrod wrote that, for him, a suitable definition of equilibrium banking policy would be 'along one of two lines'. The first line of argument he put to Robertson was as follows:

You may refer to a rate of advance that can be maintained, to which I add as a corollary that this means keeping things perpetually as they are at the bottom of a depression.

For, he continued:

As soon as you allow any revival, e.g. a drop in percentage unemployed, you have an advance exceeding the long period trend.

He went on to say:

But the long period trend limits the rate of advance 'that can be maintained', and I think I am entitled to add, subject to your correction, that the depression must get progressively worse owing to the accumulated effect of random factors of a depressing kind which are not sufficiently well foreseen to be countered by banking policy *ex-ante*. If you try to reprieve the situation afterwards, you get into a rate of advance which cannot be maintained.

Harrod then said:

> I suppose you might reply that these are offset by random expansion factors which cannot be foreseen. The trouble about these is I am not sure that I see how you prevent them, if not dealt with in advance, from producing a further slump.

He reached the conclusion, therefore, that:

> if *this* is the definition of equilibrium, I am sure that you will agree with me, it is not a suitable criterion for action. The trouble is that we may have to make our beginning in a fluctuating world.

Harrod then presented a second, alternative, line of argument for Robertson's consideration. As he put it:

> You may say that you are going to pay no attention to the *actual* world. Assume initially a condition of *full* employment *not* built on an antecedent of normal rate of advance and work out the banking policy which is then required for maintaining a normal advance.

According to Harrod, this was 'the kind of thing' he did in his *Economica* article. He went on to say 'I tried to demonstrate there that even in full employment conditions, the Hayek solution would not be right'. However, he continued 'such exercises are, I think, interesting, but one must recognize how limited is their applicability to the real world'. Harrod then added:

> I have come to think banking policy *a very weak weapon* at our disposal if we try to combat the forces set up by the acceleration cum multiplier principles.

Finally, as a postscript to his letter, Harrod wrote:

> There *is* no theory, orthodox or other, about what determines the rate of interest . . . [With regard to] supply and demand for loanable funds; apart from Maynard's point that the supply depends on the total volume of income, which itself depends on the rate of interest, there is the still more important one that you have nothing to say about the demand. *This depends on the rate of growth*. But about this you have nothing to say in part I [statics].

Harrod continued:

> With tastes and techniques remaining the same, the assumption you always have to make, in any part I [static] analysis, [is that] there is no demand for loanable funds, but there is some supply. Hence, *the rate of interest must always be zero*. Very instructive for the young.

He went on:

> You can't say anything sensible about the matter until you have your rate of growth determined, about which part I theory says nothing. You have to bring in my dynamic determinants or something similar.

Harrod then said:

> It really does shock me to see you standing there absolutely naked and imagining yourself fully decked out. Maynard offers you a temporary shift in which you can run for shelter while you make yourself something more substantial.

He continued:

> But it is no light task that lies before us. My particular system of dynamic determinants, a first feeble attempt in this field, *also assumed the rate of interest as a known*.

Harrod ended his letter by saying:

> So there is the poor interest rate, with no friends either in the static or dynamic camps. That is why I look with a kindly eye on Maynard's theory *because here, at last, is one friend for him in the static camp*. He may be a poor one, but beggars can't be choosers.[5]

A few days later, on 8 October 1937, Harrod again wrote to Robertson regarding his book and his letter of 4 October. This letter, in effect, ended his correspondence with Robertson about the book and its implications. Later on, however, in 1938, he would renew his ongoing contact with Robertson; but this time, as will be seen, regarding his 'Essay in dynamic theory'. In his letter of 8 October 1937, Harrod wrote:

I think I demonstrated in my last [letter] that according to the orthodox view, the rate of interest must always be zero. You did not reply to this. The fallacy can be approached in a number of ways. I will try this one. The orthodox (I don't know whether this is the best word to describe it) theory is wrong because it is one dimension out.

This, according to Harrod, was because:

when we consider the supply of other factors, we say what price is necessary to elicit a flow of so and so much per unit of time. The amount elicited is not a lump sum but a flow which is conceived to go on so long as the conditions are unchanged.

Harrod continued:

To meet this, we have a demand schedule depending on tastes and technique of production; so and so much will be demanded at various prices. Again, the amount demanded is a flow.

Harrod then turned to savings. As he put it:

I will not bother, for the moment, with Maynard's difficulty about supply. The crucial trouble is on the side of demand. With tastes and technique the same, there is no demand in equilibrium.

He went on to say:

There may be, of course, some delay in projects still to be done, but this is once over demand which will not go on week after week. When it is satisfied, there is nothing further. You may now be tempted to say, well, then the rate of interest will fall to stimulate demand sufficiently to absorb the supply. Quite so. But again the stimulus will only – tastes and technique being the same – provoke a once over demand. When that is exhausted, the rate will have to fall again.

Harrod then said:

In fact, we come to this. Given tastes and technique and the supply schedule, there is no sense in the question: What rate of interest will allow demand to absorb the supply? We have to ask, what rate of *fall* in the rate of interest will allow demand to absorb the supply?

But, Harrod continued:

This is not at all on focus with our treatment of the other factors. We do *not* say: What rise or fall in wages or rents is required to get labour and land used assuming constant supply schedule, but what *level* of wages or rents. This is what I mean by saying the orthodox theory of interest is one dimension out.

He went on:

Put it the other way round. We may ask: At what rate must factors other than saving increase, or alternatively, at what rate must capital using inventions proceed in order to absorb the current offer of savings at a given rate of interest?

But, he continued:

We do *not* ask, at what rate must the factors other than labour increase, or alternatively, what labour using inventions must occur in order to continue to absorb a given quantity of labour at a given price.

He then went on to say:

Put it another way. You may perceive that to bring interest theory into line with the others, one must consider the whole quantum of capital, including all past savings, however this may be measured. You have your demand for the use of so and so much capital as a whole per week, which is on all fours with your demand for so much labour per week. There will be a demand schedule corresponding to the various rates of interest. This gives you a particular rate related to each quantum of capital.

However, he continued:

It does *not* give you a particular rate related to a given amount of addition to that capital, which comes back to the same point.

> Given your tastes, technique, time preference, and all the rest of it,
> what comes out of the hat isn't a rate of interest at all, but a rate of
> fall in the rate of interest.

Harrod ended his letter by saying:

> The orthodox theory determines the rate of interest and the
> volume of saving at one blast . . . In my book, there were things
> called dynamic determinants which were supposed to determine
> *not* the rate of interest but the volume of saving . . . My thing has
> different dimensions. Constant proportion is defined as growing
> amounts. Now, this analysis by dynamic determinants is not some-
> thing which can be added on to the part I [static] theory. It washes
> it out entirely and replaces it. Do you in fact think that my dynamic
> determinants are all nonsense? Otherwise, you have to sacrifice the
> orthodox account. I may say that, in spite of a number of finger-
> posts in my book pointing at the dynamic determinants, no review
> that I have seen has paid any attention to them. I have no doubt
> that it is my fault for being too cryptic.[6]

Harrod and Henderson

In a letter dated 21 February 1936, Henderson told Harrod that he
had just finished reading the first two chapters of the draft manuscript
of *The Trade Cycle*, and provided him with detailed comments,
especially on the problem of profit maximisation and the ability of
entrepreneurs to measure the elasticity of demand and maximise
revenue. Henderson also considered Harrod's treatment of Keynes's
works to be, in his view, very clear. Moreover, Henderson said that
he liked Harrod's 'relation' much more than the 'multiplier'. Henderson also told Harrod that he viewed Harrod's treatment of savings in
an unsympathetic light.[7]

Harrod, for his part, it would seem, took Henderson's initial
criticism not to be constructive in nature, so that only two days later,
Henderson apologised in a letter for what Harrod had taken to be his
unsympathetic attitude. In this letter Henderson also took issue with
the notion of imperfect competition, which, in his view, was not a
'tool' but a 'toy'. Furthermore, he made the point, which Harrod
could not accept – as Harrod later complained to Robertson in his
letter of 21 May 1936 cited above – that it was not necessarily in the

self-interest of businessmen to attain maximum profit in the short run in the trade cycle.[8]

On 26 February 1936, Henderson again wrote Harrod, restating his critique in general of Harrod's overall methodological approach. Henderson asserted that he was, in fact, on the side of Clapham in what could be called 'the economic boxes argument'. In this letter Henderson also re-emphasised his opposition to the savings-investment equality/identity, but, interestingly enough, agreed, as he put it, with Harrod's 'management of exposition of Keynes' views' in the draft manuscript of *The Trade Cycle*, calling it a 'masterly bit of work'.[9]

As Harrod wrote to Robertson on 21 May 1936, after Henderson's initial reaction to the draft manuscript of the book during Hilary term (February 1936), Harrod had heard nothing more from him. However, some two weeks later, on 4 June, Henderson wrote to Harrod regarding the policy proposals he presented at the end of his work. According to Henderson, Harrod had overstressed the problem of disequilibrium, and Henderson also found Harrod's proposals, as he put it 'eccentric and heretical'. Once again, it seems, Harrod was upset by Henderson's critique. A week later, after a personal conversation between them, Henderson wrote to Harrod. In this letter, dated 10 June, Henderson suggested that while he still believed the tone of Harrod's policy proposals to be 'heterodox', they could, in fact, be amended to enable Harrod to 'sell' them, as he put it, to the business community.[10]

Now, the correspondence cited above between Harrod and Robertson, on the one hand, and Harrod and Henderson, on the other, raises as many questions as it answers. Thus, while Harrod's attitudes towards the various critiques of his draft manuscript and reviews of his book are made clear, and even some of Harrod's 'cryptic' remarks in the book can be understood by reference to the letters cited above, other more substantive issues are raised by a careful reading of the correspondence itself.

For example, early in his correspondence with Robertson on the draft manuscript of *The Trade Cycle*, Harrod complained about Henderson's attitude towards his work. This, in addition to some very critical negative comments made by Henderson in his correspondence with Harrod on the draft manuscript as noted, explains Harrod's statement in the preface to his book that he was 'indebted' to Henderson 'for giving me a lucid and helpful explanation of his difficulties'.[11]

Moreover, Harrod's view of the published critiques of his book made by Robertson, Robinson, and Hawtrey respectively would seem to be straightforward in light of his comments on them made in his correspondence with Robertson as cited above. However, as is evident from his correspondence with Hawtrey, which I have cited elsewhere, Harrod originally took a somewhat different line regarding Robertson's review. For, in a letter to Hawtrey dated 4 March 1937, Harrod objected strongly to Robertson's interpretation of his views and complained about Robertson's treatment of them in his review.[12]

Furthermore, in his correspondence with Robertson, Harrod focused upon what distinguished his *Trade Cycle* approach from that of Keynes's *General Theory* approach. For example, in his letter to Robertson of 25 December 1936, Harrod emphasised that, in spite of Joan Robinson's view that his work was based upon that of Keynes, he had, in fact, formulated what he took to be the central message of his book even before he saw the proofs of the *General Theory*, so that his supposed 'indebtedness' to Keynes was only limited. Moreover, in his view, the focus of his book was on a totally different problem, that is, that of 'growth' and the 'laws of growth', as he stressed in his letters to Robertson of 25 December 1936 and 4 October 1937. Now, while in the preface to his book Harrod acknowledged that his 'chief debt of gratitude' was to Keynes, he also said that only the reader 'well acquainted with his writings' would 'find traces of his influence', besides the places at which 'specific reference' to Keynes was made in the book. More important to recall here, however, is the fact that Keynes only sent his detailed comments on the book to Harrod after its publication.[13]

A careful reading of Harrod's correspondence with Robertson, therefore, enables us to pose a number of substantive questions. First, in light of Harrod's assertion that in his book 'it was only appropriate to praise those who had stimulated the particular genesis of ideas' contained in it, the question may be asked – to whom was Harrod, in fact, referring? Secondly, in view of Harrod's contention that in his book he was not dealing with the same problem as Keynes, and his emphasis upon the fundamental difference between his 'macrodynamic' *Trade Cycle* approach and what he called Keynes's 'macrostatic' *General Theory* approach, the question arises – what in fact was Keynes's role in the development of Harrod's approach and views on growth and dynamics? Finally, in light of Harrod's 'problematic' treatment of the notion of acceleration and the 'acceleration principle', the question may be asked – did the reviewers and critics of Harrod's book actually overlook his 'dynamic determinants' and the interaction between what he called the 'relation' and the multiplier, as he contended, or did they see them as the refinement of already existing approaches (for example, parallel to the 'Wicksellian process' – as Haberler put it in his letter to Harrod of 8 January 1937, cited in chapter 3 – or similar to that of Pigou, mentioned by Harrod himself, as cited above)?[14]

B. DRAFTS AND DISCUSSION: HARROD, MEADE, AND ALLEN

Over the period January to May 1936, Harrod engaged in lengthy correspondence and detailed discussion with James Meade regarding the draft manuscript of *The Trade Cycle*. Maurice Allen was also involved during this period in reading and commenting on the draft manuscript and proofs of Harrod's book. With regard to the Harrod-Meade correspondence, it became so intense after Meade's initial reaction to the draft manuscript on 12 January 1936, that during the following week (12–19 January), they exchanged letters and detailed notes on almost a daily basis. In his letter to Harrod of 12 January 1936 Meade wrote:

> May I say, first of all, that I have been reading your manuscript with great pleasure and think that it is excellent. I enjoyed the [first two] chapters very much, but think that I have myself learnt most from your discussion of the 'relation', and its relation with the multiplier at the end of your second chapter.

He continued:

> I think I agree with all that discussion, but it has made me think furiously, and for that reason I am keeping your manuscript a little longer if I may, in case I find time to re-read it.

Meade went on to say, however:

> Apart from some small points which are not worth raising in writing, but which I should like to discuss with you, there were two major points on which I have written two notes. I hope you will

forgive my first note, which is much more elaborate than is necessary to make my point, but I thought the conclusion might be of interest to you.

He ended his letter by saying:

As you will see in the first note, I am suggesting that you have omitted an important point, and in the second, that you have committed a definite error. But my second note may only prove that I have misinterpreted your point.[15]

Attached to Meade's letter of 12 January were two notes. The first ('Note I'), which was very long and detailed, dealt with Harrod's 'relation' and what Meade considered to be the modifying influences on it. The second note, much shorter, and less detailed, focused upon income and the distribution of profit, and also on what Meade saw as the problems involved in Harrod's treatment of marginal and average costs and diminishing returns. Because it is crucial for an understanding of the evolution of Harrod's thought, as well as that of Meade – in addition to being possibly one of the most important missing links in the development of the growth research programme in economics – Meade's 'Note I' on Harrod's draft manuscript of *The Trade Cycle* is cited at length here (Meade, 1936a). Meade started his 'Note I' by saying:

If technique is unchanged we can write

$$x = f(C,L)$$

where x = output of consumption goods
  C = stock of capital in consumption industries

and L = amount of 'prime' factors called labour in consumption industries.

If there are constant physical returns to both factors $L \& C$, the function is homogeneous of the first degree and

$$x = L\,\frac{\partial x}{\partial L} + C\,\frac{\partial x}{\partial C}$$

or $\dfrac{L}{x} \cdot \dfrac{\partial x}{\partial L} + \dfrac{C}{x} \cdot \dfrac{\partial x}{\partial C} = 1$ . . . (i)

$\frac{L}{x} \cdot \frac{\partial x}{\partial L}$ is the marginal physical product elasticity of labour (i.e. the proportionate increase in output ÷ proportionate increase in labour). In perfect competition $L \frac{\partial x}{\partial L}$ = the real earnings of labour so that $\frac{L}{x} \cdot \frac{\partial x}{\partial L}$ will be equal to the proportion of income going to labour.

$$\left. \begin{array}{l} \text{Let } \dfrac{L}{x} \cdot \dfrac{\partial x}{\partial L} = q \\[2mm] \text{then } \dfrac{C}{x} \cdot \dfrac{\partial x}{\partial C} = 1 - q \end{array} \right\} \qquad \ldots \text{(ii)}$$

Meade then said:

In what follows I shall call q the proportion of income going to labour and $1 - q$ the proportion going to profits of capital. But my argument does not at first depend on this and to extend it to imperfect competition q is simply defined as the marginal product elasticity of labour. In any case $1 > q > 0$

Differentiating the equation $x = f(C,L)$ we have

$$\left. \begin{array}{l} \dfrac{dx}{dt} = \dfrac{\partial x}{\partial L} \cdot \dfrac{dL}{dt} + \dfrac{\partial x}{\partial C} \cdot \dfrac{dC}{dt} \\[4mm] \text{and substituting from (ii)} \\[4mm] \dfrac{1}{x} \cdot \dfrac{dx}{dt} = q \dfrac{1}{L} \cdot \dfrac{dL}{dt} + (1 - q)\dfrac{1}{C} \cdot \dfrac{dC}{dt} \end{array} \right\} \qquad \ldots \text{(iii)}$$

This is the fundamental relation connecting the proportionate rate of increase of consumption per unit of time $\left(\frac{1}{x} \cdot \frac{dx}{dt} \right)$ with the proportionate rate of increase of employment per unit of time $\left(\frac{1}{L} \cdot \frac{dL}{dt} \right)$ and the output of capital goods per unit of time $\left(\frac{dC}{dt} \right)$.

Meade continued:

On p. 78 at the bottom you say that you are assuming at first (1) no changes in technique and (2) advances or recessions that are neutral as far as the use of capital is concerned, and this neutrality is defined as the situation in which dr/x is equal to dC/C. If we assume constant returns to all factors as well as no change in technique, my equation (ii) is applicable and it is clear that if

$$\frac{1}{L} \cdot \frac{dL}{dt} = \frac{1}{x} \cdot \frac{dx}{dt}, \text{ then } \frac{1}{x} \cdot \frac{dx}{dt} = \frac{1}{C} \cdot \frac{dC}{dt} = \frac{1}{L} \cdot \frac{dL}{dt}$$

Your neutral case is therefore essentially the case in which the proportionate rate of increase in consumption is equal to the proportionate rate of increase in employment, in which case the proportionate rate of increase in the stock of capital will have the same value also. *In other words, the ratio between the stock of capital and the volume of employment is assumed constant.*

On this assumption, everything you say on p. 79 is correct. On p. 84, you suggest two modifying influences which lessen the force of the 'Relation', $\frac{1}{x} \cdot \frac{dx}{dt} = \frac{1}{C} \cdot \frac{dC}{dt}$ i.e. that the *output* of capital goods will vary in direct proportion to the *rate of change* in consumption. May I for the moment leave out your second modifying influence and will assume tastes and techniques unchanged? I suggest that the proportion of capital to labour in producing a unit of consumption goods may change not only because of changes in the rate of interest but also because of changes in the price of capital goods in relation to the price of the prime factors, i.e. of the wage rate of labour. C, the amount of capital goods, must be measured in terms of physical units called machines. The marginal product of machines is the inverse of the increase in the output of consumption due to having one more machine. The cost of using an extra machine is the price of a machine times the rate of interest. The proportion between machines and labour used will remain constant if the cost of using an extra machine bears a constant ratio to the cost of using an extra unit of labour, i.e. if the money price of a machine times the rate of interest bears a constant proportion to the money wage rate of labour. Now, when there is an increased money demand for commodities, i.e. in a boom, we know

(1) that the rate of interest rises;
(2) that the price of machines rises more quickly than the price of consumption goods; and
(3) that the money wage rate rises less quickly than the price of consumption goods.

Meade went on to say:

All three of these factors cause the rise in the demand for machines to be less than proportionate to the rise in the rate of expansion of consumption, because all give rise to substitution of labour for capital.

Assuming perfect competition we can easily express these facts in my equations. σ, the elasticity of substitution between L and C

$$= \frac{\partial x/\partial L \Big/ \partial x/x}{\dfrac{L}{C}} \cdot \frac{d\left(\dfrac{L}{C}\right)}{d\left(\dfrac{\partial x/\partial L}{\partial x/\partial C}\right)}$$

i.e. the proportionate change in the ratio between L and $C \div$ the proportionate change in the ratio between their marginal physical products. In perfect competition the price of each factor is equal to the value of the marginal product so that $\partial x/\partial L = w/p$ and $\partial x/\partial C = Pr/P$, where w = money wage rate, p = the money price of consumption goods, P = money price of capital goods and r the rate of interest (I have already argued that the money cost of a machine which is equated to the value of its marginal product is the price of a machine × the rate of interest). Then

$$\sigma = \frac{\dfrac{w}{Pr}}{\dfrac{L}{C}} \cdot \frac{d\left(\dfrac{L}{C}\right)}{d\left(\dfrac{w}{Pr}\right)} = \frac{\dfrac{1}{L} \cdot \dfrac{dL}{dt} - \dfrac{1}{C} \cdot \dfrac{dC}{dt}}{\dfrac{1}{w} \cdot \dfrac{dw}{dt} - \dfrac{1}{Pr} \cdot \dfrac{d(Pr)}{dt}}$$

or $\left(\dfrac{1}{w} \cdot \dfrac{dw}{dt} - \dfrac{1}{Pr} \cdot \dfrac{d(Pr)}{dt}\right) = \dfrac{1}{L} \cdot \dfrac{dL}{dt} - \dfrac{1}{C} \cdot \dfrac{dC}{dt}$ ... (iv)

N.B σ *is always negative* . . .

Meade then went on to substitute the various equations and found that:

if the proportional rate of change of wage rates minus the proportional rate of change in the price of capital goods minus the proportional rate of change hence rate of interest = 0, then

$$\frac{1}{x} \cdot \frac{dx}{dt} = \frac{1}{C} \cdot \frac{dC}{dt}$$

He then said:

> But if in a boom wages are rising slowly and the price of machines
> and the rate of interest are rising fast, then the proportionate rate
> of increase of consumption will rise more than in proportion to the
> output of capital goods and this phenomenon will be more import-
> ant the greater the possibility of substitution i.e. the greater the
> numerical value of σ, and the greater is q, the proportion of income
> going to labour.

Meade then apologised for the length of his note, and made two
suggestions for Harrod's consideration. As he put it:

> I am sorry to have bored you with this long note. For your book I
> only wish to make two suggestions: (i) that you should make it
> clear that your neutral advance or recession from the point of view
> of capital is one in which the ratio between capital and labour is left
> constant so that the proportionate rate of increase in consumption
> = proportionate rate of increase in employment = proportionate
> rate of increase in capital stock; and (ii) that this will happen if the
> proportionate rate of change in the money wage is equal to the
> proportionate rate of change in the price of machines while the rate
> of interest is constant, or in other words, that your Relation
> exaggerates the situation for *two* reasons apart from changes in
> technique – both because the rate of interest rises and because the
> price of machines rises more quickly than the money wage rate,
> both of which lead to substitution of labour for capital.

Meade concluded by saying:

> I may add that I think that the rise and fall of machine prices and its
> relation with wage rates in boom and slump is one of the most
> important and stabilizing elements in the capitalist system, because
> it is the most important modification of your 'Relation'.[16]

Harrod replied the very next day to Meade's letter of 12 January
1936 and the notes he sent, adding some additional comments re-

garding Meade's second note on marginal and average costs in another short letter sent the day after. At this time, Meade was in Oxford, while Harrod was in London. In his reply to Meade of 13 January, which he sent from his London residence, Harrod said:

A thousand thanks for your notes. It is very good of you to have taken all the trouble. I have the impression that both your two points are correct, and I propose with your leave to embody them. There will be a suitable prefatory expression of indebtedness.

To get in the first point I think all I need is to insert a *third* proviso on p. 84 together with a reference forward to p. 107 where I have argued that the prices of machines are subject to greater variation than other prices. I am interested that you say that you regard this as one of the big stabilizing influences. It may well be. I confess I had not thought out this point in the clear way you put it. My inclination is to regard it as not perhaps quite so important as you suggest owing to my scepticism about how far productive methods do change in response to cyclical influences. If your point is an important one, does it not make still greater nonsense of the Hayekian view that the process becomes unduly capitalistic in the boom? (By the way how very mathematical you have become!).

The second point will give me more trouble. I confess that I had an uneasy feeling of guilt, when I was writing about the relation of marginal to average cost, and a sense that I had not paused long enough to consider what I was saying. I shall have to ponder this at length. The text will clearly have to be altered in several places. I want to achieve correctitude without going too elaborately into cost theory which would be inappropriate in an essay on the trade cycle with such a broad scope as this. I thought of referring the reader in a footnote to works on imperfect competition.

Well, I am most grateful to you for these points. They are just the kind of points which I was relying on you to pull me up on. I find that when one imagines one is breaking new ground the mind gets into a state of suppressed excitement (anyhow mine does!) in which there is a danger of the critical faculties being a little blunted.

Finally, Harrod turned to his progress on the draft manuscript and said:

I have now written the best part of Ch. 3. It is all rather negative. I have explained in my opening words that this is partly because the subjects have been well looked after by other writers and I am concerned to point out the limitations of those doctrines. I hope what I have said won't strike you as excessively irreverent, *being as you are a special patron of the rate of interest*! If there is still another loop in your coil of charity that I can draw on, I will send you what I have done, when it is typed out, rather expecting and fearing your mild displeasure . . .

In a parenthetical note to the conclusion of his letter inviting Meade to have dinner with him on the following Monday evening after his return to Oxford from London, Harrod added:

By the way, there is a trade cycle meeting on the afternoon of that day.[17]

Meade replied to Harrod the next day. In this letter, dated 14 January 1936, he enclosed an additional note on Harrod's 'relation'. In his letter Meade said:

I should very much like to read your chapter 3 when it is ready. I have been thinking over your 'relation' and enclose a few detailed considerations. I hope that you will forgive me for bombarding you with so much criticism. I am quite sure that your 'relation' is of the utmost importance, but I became increasingly convinced that there *are* situations in which it underestimates changes in the proportions between capital and labour. Anyhow, you can judge from the enclosed note. I will keep your manuscript if I may . . .

In the additional note on Harrod's 'relation' which he enclosed along with his letter, Meade wrote:

I have been considering your 'relation' further and would like to suggest the following points. I am not sure how important they are in fact.

According to *Meade*, there were four possible cases, which he outlined as follows:

Case (1) there is unemployed labour (or a growing population of workers; the important point being that there is labour to be absorbed) *and* unemployed capital (i.e. firms are closed down or working at very low capacity).

Case (2) there is *no* unemployed labour and a stationary population of workers and *no* unemployed capital.

Case (3) there *is* unemployed labour or a growing population of workers, but *no* unemployed capital.

Meade also said:

for formal purposes there is a [fourth] case of *no* unemployed labour *and* unemployed capital.

However, on his view 'it is of no theoretical importance'. Meade then said:

I suggest that it is only in case (3) that the difficulties due to your 'relation' are present in their acute form, assuming throughout constant technologies and tastes, i.e. no inventions.

He continued:

In case (1), if consumption is increasing, labour and capital are being absorbed into production and there is no change in the proportion of labour to capital. In this case, your 'relation' does not hold good, since a proportionate rate of increase in the capital stock in existence need not be equal to the proportionate rate of increase of consumption. If net investment *is* taking place at an increasing rate in order (because of the multiplier) to cause consumption to increase, then investment is only taking place to substitute capital for labour by the substitution of new types of machinery, i.e. because the rate of interest is falling or the price of machines is rising less quickly than the wage rate of labour.

Meade went on to say:

When, therefore, the point is reached at which all labour and all capital are absorbed, there need be no crisis, for the demand for new machinery does *not* now fall off because the rate of increase in consumption falls, since construction of new machinery was only taking place to substitute capital for labour, while the rate of increase of consumption was being met out of the stock of unused capital.

He then said that in this case:

To prevent a crisis, all that is necessary is that the rate of interest should go on falling as before to cause a continuing substitution of capital for labour. If, at the start, the amount of unemployed labour bears a smaller or greater ratio to the rate of unemployed capital than the amount of employed labour bears to the stock of employed capital, we shall reach a point at which all labour is employed, while some capital is still unemployed, or all capital is employed, and some labour is not employed, i.e. case (1) becomes case (4) or case (3).

Meade then continued on to say:

In case (2), since there is no unemployed labour to absorb, any increase in consumption must be due to the substitution of capital for labour, i.e. investment must be taking place because the rate of interest or the price of machinery in relation to the wage of labour is falling, and capital is being substituted for labour.

He then said:

In this case, to avoid a crisis, all that is necessary is to preserve the rate of fall of the rate of interest and the rate of substitution of labour for capital.

Meade now considered the third of his notional cases. As he put it:

In case (3), your 'relation' *does* prevent the most devastating problem, which I had never seen before. Here, at *first* there need be no substitution of capital for labour and no fall in the rate of interest or fall in the price of machines in relation to the wage rate of labour. The proportionate rate of increase in the capital stock will be, in these circumstances, equal to the proportionate rate of increase in consumption, is equal to the proportionate rate of increase in employment.

He continued:

But as soon as all unemployment is absorbed, or starting with full employment, as soon as the population of workers grows at a smaller proportionate rate of increase, the rate of increase of consumption will fall, and the absolute level of investment will therefore fall with all the consequences which you argue.

Meade went on to say:

> To preserve full employment in these circumstances it is necessary that *suddenly*, at the point at which all labour is absorbed, a demand for capital for purposes of substitution for labour should develop as great as the demand for capital which did exist to keep the proportion between capital and labour constant, while unemployed labour was still there to absorb.

He then said:

> I agree that it is quite *fantastic* to assume that the rate of interest can *suddenly* begin to fall, in fact, at a rate which will immediately have this effect.

Meade added parenthetically:

> Case 4 is in no essential particulars different from Case 2. Here again, any investment that is taking place must be for purposes of substitution of new forms of capital for labour and there is no question of *suddenly* developing a 'substitution' demand for capital to take the place of a 'non-substitution' demand.

Finally, he said:

> I conclude from this that your 'relation' has shown a very important difficulty which exists when attempts are made to cure a situation in which there is *much* unemployed labour and *little* unemployed capital, i.e. Case 3 or Case 1 turning into Case 3. But when there is either *no* unemployed labour or *as much* unemployed capital as unemployed labour, I think your 'relation' very much exaggerates the difficulties of maintaining full employment.[18]

Two days later, on the morning of 16 January 1936, Harrod replied to Meade's letter of 14 January, and his additional note on the 'relation' and possible cases of its limited application. In his letter of 16 January, Harrod said:

> I entirely agree with the point which you make by reference to four cases.
> The trouble is that after a slump though there may be some

surplus capital capacity there will not be as much as there is surplus labour. For whereas *in the slump years* the population continues to grow and possibly also methods improve in accordance with the secular trend, capital equipment does *not* do so. Therefore, in the nature of the case there will be more surplus labour than surplus capital when the revival begins. I suspect that it is difficult to get a good revival going until in most industries surplus capital is fairly well reduced by obsolescence etc. so that a substantial advance will necessitate new equipment.

I probably ought to go rather more carefully into the condition of surplus capital at the revival.

Harrod added that he had already sent Meade the completed sections of the third chapter of his draft manuscript.[19]

Meade answered Harrod that very afternoon. In his letter of 16 January, Meade wrote:

Thank you very much for your note and also for your next chapter, which came this morning. I have written a note in answer to your note. You will see that in fact I accept your main proposition . . .

Meade added:

I have just read through Chapter 3 rather hurriedly and have got your note on my four cases. I feel that the part in Chapter 3 which interests me most is the part on the rate of interest, my criticisms of which, if any are already included in my argument about your 'relation'.

He went on to say:

I have written a very short note on your 'relation' and the rate of interest in consequence of sending the first part of Chapter 3. I am afraid that I read the entire part on D.H. R[obertson] and time lags and on money generally very hurriedly as time is beginning to press heavily . . .

Meade then concluded:

But I am sure that it is with your 'relation' and the rate of interest that I feel most inclined to argue. The rest I think I fully accept.

Attached to this letter was Meade's note which he termed 'The relation and the rate of interest'. In it, he said:

> You agree with my four cases, i.e. that the absorption of unemployed labour will only lead to an unavoidable crisis if there is, at the start, a greater volume of unemployed labour than capital. Starting from the bottom of the slump, it will then always be possible to absorb any levels of unemployment without danger up to the point at which capital is fully employed.

According to Meade, however, after this point is reached, 'any . . . advance leads to the danger of collapse'. He then asked:

> Might not the danger be avoided if the rate of interest were so manipulated to control the substitution of capital for labour that the remaining unemployed were absorbed at a constantly diminishing rate?

Meade then gave the following example:

> Suppose there are 1 million unemployed to absorb. The proper policy would be so to adjust interest rates that, say, 1% of the unemployed were absorbed in each year. In the first year interest rates would be raised or lowered so to affect the capitalistic nature of replacements and new investment, and thus the volume of net investment, that the unemployed were absorbed at the rate of 10,000 p.a. At the end of the year 990,000 unemployed would remain, and in the 2nd year, the rate of interest would be adjusted so that they were absorbed at the rate of 9,900 p.a. and so on (I have taken an ordinarily low %).

He went on to say:

> By this means, each year more capital investment would have to take place to substitute capital for labour since the savings of the community would presumably be rising, and the amount of capital investment required to keep the proportion of capital to labour constant would be falling each year. Each year the rate of interest would have to fall so as to develop an increasing 'substitution' demand for investment. But this process would be gradual. A sudden need for the whole of investment to be shifted by a fall in

interest rates from that necessary to absorb unemployment to an
equal amount of 'substitution' investment would be avoided.

Finally, Meade asked Harrod:

> Would you agree that theoretically, at least, a policy of this kind
> does make it possible to absorb the unemployed without con-
> sequent price rises? If so, is not the statement on p. 153, for e.g.,
> an exaggeration of it?[20]

Harrod answered Meade on 19 January 1936. In this letter, he took
up the points Meade had made regarding the 'relation' and the
interest rate, and also other points made in Meade's earlier note on
the relation of the ratio of marginal cost to average cost to the
elasticity of average cost. With regard to the first issue, Harrod said
that he agreed 'that in recovery there is a possible behaviour of the
interest rate which would make this all right and I must put that in'.
However, Harrod added 'Paradoxically the interest rate is required
to *fall* as the boom proceeds'.[21]

The next significant exchange of letters and notes between Harrod
and Meade on the draft manuscript of *The Trade Cycle* took place
during early May 1936. Meade had received the final chapters of the
manuscript from Harrod by the end of April, and on 1 May 1936 sent
Harrod a letter in which he provided both his general view and
specific points of comment on them. Meade said:

> I have read the enclosed chapters and enjoyed them very much. I
> am afraid that I have not had time to study them as carefully as the
> earlier chapters, so that I may have missed many points which I
> should have otherwise liked to discuss.

Meade then went on to deal with Harrod's treatment of what he
called the 'Foreign balance'. As he put it:

> I think I agree entirely with the main argument, but I feel that
> more emphasis should be placed on the effect of the rate of interest
> on the proportion of saved income which is lent at home and the
> proportion which is lent abroad.
>   The balance of payments decrees an inflow of specie, but it is not
> 'the country' which determines how much shall be lent abroad to
> obtain interest earning assets. It is the individual who will decide

whether to lend at home or to lend abroad according as, inter alia, the rate of interest is higher at home or abroad. I cannot see that an inflow of specie into a country will, in itself, make foreign lending more probable.

You agree and I agree that if all the dynamic determinants are appropriate, a steady rate of growth may be maintained in a country at a given rate of interest and with fixed exchange rates and that this does not involve the absence of a movement of gold out of short term balances – and you add (p. 212, 1st para.) that the steady rate of advance may be stopped because of an . . . inclination to stop the flow of specie.

Meade then asked Harrod:

Might it not be worth adding something about the rate of interest here? If the dynamic determinants were favourable, it may be a rate of interest which will preserve steady advance. But this rate of interest, if there are fixed exchange rates need not be the rate which prevents a flow of specie. There will be another rate of interest which will do this, and this other rate may involve a recession. This I believe is implied in your analysis.

Meade ended his letter by telling Harrod that he was not happy with Harrod's argument regarding the efficacy of employment subsidies, and enclosed a note entitled 'the effect of subsidies on employment' accordingly.[22]

Harrod replied to Meade in a letter on 4 May 1936, which, in effect, closed the correspondence between them on the draft manuscript of *The Trade Cycle*. In this letter he said:

Many thanks for your comments, which I think are just. I am glad that you drew my attention to the fact that I have not done the rate of interest justice in discussing foreign lending.

With regard to subsidies, I am no longer so confident as I used to be. I have thought a certain amount about it and can't feel my way to a conclusion that is independent of complicated assumptions. The position I take in the volume is that (1) if the subsidy is general and raised by taxation I do not know what effect it would have on output but that (2) if a formula could be devised by which any increase of output under the subsidy would be accompanied by a suitable shift away from profit, then the subsidy ought to stimulate output.

Harrod then asked Meade:

> Is it your view that a general subsidy on employment financed by
> taxation would stimulate output whether it were thus carefully
> devised or not? If so, what about the multiplier? Or perhaps you
> think that even if not devised for that purpose, the result of a
> general subsidy would somehow be automatically to cause a shift
> away from profit?

Harrod concluded his letter by saying:

> My present position is that unless I get some inspiration, I am
> likely to remain in an agnostic position. Don't bother about this.
> But if you think of anything helpful about subsidies, I should be
> most glad to know.[23]

In contrast to the frequency and intensity of the Harrod-Meade
correspondence on *The Trade Cycle*, the exchange between Harrod
and Allen on the draft manuscript and proofs of the book was much
more limited both in its scope and extent. For example, after having
complained to Robertson in his letter of 21 May 1936 about Allen
being 'dilatory' in reading the manuscript, Allen wrote Harrod and said:

> I shudder to think I may have delayed the work on your book but I
> have had . . . vacation since Sunday when I could re-read the
> typescript. An accumulation of pupils and committees descended
> on me. I send back now the portions which contain James Meade's
> notes. The sections I want to look at again in the later chapters,
> and the remedies, that I have yet to read, have no marginal
> comments from him, so that I hope my holding them until the end
> of the week is not excessively inconvenient.[24]

Harrod also sent the proofs of the book to Allen for his comments.
In reply, Allen said:

> Thank you for letting me see these proofs. I hardly dare to write
> about the book, I've behaved so awfully about it. My only consola-
> tion is that reflection has removed the difficulties which at first I
> thought I saw and tried feebly and for so long to write to you
> about. I enclose two notes on the points which seem to me rather
> important in the proofs.

The notes Allen enclosed with his letter dealt, among other things with (a) the stabilising influence of plasticity of prime costs; (b) entrepreneurial anticipations (expectations) and destabilising influences on firms and future price policies; and (c) anticipations during trade fluctuations. As Allen put it:

> Further, it seems to me desirable, as a matter of general method in economic analysis, to bring anticipations into the foreground as clearly as possible.[25]

Harrod did, in fact, acknowledge the problem of 'anticipations' in his book when he said that 'Mr. W.M. Allen has properly observed that the text does not do sufficient justice to the effect of *anticipations* on present policy'. In his 1939 'Essay' and afterwards, however, Harrod was to take the effect of anticipations and expectations as cardinal features in the analysis of growth and dynamics (Harrod, 1939a).

Interestingly enough, the policy prescription for reducing unemployment suggested by Meade in his note 'the relation and the rate of interest' sent along with his letter to Harrod dated 16 January 1936 reappeared, in a more refined form, as *An Introduction to Economic Analysis and Policy* (Meade, 1936b). In the chapter of that book entitled 'The proper criterion of policy', it took the form of what Meade called 'a simple criterion for the proper rate of monetary expansion'. Meade's 'criterion', however, was not based upon a 'simple' policy rule. Rather, it emanated from his views on a number of specific problems.

These related to (a) overall systemic and price stability; (b) the existence of a 'critical point' in the economic system, that is, 'the point at which capital is fully employed' beyond which – as he wrote in his note of 16 January 1936 – 'any . . . advance leads to the danger of a collapse' and 'consequent price rises' (or as he later said in his book 'just as there are dangers in expanding beyond a certain point, so there are dangers in expanding too quickly up to that point'); and (c) his notion of a '"standard" volume of unemployment'.[26]

Meade was aware that in conditions of high unemployment or, as he put it, at 'the bottom of the slump', too rapid an economic expansion would, in fact, prove counterproductive. In his view it would first lead to rapid price rises. In order to stop this, a subsequent fall in prices would be required, which would then, in turn, increase unemployment. According to Meade, so as to determine the 'proper' monetary policy, i.e. one which would guarantee both price and employment stability, it would be necessary to first estimate what he called the '"standard" volume of unemployment'.[27]

Meade defined unemployment as 'of "standard" size when it has been just sufficiently reduced for money-wage rates to start rising at the same rate as the marginal product of labour'. The actual level of unemployment would then be compared to the 'standard' volume, and, on his view 'according as actual unemployment is greater or less than this, a policy of monetary expansion or contraction should be adopted'. The expansion or contraction would then be 'controlled', according to him, 'through the control of interest rates, of public works expenditure, and of consumer's credits'. Meade concluded 'by this means it can be judged not only whether a policy of expansion or of contraction should be adopted but also whether the rate of expansion or of contraction should be altered'.[28]

Now, this is not the place for a detailed analysis of Meade's notion of a '"standard" volume of employment' and its rationale. Suffice it to say, however, that for an economist with a Hayekian world-view, who may have been familiar especially with the 1938 American edition of Meade's textbook (edited by Hitch), the elucidation of a 'natural rate of unemployment' (NARU) hypothesis would not have been a difficult conceptual step to take, although it would have been a convoluted one. For Meade's notion seems to be closer to a Keynesian-type 'inflation gap', or even an inflation-unemployment trade off, than a Hayekian-type NARU approach.[29]

Moreover, both in his 'Note I' of 12 January 1936 on the draft manuscript of *The Trade Cycle* cited in detail above, and in his book *Economic Analysis and Policy*, Meade dealt with the idea of capital-labour substitution as a tool for use 'against the cycle' and the role and effects of changes in the rate of interest in this context. Meade was, in fact – as Harrod put it in his letter of 13 January 1936 – 'a special patron of the rate of interest'. For his part, however, in his 'system of dynamic determinants' as manifest in *The Trade Cycle*, Harrod 'assumed the rate of interest as a known', as he told Robertson afterwards in his letter of 4 October 1937 cited above. Furthermore, in his 1939 'Essay', as will be seen, Harrod took the view that 'the effects of changes in the rate of interest are probably slow-working', and thus not 'suitable . . . for use against the cycle'.[30]

Any economist familiar with both Meade's earlier book *The Rate of Interest in a Progressive State* (1933) and, say, the American edition of his textbook *An Introduction to Economic Analysis and*

Policy (1938) for example, could quite easily have put together a 'neo-classical' type growth model as a counterpoint to Harrod's 1939 'Keynesian' type of approach to growth using the ideas Meade presented in these published works. However, Meade had actually developed a '"neo-classical" growth model' in his 'Note I' on Harrod's draft manuscript of *The Trade Cycle* and this, in January 1936. Thus, in his 1961 book *A Neo-Classical Theory of Economic Growth*, Meade in fact actually only rediscovered the model he had outlined to Harrod 25 years before. As Harrod said, albeit in another context, 'of interest this for trade cycle analysis' and, in my view, also for the history of economic thought.[31]

C. DISAPPOINTMENT AND FURTHER DEVELOPMENT: THE OXFORD CONFERENCE AND 'TRADE CYCLE GROUP'

The September 1936 Oxford meeting of the Econometric Society was, in my view, a watershed in the development of Harrod's approach to the problems of the trade cycle, growth, and dynamics. The reaction at the meeting – or more correctly, lack of it – to his newly-published book, *The Trade Cycle*, disappointed him, to say the least. Moreover, there seemed to be a distinct 'non-reaction' to the call he made at the end of the 'IS–LM' paper he presented at the 'symposium' on Keynes's *General Theory* system for the development of a Keynesian-based macrodynamics which, in his view, would complement that of Frisch, Tinbergen, and Kalecki. The reason for this, as I have shown elsewhere, was that a new representation, or rather 'suggested interpretation' of Keynes's *General Theory* system had, instead, caught the imagination of those at the conference, namely, Hicks's IS–LM diagram.[32]

This brought Harrod to the realisation that something more was needed in order to get the core of his message across, both at the conceptual level and at the level of exposition and presentation. On the other hand, some of the 1936 Conference papers and activities reinforced Harrod's position on issues which had concerned him since he first started thinking about them over a decade before, besides opening new perspectives on them; enabling him to venture into new areas of thought regarding the very fundamentals of growth and dynamic theory.

Now, a number of Oxford-based economists and staff of the

Oxford Institute during the mid-1930s, who had been in contact with Harrod during the formative phase of his ideas also attended the 1936 Conference. These individuals included Meade, Hitch, Marschak, Fraser, and Shackle, and others such as Brown, Phelps-Brown, Bowley, Bretherton, Burchardt, and Hall. Most of these personalities were interested, to one extent or another, in trade and business cycle theory, and in the problems of dynamics and growth. So Harrod's idea of dynamising Keynes had, in Oxford at least, potentially fertile ground on which to develop.[33]

In order to understand the change in Harrod's outlook that occurred as a result of the September 1936 Oxford Conference, I will briefly outline here those proceedings which may have influenced him most. In my view, these were:

1. The 'symposium' on Keynes's *General Theory* system, which took place on Saturday morning, 26 September 1936, and the informal meeting that took place afterwards between Harrod and a small group of conference participants during which he discussed with them the theme of his recently published book and his ideas on dynamics and growth.
2. The papers presented by Frisch and Tinbergen, and the subsequent 'colloquium on macrodynamics' conducted by Frisch that afternoon.
3. The paper given by Neyman on Sunday morning, 27 September, in which he stressed the difference between what he called the 'empirical' and the *a priori* approaches to dynamics.
4. The paper given by Akerman on Monday morning, 28 September, entitled 'Premises of Trade Cycle Theory', in which he surveyed and characterised the development of theories of the trade cycle accordingly.[34]

I have dealt with the Saturday morning 'symposium' on Keynes's *General Theory* – at which Harrod, along with Meade and Hicks, presented their respective IS–LM papers – in detail elsewhere. However, what is relevant to Harrod's book *The Trade Cycle* and its reception deserves to be recalled here. Two conference participants – George Shackle and Arthur Brown – gave their personal recollections of what took place that morning and Harrod's later reaction to the outcome of the symposium and his informal discussion of *The Trade Cycle* afterwards.

Shackle, for his part, recounted in his book *The Years of High*

Theory (1967) the answer Harrod gave when asked what he meant when he said – at the informal discussion on *The Trade Cycle* after the 'Keynes symposium' – that 'output is increasing'. According to Shackle's published account, the questioner wanted to know whether Harrod actually meant that 'it has been increasing' or 'is expected to increase'; whereas Harrod's response was to reject the question by saying he meant that 'output is growing'. When interviewed, Shackle also recalled that:

> Harrod came to the conference with a little green leaflet about his book *The Trade Cycle*, and *The Trade Cycle* was already out . . . Harrod was explaining what you could call his growth theory or his trade cycle theory . . . they're really the same thing . . . I think it is fair to say that Harrod had come to the meeting to try and expound and present his growth and trade cycle theory.

Shackle's view of the rationale of Harrod's activities at the conference were supported by Arthur Brown's recollections regarding Harrod's reaction to the success of Hicks's diagrammatic interpretation of Keynes, to the detriment of Harrod's *Trade Cycle* approach to dynamising Keynes. In an interview, when asked whether Harrod was disappointed by the reaction to his book and upset by the success of Hicks's diagram, Brown answered:

> I'm sure . . . I'm sure he was. I mean the word went round . . . Charley Hitch remarked that Harrod was peeved that nobody in Oxford appeared to be reading his great book on the trade cycle . . . I wasn't aware of a great splash made by *The Trade Cycle* in Oxford, whereas the Hicksian IS–LM thing had made a considerable splash . . . I think . . . he was sad because the book . . . *The Trade Cycle* didn't make a bigger splash . . . But we knew where Harrod was going and he got there in 1939 in . . . 'Essay in Dynamic Theory' . . . Indeed he regarded himself as having gotten there in the trade cycle book . . . which was schematized to a higher degree in the 'Essay' in 1939. Of course that was his turn to make a splash . . . This is where his mind was . . . he'd done with the *General Theory* . . . here was his book which should have been as much regarded as the *General Theory* . . . and people should have been discussing that . . . instead of Hicks' . . . he was clearly well on the way to his dynamic system then and went further in the next two years.[35]

On the afternoon of Saturday, 26 September 1936, Frisch gave a presentation which he called 'Macrodynamic Systems leading to Permanent Unemployment'. In this, Frisch showed that a condition where 'permanent unemployment' was possible – which Keynes focused on in the *General Theory* – was, in fact, evident in macrodynamic work done over the previous decade by Kalecki, Tinbergen, and Frisch himself, among others. After Frisch's presentation, Tinbergen focused on the problems relating to what he called 'Dynamic Equations Underlying Modern Trade Cycle Theories'. In his presentation, Tinbergen surveyed what Phelps-Brown – who reported the proceedings in *Econometrica* in October 1937 – saw as 'the different attempts that have been made to describe the endogenous movements of an economic system by a complete system of equations, i.e. by a system showing as many equations as variables'. In 'a subsequent colloquium', Frisch presented what Phelps-Brown called 'an ideal program for macrodynamic studies', which consisted of both theoretical and statistical enquiry.[36]

The next day, Sunday, 27 September 1936, Neyman presented a 'Survey of Recent Work on Correlation and Covariation'. One of the types of problems Neyman dealt with in his paper was what he called 'applicational problems, in which the task is to adjust a system of hypotheses, mathematically expressed, in such a way that their consequences will conform with the available observations'. Neyman asserted that in dealing with this type of problem, there were 'two paths of approach, the empirical, and the a priori'. According to him, the development of Astronomy could be cited to illustrate this. As he put it, the difference between the two approaches:

> may be emphasized by the comparison with two different phases in the history of Astronomy. The first phase is that of Ptolemy to Kepler. Ptolemy laid down the principle that mathematicians should endeavour to represent all the celestial phenomena by uniform and circular motions. This principle was followed roughly by Copernicus, and was removed by Kepler. But all the effort in this phase consisted in *guessing* the appropriate formula and in adjusting the numerical coefficients so that it might fit the observation.

Neyman went on to say:

> That is what is being done in the empirical approach to social and economic phenomena, e.g. in the analysis of time series, which we

try to split into trend, business cycles, seasonal variations etc. In Astronomy, the new era began with Sir Isaac Newton, and with his set of hypotheses concerning not the functions representing the observable facts, but the machinery which may have produced those facts. That is what may be termed an a priori construction.[37]

The last morning of the Conference, on Monday 28 September, Akerman gave a paper entitled 'Premises of Trade Cycle Theory'. In this paper he divided trade cycle theory into four types, identifying the respective theories, the policies they lead to, and their proponents as follows:

(a) *equilibrium* theories (which lead to stabilisation policies) as advocated, in his view, by Fisher, Cassel, Keynes (1930), and Hayek (1931);

(b) *anticipation* theories (which lead to policies of 'mitigation of monetary risk') as advocated by Knight, Myrdal, Lindhal, and Keynes (1936);

(c) *cumulative change* theories (which lead to cycle-smoothing policies) as advocated by Wicksell, Schumpeter, and Robertson; and

(d) *activity period* theories (which lead to policies regulating the 'interdependence of activity periods') as advocated by Akerman himself (for example, 1928).

At the end of his presentation, Akerman concluded that 'trade-cycle analysis proper is . . . essentially an analysis of the conversion of the depression into revival'.[38]

What is important to note here is that neither in the 1937 *Econometrica* account of Frisch's presentation and 'colloquium on macrodynamics', nor in the summary of Akerman's survey of trade cycle theories as recorded by Phelps-Brown at the September 1936 Oxford Conference is Harrod mentioned, let alone his book, *The Trade Cycle*; and this, although Harrod would have been very active in discussions – even leading an informal one after the 'symposium on Keynes', as was mentioned earlier.

On 7 February 1937, some four months after the September 1936 Oxford Conference, Harrod wrote Meade a long letter in which, after other matters, he took the opportunity, as he put it, 'to raise an economic point'. Harrod said:

You remember how you emphasized the importance of the decline in the relative price of capital goods in the slump and I inserted one or two sentences in my book in deference to your views. I was convinced by your argument and I confess I have tended to assume perhaps too hastily that it was the *volume* of capital goods output that was all important.

Harrod continued:

At our Trade Cycle group the other night Hitch made a point which if right is surely important. He argued that it is the *value* not the *volume* of capital goods output which is important as touching the absorption of saving.

Consequently he held, that since the demand for constructional goods as a whole is probably inelastic in a slump, arrangements tending to hold up their prices were beneficial in mitigating the severity of the slump. We argued your point against him that a drop in capital goods prices is helpful in tending to make the productive process more capitalistic at a moment at which it is all important that investment should be stimulated, but he argued that the drop in prices with an inelastic demand reduces net investment even if it does lead to some substitution.

Harrod then presented the following case for Meade's consideration. As he put it:

Suppose consumption goods industries B have to pay capital goods industries A £1500 instead of £1000 for replacements. The extra £500 comes out of the reserves of B and is distributed as income in A. Thus it is a factor mitigating depression. He [Hitch] admitted that some of the £500 might have been wrongly – if not expended – distributed as income in B or if received in A might merely be used to repay overdraft which does no good.

Harrod concluded:

But these he [Hitch] claimed were secondary matters, the primary effect being reflationary. Do you agree?[39]

Interestingly enough, in his book *Economic Thought and Language* (1937), Fraser – who both attended the September 1936 Oxford Conference and was in contact with Harrod after leaving Oxford for Aberdeen in 1935 – made a similar point as that made by Hitch at the meeting of the 'trade cycle group' which Harrod wrote to Meade about. Fraser, who had an ongoing interest in the problems of the trade cycle – and even reviewed Macfie's textbook survey entitled *Theories of the Trade Cycle* (1934) in the *EJ* in June 1935 – wrote:

> For the understanding of the trade cycle what matters is the volume of funds available as capital purchasing power [i.e. value], and the amounts of that purchasing power which are in fact used for the acquisition of equipment and/or claims.[40]

Now, while Harrod may have left the September 1936 Oxford Conference feeling disappointed at the reception, or lack of reaction, to his proposed dynamisation of Keynes and his 'dynamic determinants', as he later acknowledged in a letter to Robertson in October 1937, this problem may, in fact, have resulted, at least in part, from the 'cryptic' way in which he presented his ideas in his book. Perhaps the most problematic aspect is that while he had, in fact, almost completely spelt out his subsequent approach to growth in his book, this also went unnoticed by his critics. At this point, then, let us turn to what Harrod's critics actually said about *The Trade Cycle*.[41]

D. CRITIQUES, REVIEWS, AND REVIEWERS

While it did not make the positive impression he expected at the September 1936 Oxford Conference, Harrod's book still received widespread critical attention. Moreover, despite Harrod's assertion to the contrary – in his letter to Robertson of 8 October 1937, as cited above – most of the reviewers of his book, in fact, focused their attention on the problematic aspects of (a) his 'dynamic determinants'; (b) his interpretation and application of the 'relation' ('acceleration principle') and its interaction with the 'multiplier'; and (c) his aversion to using 'time-lags' in explaining the cycle.

The difficulty in putting the critiques and reviews of *The Trade Cycle* in their proper perspective, however, does not necessarily relate to the negative position a number of them took regarding the book as a whole or specific aspects of it. Rather, although these negative points of criticism must be recalled here, what may be more interesting and important are the points of constructive criticism of the book that may have influenced Harrod on the road to his 1939 'Essay'.[42]

For example, while on the one hand Joan Robinson – in her review of the book that appeared in the December 1936 issue of *EJ* – termed Harrod's initial use of his 'dynamic determinants' an 'odd . . . and fanciful method of exposition', on the other hand she asserted that his book was 'a considerable addition to the theory of the trade cycle'. According to her, Harrod's 'main contribution to the theory of the trade cycle lies in his combination of the principle of the Multiplier . . . with the principle of the Relation'. She also recognised that, in Harrod's view, as a result of the outcome of this interaction, 'a steady rate of expansion can . . . never be achieved'. According to her 'this conception is an important addition to the theory of employment' since, as she admitted 'Mr. Keynes has somewhat neglected the Relation'. However, as she put it, while 'steady advance' was discussed by Harrod, this, in her view, had 'no bearing on the trade cycle', since in her opinion, Harrod's approach here was 'based on unnatural assumptions . . . and its sole purpose' according to her, in his 'scheme is to show that a steady advance cannot occur'.[43]

In his February 1937 review of Harrod's book, Robertson first focused upon what he saw as the problematic and 'somewhat arbitrary' nature of Harrod's assumptions. Robertson went on to assert that, in his view, the 'main theme' of the book was, in fact 'the phenomena of growth', although, as he noted, according to Harrod 'even if we start with full employment, a steady rate of advance . . . in total output can never be maintained'. Interestingly enough, Robertson also agreed with Harrod as to the importance of the acceleration principle in trade cycle analysis and in explaining specific aspects of the cycle itself, as he put it 'even in the absence of that chronic tendency to oversaving which is implied by Mr. Harrod's analysis of the obstacles to a steady rate of advance'.[44]

Another review of the book appeared in the first issue of the *Manchester School* for 1937, this time by Stafford. In his review, he focused upon the 'dynamic determinants' by saying that:

> the interest of these determinants is not that they determine what the level of output shall be (for being dependent functions of that level they cannot do this), but that for Mr. Harrod's purpose they facilitate the analysis of the conditions under which different outputs can be put forward.

Stafford also referred to Harrod's proposed interaction between the 'multiplier' and the 'relation', but took issue with his dismissal of monetary policy, for example, short-term interest rates and credit conditions as factors in 'easing readjustment' over the cycle. As Stafford put it, in Harrod's book 'monetary policy is not given the dignity of a determinant'. According to Stafford, Harrod's:

> dynamic determinants are influenced by monetary policy – the propensity to save is greater with a stringent credit policy, both for the large investor and the public company, the shift to profit, which is a function of the rate of advance, and the capital ratio which is a function of credit policy.

In Stafford's view 'there is something – credit policy – behind the facade of the determinants which is too important to be hidden'.[45]

In his review of Harrod's book in the March 1937 issue of the *American Economic Review*, Wynne noted that others had preceded Harrod in 'linking the cycle' with the 'process' he described in *The Trade Cycle*. According to Wynne, however, Harrod claimed that other theories of the cycle had missed the 'necessary links', which gave his theory, as Wynne put it, the nature of 'an intelligible and self-consistent whole'. Wynne asserted that Harrod had made 'high claims' for his theory, but he continued 'whether they are accepted or not, there can be no doubt of the importance of the book'.[46]

In May 1937 two reviews of Harrod's book appeared, one by Hansen in the *Quarterly Journal of Economics* – which, in fact, was reprinted, with modifications, in his book *Full Recovery or Stagnation* a year later – and the other by Tinbergen, in *Welt. Archiv*. In his review Hansen also focused on the problematic aspects of Harrod's 'dynamic determinants' and the interaction between his 'relation' and the 'multiplier'. Hansen claimed that there was a lack of 'supporting evidence' for Harrod's assertion that his approach was better at explaining the trade cycle than others. He also stated that Harrod's 'relation' was, in fact, 'the well known principle of acceleration', albeit, in his view, incorrectly formulated. Moreover, Hansen asserted that Harrod seemed to have 'missed' those published papers in which the 'acceleration principle' was, in his view, correctly presented; otherwise, as Hansen put it 'he would certainly not have made the mistake all over again'. In addition, according to Hansen, 'far from being neglected by cycle theorists', as Harrod maintained, the 'acceleration principle', on Hansen's view, had received 'more prominence than it deserves'. He went on to cite Kuznets and Tinbergen to the effect that fluctuations in capital goods output were, in fact, much less than could be expected from the 'acceleration principle', and those that occurred could be explained, for the most part, by reference to other factors. In Hansen's view, then, 'the fundamental explanation lies elsewhere'.

Hansen then maintained, in contrast to Harrod's view, that what he called the 'true "dynamic determinants" of growth and progress' were factors such as 'inventions, the discovery of new resources', and 'changes in the efficiency of the factors of production', along the lines outlined, for example, by Spiethoff, Cassel, Robertson and Schumpeter. He concluded his review of Harrod's book by saying that the use Harrod made in it 'of the Relation and of the Multiplier is neither precise nor accurate. The Relation, *when correctly stated*, is surely not without significance but' in *The Trade Cycle* was 'made to carry a load well beyond its powers'. Hansen then said that in the book 'The Multiplier suffers from the same defects exposed by Haberler in his criticism of Keynes'. Finally, Hansen ended the review by saying 'with respect to the determinants, Mr. Harrod has bravely endowed ordinary commoners with distinguished titles'.[47]

In his review of the book in the May 1937 issue of *Welt. Archiv*, Tinbergen first pointed out that Harrod's 'relation' was synonymous, as he put it, with the 'acceleration principle of Clark and Haberler'. He also went on to question whether the interaction of Harrod's 'relation' and Keynes's 'multiplier doctrine', as he called them would, or could, produce a cyclical movement without the introduction of a lag. Moreover, Tinbergen showed, in his view at least, that 'without introduction of a lag, the formulae for the two relations Harrod mentions do not produce a cyclical movement of the variables'.[48]

Haberler, in his review of Harrod's book published in the *Journal of Political Economy* in October 1937, first questioned whether Harrod's '*Trade Cycle* approach' was 'an entirely new theory of the cycle' or not. In Haberler's view, almost all of the factors Harrod used were, as he put it, 'well known', having had 'found their place in other theories of the cycle'. However, as he admitted, Harrod put 'them together to form a closely reasoned theory' which could be called 'eclectic', and further, as Haberler said, it was 'the only possible procedure' that Harrod could have taken.

Haberler went on to term Harrod's account of the downturn resulting from the interaction between 'the relation' and 'the multiplier' as, in his words, 'the familiar description of a "Wicksellian" process of contraction'. He then asserted that Harrod either did not 'realize', or did not mention that this interaction was, as he put it, 'in reality a common feature of almost all trade cycle theory'. In Haberler's words:

the lack of any indication of this fact is unfortunate, because it conceals the continuity of thought in this field and creates or intensifies the impression of deep-rooted dissensions between different groups ('schools') of writers which is so discrediting for the reputation of economists.

It is not surprising, in light of their earlier correspondence and his initial reaction to the book as cited above, that in addition to the works of Clark and Slichter, Haberler mentioned his own *Prosperity and Depression* in this regard.

Interestingly enough, Haberler also focused on the problem of Harrod's objection to the use of time lags in explaining the cycle. As Haberler put it:

> I find it . . . difficult to reconcile Mr. Harrod's description of the interaction of 'Relation' and 'Multiplier' with his outspoken aversion for using time lags in the explanation of the cycle . . . it would seem that 'Relation' and 'Multiplier' if interpreted so as to refer to the same period, would contradict one another. Mr. Harrod can avoid this only by introducing (implicitly) time lags: investment today entails consumer's demand tomorrow, which, in turn, stimulates investment on the next day.

Finally, Haberler also focused upon Harrod's 'dynamic determinants', and said that he found it very hard to comprehend how they 'decreed' the slowdown and reduced activity.[49]

Gaitskell's treatment of Harrod's book in the November 1937 issue of *Economica*, although the last of the major reviews, also dealt with its 'outstanding' problematic aspects. On Gaitskell's view, while Harrod's 'terms' were 'new', as he put it 'the concepts are familiar'. He cited the example of 'the relation' which, as he said was the 'term given by Mr. Harrod to what is more widely known as "the acceleration principle"'. After dealing with the interaction between Harrod's 'relation' and 'the multiplier', and Harrod's 'dynamic determinants', Gaitskell said: 'Even if one disagrees at certain points with the emphasis he places on "the relation", there can really be no doubt that it is a phenomenon which no serious analysis can possibly omit". However, Gaitskell went on to say, as Tinbergen and Haberler before him, that 'here surely the time sequence must not be overlooked'.[50]

Two additional critiques of Harrod's book must also be mentioned here. The first was that of Hawtrey, published in his *Capital and*

Employment in 1937. The second, and possibly the critique that influenced Harrod most, was that of Keynes, which consisted of his 'miscellaneous' and 'lecture' notes and his correspondence with Harrod on the book after its publication. I have dealt with the Hawtrey critique and the Harrod-Hawtrey correspondence on it in detail elsewhere. Suffice it to say here that Harrod's presentation of the 'relation' and 'dynamic determinants' was seen as being too 'mechanical', and his negation of the efficacy of monetary policy was considered to be 'unsatisfactory' by Hawtrey.[51]

While Keynes's considered reaction to Harrod's book would seem to be the 'two resulting documents' he sent Harrod on 31 March 1937 as a result of having 'read' the book 'carefully' – that is, his 'miscellaneous' and 'lecture' notes on *The Trade Cycle* – there is some indication that he actually discussed the problems of what can be called the '*Trade cycle* approach' with Harrod as early as mid-February 1937. For example, in a letter to Harrod dated 18 February 1937 found in the Harrod papers, Keynes dealt with what he called Harrod's 'conundrum', which, although he thought it very interesting, he was also not sure how much it emanated from semantic considerations.

In this letter Keynes went on to provide Harrod with a numerical example to illustrate his belief that an increase in the value of capital was necessary to keep up with output, and that this increase would need to be somewhat more than the increase in the value of output, as a result of longer periods of production required. Keynes referred to his 'debate' with Harrod on this point, and that the assumption of a 'steady' rate of interest would 'facilitate' it. According to Keynes, his 'argument' was that, on the assumption of a 'steady' interest rate, one of the characteristics of technical innovation was to bring about an increase in the amount of capital required per worker. However, in his view, this rise in capital requirement was not much larger than 'in proportion to the output'. Keynes concluded his letter by saying, among other things, that if there would be capital shortfall, in this case, less than the 'normal' savings level, then it would be necessary to bring about an increase in capital utilisation by a considerable decrease in the interest rate.[52]

In any event, on 31 March 1937, Keynes sent his two 'notes', to which Harrod initially replied on 6 April. In his letter Harrod emphasised that Keynes, in his criticism of the book was 'still thinking of *once over* changes'. This, Harrod regarded 'as a static problem', whereas his own 'technique', as he put it, related 'to steady growth'. Moreover, Harrod continued:

You may suppose that population or efficiency *in fact* shows an arithmetic increase. That may be so. If it is we *must* have a cycle to allow things to get into arrears and then go forward for a time in a geometric spurt. It is in some respects the converse of the difficulty which Malthus feared, population increasing in arithmetic ratio and the means of subsistence (stock of capital) increasing in geometric ratio![53]

The next day Harrod again wrote to Keynes regarding his critique of the book, replying this time in much more detail. In his letter, besides answering Keynes's criticisms point by point, Harrod wrote:

I quite see why you were worried by my assumption that the stock of capital and investment were increasing at the same rate. I am right in saying that they *must* be increasing at the same rate if the increase in the stock of capital is steady. Nor is there anything unrealistic about the idea that they will increase at the same rate except in the revival. Here of course the increase of investment is greater, which entails that the increase of stock is *accelerating*. I did not want to trouble the reader's heads with acceleration when I was trying to get across unfamiliar stuff about the rate of growth (I notice that you define the relation in your notes in a most undesirably static way. It makes me feel about you slightly as you feel about critics of the *General Theory*! – namely that you won't re-orient your mind to the dynamic point of view.)

But the main point is that even if the rate of increase of investment exceeds the rate of increase of stock throughout the boom, this still makes no difference to the point that once the increase of consumption and so of stock required slows down, investment is no longer required to increase at all. Your arguments do not invalidate this in the slightest degree.[54]

Keynes replied to Harrod on 12 April 1937, and said that he had, in fact, misunderstood Harrod's theoretical approach to the trade cycle as put in their correspondence. However, he went on to say:

But the odd thing is that, having invented so interesting a theory, you should not have mentioned it in the book! . . . Indeed, I should doubt whether any reader who has not talked or corresponded with you could be aware that the whole of the last half of the book was intended to be in relation to a moving base of steady progress . . . you put your readers off the track by calling your book *The Trade Cycle*, and arguing as though your thesis principally related to that. For it seems to me that your theory has little or no bearing on the trade cycle, though none the less interesting for that. The phase of the boom is most certainly not a phase of steady growth. Yet you seem to be assuming that it is when you are considering the transition from the boom to the slump . . . It is necessary to explain whether by steady growth you mean steady growth of capital or steady growth of income. For the two are only the same on the assumption that the relation is constant.

Keynes also said that:

Since in fact the growth of population and the growth of technique are not steady, there is no presumption of steady growth, although probably there has been one in recent conditions in favour of growth. If there is continuous full employment, then there will be as high a rate of (unsteady) growth as is compatible with other factors . . . Thus steady growth and full employment are different criteria of policy. Full employment may require unsteady growth and steady growth may involve unsteady employment.

On this basis, Keynes concluded that:

You have shown, I think, that steady growth can only occur as the result of a miracle or intense design. But this is essentially a long-period problem, and steady growth a long-period conception. As I have said above, I do not see that the theory has any application worth mentioning to the trade cycle. The maintenance of steady growth is at all times an inherent improbability in conditions of *laissez-faire*.[55]

Harrod answered Keynes in a letter dated 15 April 1937, in which he said, among other things, that he would try to 'develop' his 'ideas for a form suitable for publication' in view of Keynes's 'reaction' to his book. In this letter, Harrod also wrote that he agreed with Keynes 'that steady growth and full employment do not provide the same criterion'. Harrod went on to say:

As between them I do not favour steady growth. On the contrary I say several times that, starting with the slump, to damp growth down to what could be steadily maintained would involve perpetuating existing unemployment, which would be intolerable.[56]

Finally, in the letter which closed the correspondence between them on 20 April 1937, Keynes said that he was not planning 'to write anything' on the points he raised in his critique of the book and the correspondence on it, until Harrod had 'carried' his 'ideas a stage further', which Keynes hoped Harrod would 'soon do'. It took over a year for Harrod to formally specify and set down his new ideas on growth and dynamics in writing, and this only after he discovered what he called the 'fundamental growth equation', or 'fundamental relation'. It is to the process involved in what Harrod called this 'mental revolution' and the influences upon it that we now turn.[57]

5 From the Trade Cycle to the 'Essay', 1935–39

In March 1945 Harrod and Robertson, as other economists of the time, were preoccupied with the questions of the post-war economic situation and reconstruction. Harrod, for his part, was especially concerned with the re-establishment of economic advance and growth. Thus, it is not surprising that he discussed the theoretical problems involved in an exchange of letters with Robertson. In a letter to Harrod dated 15 March 1945, Robertson said:

> I agree that your sense of the word dynamic is the most natural one to start with (though I wouldn't go so far as to say that the Hicksian stuff 'isn't dynamics at all'). I believe Marshall's system to be dynamic in your sense (see *Principles*, V.5. para. 3); also Cassel's *Theory of Social Economy* (1st English translation, vol. I, para. 6, p. 149 etc.). But how far, once one *departs* from the simplest assumption of steady progress, there is a hope of *discovering* the laws of such a system, I do not know. The multiplier seems to me wobbly enough as a short answer. But the principle of acceleration is worse. I am not optimistic about the claims of Economics to be a real science.[1]

To this, Harrod replied on 20 March 1945, starting his letter by asking Robertson:

> Have you yourself written anywhere, or can you refer me to someone else's writing that you have in mind when you say that the acceleration principle is worse? That is my sheet anchor. You cannot, of course, expect to find it modified in the short period, i.e. inside the trade cycle, because we are then scarcely at a steady rate of advance.

Now, it would seem that Robertson actually returned Harrod's letter of 20 March to him and, instead of formally replying, answered Harrod by means of jotting down his own comments on what Harrod had said in the margin of Harrod's original letter. Thus, in a marginal pencil note, appended in brackets to the text of Harrod's letter of 20 March, Robertson wrote in answer to Harrod's query:

There is a largish article literature by Frisch, Kuznets, Tinbergen, J.M. Clark etc., but it's not one of the subjects I've tried to do since my return to academia.

Harrod went on to say in his letter of 20 March:

I don't regard the multiplier principle as belonging to dynamics . . . The multiplier defines the relation between certain magnitudes in the static equilibrium. It has no dynamic component in it. There is no rate of increase or decline.

In answer to this, Robertson appended in the margin:

I agree, but it's apt to be used, e.g. by you in *The Trade Cycle* in analyzing dynamic processes . . .

Harrod then continued to say in his letter:

It is quite true, as has been pointed out, that in order to trace the movement from one static equilibrium to another, you may need to know some dynamics. That is a further reason for learning or devising some. It may be very important if the forces governing static equilibrium give an indeterminate result as between two or more possible positions.

Harrod then said:

I think your citation from Cassel more relevant than Marshall. Both only touch the problem. Aren't the concluding chapters in Marshall more relevant? I think the 'Classics' were full of dynamics. Ricardo's tendency of rents to rise, profits to fall etc. Ricardo was almost as much dynamic as static. But in refining upon the old dynamic theory with the apparatus of marginalism and simultaneous equations, it is always static theory that gets more and more precise, and the dynamic part has been forgotten.

Harrod concluded his letter to Robertson of 20 March 1945 by saying:

I am afraid my dynamics wouldn't be very scientific in the proper sense. I am still thinking rather in terms of a geometry of a system of relations which can be defined by pure thought. I am not altogether pessimistic about the Tinbergen type of empiricism, but that is beyond me. What I have in mind is something more simple. I shall evidently have to try to put it down on paper and I shall burden you with my questions.[2]

This frank exchange with Robertson raises a number of interesting questions regarding the nature and characteristics of the 'mental revolution', as Harrod put it, involved in the formulation of the system he outlined in *The Trade Cycle* (Harrod, 1936a) and later on, in his 'Essay' (Harrod, 1939a). First of all, to what extent was he influenced by both earlier and contemporary writings on the 'progressive' economy, the acceleration principle, macrodynamics, and 'optimum' saving, such as those of Cassel, Tinbergen, and, for that matter, Kalecki and Lange? Secondly, between 1935 and 1939, Harrod both reviewed the works of other economists who dealt with macroeconomic problems, such as Durbin, Robinson, and Lundberg, and also corresponded with some of them regarding his views on these problems, such as Durbin. To what extent, then, did this process influence the development of his thought over the period? Thirdly, as is well known, Harrod engaged in a long exchange with Keynes on his 'Essay'. But, as will be shown, he also sent a copy of the draft of his 'Essay' to Robertson for comment, and also corresponded with him regarding it. To what extent, then, was Harrod influenced by Keynes *and* Robertson when finalising his 'Essay'? Finally, as will be seen, besides sending the draft of his 'Essay' to Keynes and Robertson, Harrod, it seems, also asked Marschak to read and comment on it. To what extent, then, was Harrod influenced by Marschak's diagrammatic representation of his approach and detailed comments on it?

A. THE CASSEL-KALECKI-TINBERGEN-LANGE CONNECTION: READINGS, REFLECTION, AND INTROSPECTION

Cassel's influence on Harrod

The first English translation of Cassel's book, *The Theory of Social Economy* (1918) by McCabe was published in 1923, and cited repeatedly by Robertson in his book, *Banking Policy and the Price Level* (1926). Harrod, for his part, reviewed Robertson's book in 1927, and thus, had he been directly influenced by Cassel's book at the time, could have no doubt arrived at what has been called by Brems the 'Cassel-Harrod growth equation' over a decade before it actually appeared in print. Moreover, in his 1938 'Scope and Method' paper, Harrod mentioned McCabe's 1923 translation of Cassel's book, and in his 're-appraisal' of Walras, Harrod recalled reading Cassel, as he put it, 'on monetary questions'.[3]

In fact, Harrod was also familiar with Cassel's earlier works, including his *Fundamental Thoughts on Economics*, which Harrod also mentioned in his 1938 'Scope and Method' paper, and Cassel's *Nature and Necessity of Interest*, on which Harrod had made detailed notes while still a student. Therefore, if Harrod *had* focused upon Cassel's equational representation of a 'progressive economy' as manifest in his book, he would have been able to present his version of the growth equation as early as September 1938 in the published version of his 'Scope and Method' paper, rather than some six months later, in March 1939. As will be shown below, Harrod discovered his growth equation independently of Cassel's equational representation of growth in a 'progressive economy'.[4]

Now, Harrod's equation can be derived from Cassel's equational system, as will be shown below, however, in order to do this, both a sophisticated gedanken (thought) experiment and suitable algebraic manipulation are required. For Harrod to have derived his equation from Cassel, he would have had to first start with Cassel's notion of the 'degree of saving' or 'relative saving of the community'. A proportional relationship was defined by Cassel of the form:

$$1/s = S/Y \tag{1}$$

where Y is income, S is savings, and $1/s$ is 'annually the proportion' – in absolute amount Y/s – of income that 'is saved' that is, the 'degree of saving', or 'relative saving of the community'.[5]

If Harrod took $S = I = \Delta K$, then

$$Y = s\Delta K \tag{2}$$

and

$$Y = Y/S \cdot \Delta K \tag{3}$$

Given that this was the case, Harrod would have obtained

$$Y/\Delta K = Y/S \tag{4}$$

since, by definition, $Y/S = Y/I$, or $S = I$.

Up to this point, things are relatively simple. The key equation here would be equation (4), since it could have been further transformed into his growth equation. In other words, if equation (4) was inverted and both sides multiplied by the algebraic equivalent of unity, that is, $\Delta Y/\Delta Y$, Harrod would have arrived at the following equation:

$$\Delta Y/\Delta Y \cdot \Delta K/Y = S/Y \cdot \Delta Y/\Delta Y \tag{5}$$

From this, he would have obtained, after rearranging terms:

$$\Delta Y/Y \cdot \Delta K/\Delta Y = S/Y \tag{6}$$

This would have given Harrod his growth equation, where $\Delta Y/Y$ is G, $\Delta K/\Delta Y$ is C, and S/Y is Harrod's 's', that is, the propensity to save:

$$G \cdot C = s \tag{7}$$
$$\text{or, } G = s/C \tag{8}$$

The algebraic manipulations and transformations outlined above, however, could be said, on Harrod's own account, to be a bit 'beyond' his mathematical ability. Thus, it is indeed doubtful whether he would, or could have actually reached his growth equation by such a circumspect route.[6]

Kalecki's Influence on Harrod

With regard to Kalecki, it is well known that he published a number of important papers on the 'business' and 'trade' cycle over the period in question, such as 'A macrodynamic theory of business cycles' in the July 1935 issue of *Econometrica*, and 'A theory of the business cycle' in the February 1937 issue of *RES*. Whether Harrod, in fact, took any notice of Kalecki's work has been, up to now, a moot point, since no evidence of any direct influence has ever been discovered. However, a decade before their retrospective exchange of views in March 1945, Harrod, in a letter to Robertson dated 3 October 1935 – parts of which have already been cited above – also wrote:

> I have before me *Econometrica* with its Tinbergen and Kalecki. I suspect that Kalecki is saying something that I have been feeling towards, and I have got to try and find out. But what a paper it is![7]

Moreover, in a letter to Keynes some three years later, Harrod again mentioned the contributions of Kalecki and Tinbergen; this time, also bringing in Lundberg's work (the importance of which will be dealt with below). In his letter, dated 18 September 1938, Harrod wrote:

> The introduction of a lag into an otherwise smoothly working system may set up an oscillation. Tinbergen reviews a number of theories of this sort in *Econometrica* 1935. Kalecki, Lundberg and others have been working on them.[8]

Now, this is not the place for a detailed analysis of the similarities between the approaches of Harrod and Kalecki to the problems of the trade cycle, growth, and dynamics. Suffice it to say, however, that according to his letter to Robertson, at least, as early as October 1935, Harrod was both aware of and impressed by Kalecki's work and thus could indeed have been influenced by it.

Tinbergen's Influence on Harrod

The question of Tinbergen's possible influence on Harrod is somewhat problematic, to say the least. Moreover, it is also complicated by what in my view is an anecdotal myth regarding the effect of Tinbergen's review of Harrod's book, *The Trade Cycle*, upon the development of Harrod's thought. This has, in turn, obfuscated what may have been the actual effect of Tinbergen's work – especially his 1935 *Econometrica* and 1938 *Economica* papers, the latter entitled 'Statistical evidence on the acceleration principle' – upon Harrod. Now, I have dealt in detail with the problem surrounding Tinbergen's review of Harrod's book and Harrod's reaction to Goodwin's contention regarding its influence upon him elsewhere, so this will not be repeated here. Suffice it to say, however, that while Harrod expressed both his ongoing interest in and appreciation of Tinbergen's work during the years in question, he never acknowledged having been influenced by Tinbergen's 1937 review of *The Trade Cycle*.[9]

On the other hand, over the period July-September 1938, Harrod corresponded intensively with Keynes regarding Tinbergen's appraisal of the general validity of the acceleration principle and his overall approach to the problem of the cycle. For example, in a letter to Keynes dated 6 July 1938, among other things, Harrod mentioned Tinbergen's statistical work on the acceleration principle. He dealt in detail with Tinbergen's contention that it did not hold and did not, therefore, have the influence he had ascribed to it. He wrote:

> I feel that Tinbergen may be doing very valuable work in trying to reduce this part of theory to quantitative terms . . . The matter has a personal interest as well as a purely academic one to me . . . I make a statement about the 'acceleration principle'. Then Tinbergen comes and says that the facts do not suggest that it had the influence I ascribed to it. Surely one ought *not* to leave the matter there. To Tinbergen, the statistics merely *suggest* a negative result. To me, if I applied his technique, they might suggest a refinement of my concepts or a restressing of the importance of one at the expense of the other. I confess all this frightens me a little.

Keynes replied to Harrod's letter on 16 July, and among other things, said:

> My point against T[inbergen] is a different one. In Chemistry and Physics and other natural sciences the object of experiment is to fill in the actual values of the various quantities and factors appearing in an equation or a formula; and the work when done is once and for all. In economics that is not the case, and to convert a model into a quantitative formula is to destroy its usefulness as an instrument of thought.[10]

The correspondence between Harrod and Keynes regarding Tinbergen's work continued on through August-September 1938, and focused, in the main, on Keynes's reaction to the draft manuscript of Tinbergen's League of Nations study, which had been sent to him for evaluation, and which Keynes eventually also reviewed in the September 1939 issue of *EJ*. In the course of this correspondence Harrod told Keynes – in a letter dated 3 August 1938 – that he had met Tinbergen in Cambridge during July 1938 and, in his letter to Keynes regarding Tinbergen's draft manuscript sent on 18 September, said that he had also discussed the manuscript with Tinbergen during his visit to Cambridge. As Harrod put it in his letter to Keynes of 18 September 1938: 'You think that his book is in effect a study of the oscillatory consequences of assuming a lag. I think it is and Tinbergen agreed when I put it to him'.[11]

What is interesting to note here is that, in a letter to Harrod dated 11 August 1938, among other things, Keynes admitted that he had not studied Tinbergen's work 'as carefully' as Harrod had, and on 20 September Keynes wrote Tinbergen to the effect that the statistical analysis and methodology of his draft manuscript might be limited in its applicability or not applicable at all to the 'broad problem' of the 'credit cycle' and the 'general theory' of the 'trade cycle', and that he was sending a copy of this letter to Harrod, as he put it, 'for information'.[12]

It would seem, therefore, that Harrod, for his part, was more concerned with Tinbergen's results than with his method, for in his May 1938 *Economica* paper, Tinbergen had called into question both the analytical and empirical validity of Harrod's 'Relation' (acceleration principle). In his paper, Tinbergen wrote:

> Much attention has recently been given to the so-called 'acceleration principle' or 'the Relation' as Mr. Harrod calls it . . . Mr. Harrod regards the acceleration principle and the multiplier principle acting in combination as the chief forces in trade cycles.

After presenting his 'statistical evidence', Tinbergen concluded, however: 'it may be said that the acceleration principle cannot help very much in the explanation of the details in real investment fluctuations.'[13]

Tinbergen's 'assault' on his 'Relation' (the 'acceleration principle') – the 'sheet anchor' of his *Trade Cycle* approach, as he called it – would seem to have upset Harrod at the time, as he admitted in his letter to Keynes of 6 July 1938. Harrod probably started reorganising his thoughts on the problems of the trade cycle, growth, and dynamics, therefore, sometime after reading Tinbergen's May 1938 *Economica* paper. And it may have been Lange, in the previous issue of *Economica*, who actually provided Harrod with the solution to his 'conundrum', in the form of his concept of 'optimum' saving.[14]

Lange's Influence on Harrod

In the February 1938 issue of *Economica* (Lange, 1938a), Lange published a paper entitled 'The rate of interest and the optimum propensity to consume'. In this paper, he also introduced the notion of an 'optimum propensity to save' which, in his view, depended on 'the shape of the liquidity preference and of the investment functions'. According to Lange, this imposed 'a maximum limit on investment per unit of time and any attempt to exceed it by raising the propensity to save above its optimum frustrates itself by leading to a diminution of investment'.[15]

Now, in the same May 1938 issue of *Economica* in which Tinbergen's 'result' effectively undermined the very foundation of Harrod's *Trade Cycle* approach, Lange's review of Lundberg's *Studies in the Theory of Economic Expansion* appeared (Lange, 1938b). Harrod, for his part, had also reviewed Lundberg's book in the August 1937 issue of *ZFN* (Harrod, 1937c), a review which will be dealt with in detail below. It is extremely likely, therefore that Harrod also read Lange's review of Lundberg. While brooding over the problem raised by Tinbergen's attack on his 'Relation', then, Harrod may have recalled Lange's earlier February 1938 *Economica* paper, which it is almost certain he had read, and thus recalled Lange's notions of the 'optimum' propensities to consume and save respectively.[16]

It is clear that acceptance of the 'tautological' condition that *I* (Investment) must always equal *S* (Saving), when combined with Lange's notion of the 'optimum propensity to save' in fact generates – 'in a split second', as Harrod later put it, albeit in another context – his 'fundamental relationship'. After reading Tinbergen, and recalling Lange, Harrod could have, therefore, conducted the following thought experiment:

Multiplying both sides of $I=S$ by the growth rate ($\Delta Y/Y$) would have maintained the equality/identity $I=S$, as in equation (1) below, that is,

$$I \cdot \Delta Y/Y = S \cdot \Delta Y/Y \tag{1}$$

Following from this, and rearranging the left-hand side of the equation, he would have obtained

$$I \cdot \Delta Y/Y = S/Y \cdot \Delta Y \tag{2}$$

which can be rewritten as

$$\Delta K \cdot G = s\Delta Y \tag{3}$$

where $\Delta K = I$; $G = \Delta Y/Y$; and $s = S/Y$.

Now, by defining $\Delta Y/\Delta K$ as $1/C$, Harrod would have immediately obtained:

$$G_w = s/C \tag{4}$$

where G_w is 'warranted growth'. Furthermore, by defining $\Delta K/\Delta Y$ as Cp, that is, 'the value of the increment of capital per unit increment of output actually produced', if $C = Cp$, then $G = G_w$.

In other words, then, Lange's optimum propensity to save would be that which maintains the condition $I = S$, that is, that which is 'warranted'.[17]

Interestingly enough, in his review of Lange's *Price Flexibility and Employment* (1945) in the March 1946 issue of *EJ* – a year after his first post-war exchange with Robertson on the nature of dynamic economics and growth theory cited above – Harrod returned to the question of what constituted 'true' economic dynamics. According to him, Lange's equational approach in his 1945 book was 'genuinely dynamic', since his equations referred 'to rates of the movement of prices. They define conditions in the field around a postulated equilibrium of the system'. However, Harrod continued:

> But they only touch the fringe of economic dynamics. We shall not have got a genuine dynamics of the subject, until the variables, the values of which are determined by the fundamental equations of the equilibrium, are not rates of production per unit of time, but rates of increase of production, rates of capital accumulation, etc., per unit of time. The introduction of dynamic considerations into the analysis of what happens when the system is in disequilibrium is an advance; but we shall not have reached our goal until we can define the normal condition of the system as being one of motion, a state of rest being a special and improbable case.[18]

Now, whether or not Harrod actually conducted the thought experiments outlined above, it is clear that the possible influence of Lange's ideas upon Harrod must also be taken into account.

Moreover, Tinbergen's influence must not be relegated to the realm of anecdotal myth by referring only to his 1937 review of *The Trade Cycle*, for it is clear that his ongoing influence upon the development of Harrod's thought – especially the effect of his May 1938 *Economica* article – was significant, and may even have catalysed the discovery of Harrod's 'fundamental equation'.

B.   THE DURBIN-ROBINSON-LUNDBERG CONNECTION: REVIEWS, CRITICISM, AND CORRESPONDENCE

Over the period in question, Harrod reviewed a number of works, the process of which may have also influenced the development of his thought. The first of these was Evan Durbin's book *The Problem of Credit Policy*, of which Harrod was, for the most part, critical in his review of it in the December 1935 issue of *EJ* (Harrod, 1935b). Harrod's review prompted an ongoing correspondence with Durbin over the next two years, during which Durbin also turned to Robertson for intellectual support; for, as Robertson put it in a letter to Durbin dated 29 July 1935, he was in 'accord' with Durbin's 'main conclusions'.[19]

Perhaps the most interesting letter in the Harrod-Durbin correspondence is one from Durbin to Harrod dated 15 June 1937, after discussion between them, in which Durbin focused upon what he took to be Harrod's central concern, which, in his view, was the growth rate. In order to illustrate his point, Durbin drew a series of diagrams in which he showed what he thought the message of Harrod's *Trade Cycle* actually was. Durbin's first diagram consisted of a curve showing the transition from the initial stage of recovery to the later period in terms of a change in slope in the growth rate in output 'from the high rate of growth set up early in the boom to the secular rate of growth appearing when full employment is reached'.

The second diagram Durbin drew showed a steeply-rising curve of net money income, along with a less-steeply-rising curve of consumption expenditure, both of which are rising faster than the physical output of consumption goods, so that 'after a time prices will rise as expenditure is rising more rapidly than the output of consumption goods'. This, Durbin took as the 'later period of recovery', which involved inflation. According to Durbin, if 'after a time it is decided to check the inflation', this will bring about, in turn, a contraction in economic activity that 'will be cumulative and severe' due to the combined action of the accelerator and multiplier.

Durbin concluded, however, that the acceleration principle could only be utilised for explaining 'the relative movements of capital and consumption goods production' in the trade cycle 'and not as an explanation of the "inevitable" crisis'. The seeds of doubt regarding his 'Relation', then, were sown in Harrod's mind as early as mid-June 1937; but, at the same time, his attention was also being focused in on the problem of maintaining a 'secular' growth rate of output without the threat of inflation, on the one hand, and contraction, on the other.[20]

Harrod reviewed Joan Robinson's *Essays in the Theory of Employment* in the June 1937 issue of *EJ* (Harrod, 1937b). In it Harrod focused on what he called the 'pièce de résistance' of her book, which, in his view, was her essay on 'the long period theory of employment'. While Harrod thought the 'general' approach of Keynesian-based long-run macrostatics employed by Robinson in her book – and especially in this essay – valid, it was only one 'method', as he put it, 'among alternative procedures'. By focusing on the limitations of her method, Harrod said:

> But it may serve also to increase our impatience for the elaboration of a dynamic analysis. It is high time that we had a method of dynamic analysis, not in substitution for but in addition to Mrs. Robinson's method, which considers the conditions pertaining to *rates of growth*. Static analysis is concerned to determine the magnitude of prices, employment, etc. consistent with certain basic conditions. Dynamic analysis should be concerned to determine what rates of growth or decline of these magnitudes are consistent with rates of growth or decline in the basic conditions and with one another. If the reader feels that Mrs. Robinson's methods in this essay are unduly artificial he is probably wrong; but I suggest that he is right if he feels that it reveals a great gap in economic theory which urgently needs filling.[21]

On the level of private criticism, Harrod expressed his disagreement with both the Robertsonian and Robinsonian positions regarding the determination of the long-run rate of interest in a letter to Robertson dated 22 January 1938. In this letter he wrote:

> I am so far unrepentant about the rate of interest in a stationary state. Current new investment involves an increase in the means of

production but this contradicts the static assumptions. If you are prepared to waive this and allow growth of capital in an otherwise stationary state, then the laws of supply and demand give you not a rate of interest but a rate of fall in the rate of interest with nothing said as to the absolute level of the rate of interest. The ordinary analysis does not provide any account of what determines the absolute level.

Harrod continued:

In her last book [*Essays in the Theory of Employment*] Joan Robinson says that the rate of interest must always be falling. That is only true as a general statement, if you are dealing with a static state. But how foolish to assume that in a book on unemployment and the trade cycle.[22]

In his treatment of Joan Robinson, then, Harrod was again 'throwing out' one of the many 'hints' – as he called them in a letter to Keynes on 3 August 1938 – 'of the possibility of formulating a simple law of growth'.

Harrod reviewed Lundberg's book in the August 1937 issue of *ZFN* (Harrod, 1937c). In Harrod's opinion, Lundberg's work was 'an extremely important contribution to economic studies'. In his review Harrod took issue, however, with Lundberg on two major points. The first concerned Lundberg's problematic treatment of certain aspects of Keynes's *General Theory*. Among these were what Harrod saw as Lundberg's misinterpretation of Keynes's approach to saving and hoarding, and Lundberg's views regarding the limits of Keynes's notion of liquidity preference in interest rate determination. The second point Harrod raised related to whether Lundberg's method was 'the only alternative', as he put it 'to the methods of static analysis'.[23]

As for the first point, interestingly enough, while in his later review Kahn also focused on Lundberg's interpretation of Keynes's liquidity preference relation and approach to interest rate determination (Kahn, 1938), Harrod was much more sympathetic than Kahn to Lundberg's critique of certain shortcomings in Keynes's *General Theory*. For example, Harrod maintained that Lundberg's 'criticism that the curve of the marginal efficiency of capital may be expected to shift during an "adaptation process" . . . is better founded', in Harrod's view, resulting from the fact, as he put it, 'that this matter is not analysed by Mr. Keynes'. Harrod also asserted that while the 'critical sections' of Lundberg's book 'contain a vast amount of interesting matter . . . with the exception of a brilliant interlude in Ch. IV, they are rather overloaded with methodological matter'. Lange, in his review of Lundberg's book, was not as impressed by chapter IV, and in his review wrote that it 'would have gained in clarity by the use of some calculus and greater generalisation'. Be that as it may, Harrod still continued on to say that 'the reader will be wrong if he is disappointed; let him persevere'. As the later reviewers noted, Lundberg's chapter IX, in which his 'model sequences' appeared was, as Harrod put it, 'the meat of the volume'. In Harrod's view, however, if Lundberg 'had placed this earlier in the volume, his critical sections would have been much more telling'.[24]

With regard to the second point, Harrod asserted that Lundberg's 'model sequences' were 'done with great care and ingenuity', and went on to outline what he called the 'determining factors' in Lundberg's 'method of dynamic analysis'. According to Harrod, these factors included 'the proportion of income saved' and 'the proportion of costs which do not generate incomes'. Moreover, Harrod stated that the results of Lundberg's approach 'are based on the division of production into . . . consumption and capital goods, the application of the "acceleration principle" to part of . . . capital production and, in a roundabout way, the operation of the multiplier'.[25]

In addition, Harrod referred to the importance of Lundberg's notion of 'the length of the unit period' which, in Harrod's view, constituted a 'reaction time' upon which, in his words 'much depends'. Harrod then distinguished between Lundberg's 'alternative to the methods of static analysis' and his own; but more about this below. Finally, Harrod concluded his review by stating that 'Lundberg's book is one which all students of the trade cycle should study. It breaks new ground, and displays high qualities of intellectual insight and grasp'.[26]

Now, in my view, in his review of Lundberg's book Harrod gave what was the first explicit – albeit verbal – formulation of his notion of 'warranted growth'. As Harrod wrote in his review:

> I suggest that it may be possible to construct a method of dynamic analysis more closely analogous to the dynamics of mechanics. In place of the static question, what rate of production of eggs per day will be consistent with the maximization of the advantage of egg producers, we ask, what rate of increase in the production of eggs

per day will lead to this result? This is a natural extension of the static theory, appropriate to an expanding economy. At what rates of increase (or decrease) must all members of the system pursue their operations so that, when they all do this, no one shall find it to his advantage to do otherwise than continue expanding at this rate? A system of equations in which these rates of increase (or decrease) are unknowns should be elaborated, on lines similar to those of traditional static systems, with sufficient unknowns to determine the values of the additional unknowns also.[27]

After introducing his alternative to Lundberg's method in the form of the 'dynamic' question he posed as cited above, Harrod went on to say that:

> if a dynamic system of this kind could be established, the considerations introduced by reference to 'sequences' could be superimposed as corrections. My complaint of the sequence analysis is that it seeks to introduce the corrections, before the dynamic principles themselves are established . . . changes may occur in a system that is not expanding. The existence of change reduces *pro tanto* the applicability of the static analysis to the real world. It gives rise to problems of profit, which to some extent disrupt the traditional static system. It may be that a sequence analysis is the best method of coping with these problems. But they have no direct connexion with the problems of growth.

Harrod continued on to say that:

> the former set of problems, because they involve arbitrary decisions, may prove amenable to sequence analysis. The latter should be solved by a system of equations relating to a given point of time but containing terms expressing rates of growth.

Harrod concluded his presentation of what he called his dynamic 'alternative' to Lundberg's approach by saying that:

> A sequence analysis is especially attractive to students of the trade cycle, because it is not difficult to make reasonable assumptions which generate a cycle. None the less I incline to the view that the real secret of the cycle is to be found in a dynamic analysis, of the kind here contrasted with the sequence analysis.[28]

It seems, therefore, that in terms of the evolution of his growth and dynamic theory, Harrod's review of Lundberg's book is indeed a 'missing link'. For, in this review not only did Harrod, in my view, explicitly formulate his notion of 'warranted growth' – shifting the emphasis of his thought to that of 'dynamic analysis' as being 'the real secret of the cycle' – but as noted above, he also specified the length of what Lundberg called the 'unit period' as a 'reaction time'; the importance of which is quite evident in his 1939 'Essay' (Harrod, 1939a). Almost all the pieces of Harrod's growth and dynamics jigsaw were now in place. One piece, however – the notion of inherent systemic instability – was still missing. And it may be that Lundberg's book – especially chapter IV, which introduced this notion and which Harrod called 'a brilliant interlude' in his review – actually supplied it.[29]

C. THE KEYNES-ROBERTSON CONNECTION: INTERPRETATIONS, CLARIFICATIONS, AND CONSTRUCTIVE CRITICISM

The close intellectual and personal relationship between Harrod and Keynes is well known. Moreover, Harrod saw Keynes, and Keynes also saw Harrod, as a sounding-board for the sympathetic – albeit objective – critical evaluation of ideas, and thus the ongoing exchanges between them during the period in question. What is much less known – if at all – is that Harrod saw Robertson in a similar light, that is, as a constructive critic and objective sounding-board for his new ideas. Now, this is not to say that Harrod was as close to Robertson as he was to Keynes. However, as has been shown above with regard to *The Trade Cycle*, and will now be shown by reference to the early correspondence surrounding his 1939 'Essay', Harrod relied upon Robertson, to at least the same extent as he relied upon Keynes, to provide him with objective and constructive critical evaluation of his ideas.

For example, in his letter to Keynes dated 6 July 1938, Harrod told Keynes that he had put what he called his dynamic theory 'into a much better form' than in *The Trade Cycle*. He also went on to tell Keynes that he hoped to be able to send him 'a short article quite soon'. The day before, on 5 July 1938, Harrod sent a letter to Robertson, in which he said that he 'found' his 'mind unduly excited'. This was because, as he told Robertson:

I have in my head, though not yet written out, what I believe to be a satisfactory formulation of the problem of a normal increase in terms of a law of growth, a fundamental equation governing the normal rate of growth. I hope to publish this as soon as Maynard lets me. I should like you to see it in type before that, if you would care to. I say as soon as Maynard lets me because the next number of the Journal will be swollen by a large screed constituting my presidential address [Section F of the British Association, published as 'Scope and Method of Economics' in *EJ*, September 1938].[30]

About a month later, on 3 August 1938, Harrod again wrote to Keynes, this time to tell him that he had 'just finished writing' what he called his 'restatement' of dynamic theory, which, on his view was 'a great improvement' on *The Trade Cycle*. Harrod hoped that Keynes would 'find it interesting', and told him that he had sent it on to be typed. Harrod then said that it would be ready to send to Keynes a few days afterwards. Harrod added that he would have liked the article to be published in the *EJ* 'as soon as' Keynes – who was editor at the time – could 'find room for more' by him, and suggested the December 1938 issue as a possibility. Harrod went on to say that the reason for this was not only that he had not 'taken up any space for several years', but that as he had 'been throwing out hints in a number of places of the possibility of formulating a simple law of growth', he wanted 'to substantiate the claim'.[31]

The same day as he wrote to Keynes – on 3 August 1938 – Harrod also wrote to Robertson, and said:

I have now completed my article which is in the hands of the typist. I think it is jolly good! I do hope you will like it.

Harrod went on to tell Robertson how he stood regarding Robertson's 'fundamental objections' to his approach, that is, that it didn't take into account 'lags' and that its concepts were not clearly defined. Harrod wrote:

I agree that the theory of the *General Theory* is *fundamentally static* for lack of incorporation of the 'acceleration principle' or something of the sort. On the other hand, I am in sympathy with the main contention that orthodox static theory [e.g. Marshall] does not give us all we want in the way of a framework of explanation of phenomena *before* we begin to play about with lags. In the end we have got to face the question of lags. But we can only do so profitably if *we are sure* that we are using lag hypotheses in a framework of concepts which does justice to the forces determining *normal* equilibrium or *normal* trend. I don't think we are yet in that position. I think JMK is right to suppose that we need a further clearing up of the *General Theory*, but he has not gone far enough.

As for the issue of what he meant by 'long period normal', Harrod said to Robertson:

> I have the fear that by long period normal you are still thinking in static terms; that you mean the long period of Marshall. But I don't think *that* conception is of any use for our purpose. What I want to find is a *normal* trend, and I don't think you get that by thinking in terms of successive adjustments to a long period static equilibrium.

Harrod concluded his letter to Robertson by saying:

> Joan R[obinson] tries this in her long period theory of employment and I think the result unsatisfactory.[32]

Now, the Harrod-Keynes correspondence on Harrod's 1939 'Essay' has been dealt with in a number of places, and I have also surveyed it in detail elsewhere, so this extensive exchange – which, in effect, began on 17 August 1938 – will not be analysed in depth here. Suffice it to say, however, that in my view, it was, in fact, Keynes who set Harrod straight as to the nature of what Harrod called the 'fundamental relation' or 'fundamental equation', and the 'warranted rate of growth'.[33] For, as Keynes pointed out to Harrod, while

> a warranted rate is *theoretically* possible . . . with a stationary population, peace and unequal incomes, the warranted rate sets a pace which a private risk-taking economy cannot normally reach and can never maintain.

Therefore, in order to maintain a growth rate consonant with full employment, Keynes suggested 'a drastic change in the distribution of incomes so as to reduce a[s] [the propensity to save]', among other measures, since, as he wrote to Harrod in his letter of 26 September

1938, which, in effect, wound up the correspondence between them on Harrod's 1939 'Essay':

> With stationary population, no abnormal government expenditure, and an unequal distribution of incomes, I doubt if the warranted rate can be attained in practice.[34]

But Keynes's doubts went much deeper than this, for, as he said to Harrod in his letter of 26 September 1938:

> As a result of your last letter [22 Sept.], I have, at last, seen in a flash what it is all about. My intuition told me that your conclusion could not be true *in general* but only subject to specified conditions . . . Your argument as now expounded shows, quite correctly, that *if* there is a warranted rate of growth, an increase in excess of this rate will lead to the results you indicate. But this assumes that there *is* a warranted rate. That is the basic assumption I have been allowing you to get away with. In general there is no warranted rate, and special conditions are required for a warranted rate to be possible . . . In actual conditions, therefore, I suspect the difficulty is, *not* that a rate in excess of the warranted is unstable, but that the warranted rate itself is so high that with private risk-taking no one dares to attain it, except momentarily by accident.[35]

D.　THE MARSCHAK CONNECTION: 'REMARKS' AND DIAGRAMMATIC-EQUATIONAL REPRESENTATION

Perhaps the most interesting – albeit up to now unknown – of the pre-publication comments on Harrod's draft manuscript of his 1939 'Essay' was that of Marschak. In his handwritten 'Remarks to R.F.H's "Essay in Dynamic Theory"' – which was found in the Harrod papers – Marschak not only provided Harrod with a diagrammatic and equational representation of what he took as the four rates of growth in Harrod's 'Essay', but gave Harrod a detailed page by page – and in some places, line by line – analysis and critique of the axiomatic basis of his approach to growth. Marschak divided his 'Remarks' on the draft manuscript of Harrod's 'Essay' into ten parts, which he called sections A-K respectively.

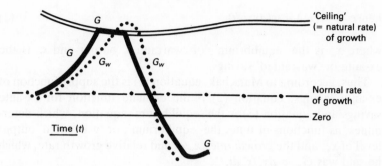

Figure 5.1   Marschak's 'chart' of the 'time shape' of Harrod's *four* growth rates

Source: Harrod papers, file V–113a.

Marschak opened his section (A) with a 'chart' in which he attempted to show what he saw as the 'time shape' of the four growth rates in Harrod's 'Essay'. These were, on Marschak's view, the actual rate of growth of output (G); what Harrod called the 'warranted rate' (G_w); the 'natural rate'; and what Marschak called the 'normal rate'. In his 'chart', Marschak called the 'full drawn' line – G; the 'dotted line' – G_w; the 'double line', the 'ceiling', or 'natural rate'; and the 'broken line', the 'normal rate', lying between the level set by G_w and zero, as illustrated in Figure 5.1.

According to Marschak, while the definitions Harrod used for the actual and natural rates of growth were not difficult to comprehend, his definition of the warranted rate was not that easy to understand. As Marschak put it, if output was denoted as x, then the actual growth rate was $g=dx/xdt$, so that the natural rate was the highest value of dx/xdt, given full employment and the state of technology. On the other hand, while G_w, the warranted rate, also depended on a given state of technology, the full employment condition was relaxed by Harrod and in its place was substituted the condition that G_w is that rate which 'will leave all parties satisfied'.

In his section (B), Marschak went on to outline what he took to be the equational structure underlying the 'axiomatic basis' of Harrod's approach in order to make the notions of 'warranted' output, 'warranted rate of growth', and 'relative rate of growth' more easily understood. In his view this could have been achieved by specifying a three-equation system of the form:

$$s_w x_w = f(x_w) \tag{1}$$
$$s_w x_w = \varphi(dx_w/dt) \tag{2}$$

hence $f(x_w) = \varphi(dx_w/dt)$ (3)

where x_w is the 'equilibrium', or 'warranted' output and s_w is the ex-ante or 'warranted' savings.

Thus, according to Marschak, equation (1) is the supply function of ex-ante savings, equation (2) is the demand function for ex-ante savings and equation (3) is the 'equilibrium' equation, which determines, as functions of time, the 'equilibrium', or 'warranted' output level of x_w, and the *growth rate dx_w/dt* and relative growth rate, which he said was $G_w = dx_w/x_w dt$.

In Marschak's view, a time shape for G_w would be obtained according to the shape of the supply and demand functions as long as functions (f) and φ did not change. He went on to say that in the simplest case, demand function φ could be a simple 'proportionality law' of the form:

$$s_w x_w = C(dx_w/dt)$$ (2a)

where constant C here would be identical with the 'C' in Harrod's equation (1); where Harrod's equation (1) is derived from his equation (2a) by dividing through by Cx_w so that

$$s_w/C = dx_w/x_w dt \, (\equiv G_w)$$ (4)

According to Marschak, in this case, his equation (3), the 'equilibrium' equation, takes on the form:

$$f(x_w) = C(dx_w/dt)$$ (3a)

so that dividing through by $x_w C$, one would obtain:

$$\frac{f(x_w)}{x} \bigg| \, C = G_w$$

which, in his view, gives expression to the 'fact' that G_w is dependent upon both (a) the schedule of the propensity to save, that is, $f(x_w)/x$, a function of output, and (b) the value of C, which is a constant.

On Marschak's view, C expressed 'expected technological conditions', and was not dependent upon the propensity to save or anything else but was, in fact, an independent factor which, together with the propensity to save, determined G_w.

In section (C), Marschak continued on to say that his differential equation (3), or the simpler case of equation (3a) will not, in general, yield a suitable solution, that is, a periodical one, although in the latter case it may be constrained. Marschak also noted that in the case of the simple form for function f (the linear form), a non-periodical function of 'explosive' form would be obtained.

In section (D), Marschak went on to say that in order to explain G, some additional postulates were necessary, although he also recognised that the equational relation $C_p = s/G$ was not a postulate, but rather a definition of C_p. Here Marschak commented that he found it hard to understand the core of Harrod's 'Essay' until he realised that the equational relation $C_p = s/G$ was, in fact, a definition of C_p, while the equational relation $C = s/G_w$ was the equilibrium relation for saving, that is, the equality of supply and demand. After this, Marschak asked Harrod whether he agreed with his interpretation of C_p and C.

According to Marschak, the additional postulates needed in Harrod's approach – so as to fully explain G – appeared in the draft manuscript of his 'Essay' in the following passages: (a) when the divergence between G and G_w, which would induce non-periodicity in specific activities was discussed; (b) when the notion of a 'ceiling' was introduced; and (c) when the possibility of negative values for the rates of growth of both G and G_w was dealt with.

In section (E), Marschak suggested that the reaction to the divergence between G and G_w as Harrod postulated it in the draft manuscript of his 'Essay', and which Marschak called 'the cumulative process', could be written as:

$$dG/dt = h(G - G_w) \tag{5}$$

h being an increasing function. Marschak then asked Harrod whether he was correct in understanding this to empirically describe the condition of both boom and depression, and not as an equation that simply followed from the others.

In Marschak's view, the opposite case could be imagined, that is, that in which a shortfall of capital equipment would be accompanied by a reduction in output and not an increase. He went on to say that Harrod's notion of 'unstable equilibrium' implied specific empirically-based postulates with regard to the psychology underlying entrepreneurial reaction to the current profit in the capital goods sector. Marschak then asked if Harrod could explicitly state this postulate in the final version of the 'Essay'; and also asked him to specify which postulate enabled him to conclude that G would increase more rapidly than G_w.

In section (F), Marschak then specified what he called the 'ceiling' relationship, which he took to be of the form:

$$G \leq G_{naturalis} \tag{6}$$

In his view, if it could be postulated that G_w continued rising after it intersected the 'ceiling' (analogous to 'inertia' of some sort), then the reversal of G would not result from what he called 'the postulate of cumulative process'. According to Marschak, this was 'one of the most interesting points' in the draft manuscript of the 'Essay', and he agreed with Harrod as to his assumption that the 'lag' this involved was 'infinitely small'. But Marschak then asked: 'What about G_w?'; and referred Harrod back to his section (C), in which he stated that functions representing demand and supply would not 'produce a periodicity' in general.

Marschak added that he presumed Harrod had postulated a change in the form of the functions, since Harrod did discuss possible changes in his parameter C. Marschak then asked Harrod to explicitly state in the final version of his 'Essay' the postulate concerning the reaction of C to changes in G. He said that Harrod had assumed, in a manner similar to the assumptions underlying the 'cumulative process' affecting G, that entrepreneurs expectations would react to their realisation, and gave, as a possible example, a change in expected technological productivity.

Marschak then summed up his sections (A) to (F) by saying that they implied a 'set-up' of the following sort:

1. An ex-ante supply function for savings (and the propensity to save).
2. An ex-ante demand function for savings, which involved a parameter C which changed.
3. A postulate which described the changes in C as a function of either G or $G - G_w$ thus giving a periodic form for the curve for G_w.
4. A postulate which explicitly stated the reactions giving rise to progressive growth in the absolute value of the difference between G and G_w.

According to Marschak, in the draft manuscript of Harrod's 'Essay', elements (1), (2), and (4) were more explicit than (3), but, on Marschak's view, not necessarily explicit enough.

In section (G), Marschak went on to deal with the state when both G and G_w were below zero. He said that while it was proven in the draft manuscript of the 'Essay' that they could fall below zero, this was necessary but not sufficient to bring about the intersection of the curves for G and G_w below what Marschak called 'the zero line'. According to Marschak, Harrod needed to prove, either theoretically or empirically, that while G increases more rapidly than G_w during the expansion, it decreases less rapidly than G_w in the contraction. Marschak then gave, as an example, equation (5) in his section (E), which, in his view 'could be replaced', in this case, by an equation of the form:

$$d(G - G_w)/dt = h(G - G_w) \qquad (7)$$

In this case, as Marschak put it, the 'rate of increase' of the difference $(G - G_w)$ 'is positive when the difference is positive, and negative if the latter is negative'. However, Marschak stated that the 'economic implications' of this were not 'clear' to him, although he acknowledged that he may have 'overlooked' Harrod's 'proof of the existence of the intersection'.

In his section (H), Marschak stated that in the case of 'empirical verification', the ex-post quantities involved, such as G and ex-post savings would not necessarily present difficulties, except for technical ones. However, in the case of the ex-ante magnitudes such as G_w and C, difficulties of principle would be involved, since, as Marschak put it, these are not 'recorded statistically'. Marschak then asked Harrod if these ex-ante values could be replaced by indices of expectations based, for example, on current profits; although, in his view, this would imply the need for Harrod to reformulate 'certain postulates'.

In section (J), Marschak told Harrod that he agreed with him that dynamics was not 'identical' with the 'theory of lags'. According to Marschak, velocities and accelerations without finite lags were sufficient 'to have dynamics'. In his view, the notion of velocity involved, by definition, a comparison between two points in time, but these could be as close to each other as one chose to make them. Marschak maintained that Harrod's statement regarding 'those who define dynamic as having a cross reference to two points of time' was 'a little too polemic', as he put it, since this did not necessarily involve lags; and those who defined dynamic in such a way would, without a doubt, support the view that Harrod's equation (1) was, in any case, dynamic, since it implied a velocity in the form of a growth rate.[36]

In the final part of his remarks, section (K), Marschak suggested a considerable number of what he called 'small alterations' to the draft manuscript of Harrod's 'Essay', which reflected his careful line-by-line reading of it. This is evident from the fact that in this section he not only provided Harrod with suggestions on how to upgrade the technical presentation of his 'Essay' by making suggestions to improve or alter specific pages and lines, but, in addition, also noticed a number of typographical errors in the draft manuscript of the 'Essay' and pointed them out to Harrod accordingly. In this section, for example, Marschak suggested avoiding the use of the phrase 'the warranted G, G_w', since, in his view, Harrod needed to make clear to the reader that G and G_w were two separate variables, which were not necessarily equivalued, although they could be, and thus G_w was not, in fact, a particular value of G; as, for example, the term x_1 was a particular value for output x.[37]

Now, while Harrod may have incorporated a number of Marschak's suggestions into the final version of his 'Essay', more important, perhaps, was the fact that Marschak's 'Remarks' clearly established for Harrod what the mathematical basis for his approach really was, namely, a system of differential equations which could be utilised to represent actual growth paths and provide at least the basis for a partial explanation of the complex and dynamic processes of economic growth. In other words, as I have tried to show in the chapters above, the foundations for the growth research programme (GRP) in economics had been laid by both Harrod and Meade, with a 'little help from their friends' over the period 1924–39. In 1936 Harrod's book *The Trade Cycle*, and Meade's comments on it, as reproduced above, can be said to have implicitly initiated the GRP. By 1939, with the publication of Harrod's 'Essay', the GRP had been formally and explicitly specified, although its 'take-off' only ostensibly occurred a decade later, after the publication of Harrod's *Towards a Dynamic Economics* (1948), and the appearance of Domar's articles (1946–52), but more about these issues in chapter 6.

6 Overview and Conclusions – Harrod, Meade, and the Growth Research Programme

In this chapter, I will try to draw together the various strands in the foregoing chapter regarding the origins and development of the growth research programme (GRP) in economics. This will be done by focusing upon the three key areas of concern that emerge from the material presented in the previous chapters regarding

  (i) antecedents, precedence, discovery, and formalisation;
 (ii) concept formulation and construction, and cross-fertilisation and sequential conceptual synthesis; and
(iii) the central message, core concepts, problems, and prospects of the ideas and models manifest in the growth research programme (GRP), as originally set out by Harrod and Meade between 1924 and 1939.

What is meant here by the GRP then, is not only Harrod's approach to growth and dynamics – as seen in his early, unpublished essays (1924–33), *Economica* paper (1934a), *Trade Cycle* (1936a), and 'Essay in Dynamic Theory' (1939a), the outcome of which eventually became known as the 'Harrod-Domar model' – but also that of Meade. Meade's approach to growth, as shown in the foregoing chapters, can be seen first in his book *The Rate of Interest in a Progressive State* (1933) and then, in much greater detail, in his 1936 unpublished 'Note I' (Meade, 1936a) on Harrod's *Trade Cycle*, as reproduced in Chapter 4 above (which in my view, is a neoclassical approach to growth pre-dating that of Solow and Swan by two decades). Moreover, Meade only 'rediscovered' and 'reworked' his own ideas for his 1961 book entitled *A Neo-Classical Theory of Economic Growth*; and this, some 25 years after originally setting them out for Harrod's consideration.[1]

Now, I would maintain that three periods in the development of the growth research programme (GRP) can be identified:

1. The 'formative' period, covering the years 1924 to 1939.
2. The 'take-off' and 'establishment', or 'progressive' period, between the years 1948 and 1963.
3. The 'decline' and 'retrograde', or 'degenerative' period, from 1964 onwards.

Over the first two of these periods, there were a number of people who took part in the sequential conceptual synthesis that characterised the intellectual activity that took place. In the 'formative' period, from 1924 to 1939, the main actors in the process of what can be called 'cross-fertilisation' of ideas and their sequential conceptual synthesis were Harrod, Meade, and other members of the *Trade Cycle* group, such as Maurice Allen, along with other economists such as Dennis Robertson and Hubert Henderson, as was shown above.

In the 'take-off' and 'establishment', or 'progressive' period of the growth research programme (GRP), the number of actors grew significantly. Two of the most important of these were John Hicks and Robert Solow. In addition to Harrod, who never left the stage he created, Meade also re-entered the realm of the growth research programme by re-discovering what he had already done in his comments on the draft manuscript of Harrod's *Trade Cycle*; but more about this below. Let us now turn, therefore, to the first area of concern, that of the actual origin of the GRP.

A.   HARROD-DOMAR OR HARROD-MEADE?

Antecedents and Precedence

In a paper presented at the American Economic Association meetings in December 1951, and first published in the *AER Papers and Proceedings* in May 1952 surveying what he called the 'econometric approach' to growth, Domar wrote:

> In economic literature, growth models, interpreted broadly, have appeared a number of times, at least as far back as Marx . . . Among recent Western writers, Cassel, Foster and Catchings, Kalecki, Lundberg, Paul Sweezy, Harrod, Fellner, Hicks, Schelling, Tsiang, Baumol, Hawkins, Alexander, and others have done substantial work.

Domar went on to say:

> I have not tried to delve into the early growth models; it seems that we were not ready for them in any case until we had digested the consequences of the Keynesian revolution. Otherwise, it would be hard to explain the complete disregard by the profession of a growth model published by Eric Lundberg in 1937 – a model not in any way inferior to Harrod's now famous creation of 1939, which in turn had to wait for almost a decade and to be repeated in his book [*Towards a Dynamic Economics*] to receive its deserved recognition.[2]

More recently, Brems has linked Cassel's equational approach to 'the evenly progressive economy' with that of Harrod; going so far as to rename 'Harrod-Domar' the 'Cassel-Harrod' growth model. Now, Brems bases his contention regarding the Cassel-Harrod linkage on the supposition that Cassel's *Theory of Social Economy* may have been the 'source' of Harrod's approach to growth and his 'growth equation'. According to Brems, the first English translation of Cassel's book (by Barron) was only published in New York in 1932, and thus seemingly appeared at about the same time Harrod was formulating his ideas, thereby influencing him at this crucial stage in the development of his approach. However, as was shown above, Cassel's book had, in fact, been translated by McCabe almost a decade earlier, and was published in London by Unwin in 1923.[3]

Moreover, the 1923 McCabe translation of Cassel's *Theory of Social Economy* was repeatedly mentioned and referred to by Robertson in his book *Banking Policy and the Price Level* (1926), which Harrod reviewed in 1927. Furthermore, not only is the 1923 McCabe translation of Cassel's book cited in Lundberg's 1937 book, which Harrod also duly reviewed, but Harrod himself mentions the McCabe translation of Cassel's book in his 1938 'Scope and method' paper. If Brem's logic regarding Cassel's direct influence upon Harrod's thought is accepted, then Harrod should have both developed his approach to growth and derived his 'growth equation' by 1930 at least, that is, some two years before the appearance of the translation Brem's himself cited as having influenced Harrod!. Finally, as I have pointed out above, the direct derivation of his 'growth equation' from Cassel's equational approach would have been very difficult for Harrod, since it would have involved sophisticated algebraic manipulation and a thought experiment a bit beyond the mathematical ability – on Harrod's own account – he was able to muster at the time.[4]

The question of Lundberg's possible influence upon Harrod has already been discussed, and the points made there need not be repeated. Since Domar himself raised the Lundberg 'connection', however, it deserves reconsideration here, especially as far as the possible influence of Lundberg upon Domar's work is concerned. Now, in this case – in contrast to that of Harrod – the matter seems, at first, somewhat more difficult to pin down. However, the key here is that Lundberg was influenced by Cassel, and Domar was influenced by Cassel, Lundberg, and Harrod.

Now, Cassel's influence – as that of Wicksell – can be seen throughout Lundberg's book, as manifest in its focus upon the expansion of a progressive economy, that is, growth, by the method of sequence analysis. The influence of both Cassel and Lundberg on Domar can clearly be seen in Domar's papers published in 1946 and 1947 respectively; the former entitled 'Capital expansion, rate of growth, and employment', the latter 'Expansion and employment'.[5]

In these papers, while Domar assumed that 'no lags are present', he focused upon what he called 'the problem of growth' by applying the principle developed by Cassel 'that in the evenly progressive economy the income increases in the same percentage as the capital'. For example, in his 1946 article Domar stated that he had 'shown that a state of full employment can be maintained if investment and income grow' at the same annual rate, while in his 1947 paper, he wrote 'the maintenance of a continuous state of full employment requires that investment and income grow at a constant annual relative (or compound interest) rate'. As for the direct influence of Lundberg on Domar's work, the following may be said. While Harrod's growth equations can be, after suitable manipulation, derived from the equational system set out by Lundberg in his 1937 book, Domar's equational approach – as presented in both his papers on growth – is directly equivalent to that outlined by Lundberg a decade earlier.[6]

The issue here, however, is whether the GRP emanates from the 'Harrod-Domar' approach – if Domar's approach is, in itself, the result of independent discovery – or if the GRP is actually the outcome of the joint effort of Harrod and Meade over the period 1924–39. As I will now show, the relation between Harrod's work and that of Domar is quite problematic. For, when considered in comparative perspective, it is clear that the issues surrounding what has been termed the 'Harrod-Domar' approach to growth are similar to its 'Hicks-Hansen' IS–LM counterpart, that it to say, the downgrading of both Harrod's originality and the significance of his work by either linking his fundamental contribution to work that followed his by almost a decade in the former case, or overlooking it entirely in the latter case. Now, some observers credit Domar with independently developing his approach to growth as published in a series of articles between 1946 and 1948, Domar simply having 'overlooked' Harrod's 1939 paper. One observer even went so far as to cite what he took to be 'the particular circumstances of the time – the intervening world war and its disruptions of normal academic exchanges' in order to 'explain why Harrod's pioneering article was overlooked by Domar (and others)'. This observer even went on to say that 'most economists became aware of the Harrod and Domar theories . . . at roughly the same time'.[7]

But, while this version of events would be convenient for the 'conventional wisdom' of the history and historians of economic thought, it simply does not make any historical sense at all. For, if this account was taken at face value, then works such as Hicks's *Value and Capital* or Samuelson's famous 'Multiplier-Accelerator' article – published in the same year as Harrod's ' Essay' – should also have been 'overlooked' until after the Second World War. Moreover, if the Second World War disturbed 'academic exchange' in economics, then why was 'academic work' itself not disturbed? Evidently, on this version of the effect of the Second World War on the 'ivory towers' of Anglo-American academia, works such as, for example, Modigliani's classic 1944 *Econometrica* paper, or von Neumann and Morgenstern's *Theory of Games and Economic Behaviour* (1944) were simply 'flukes', and not representative of the serious academic work undertaken by Domar himself, along with Hansen, Hicks, Kaldor, Kalecki, Klein, Lange . . . Samuelson, Scitovsky, Stigler, Tinbergen . . . among many others, and the degree to which academic exchange actually took place.[8]

In addition, it is indeed hard to believe that Hansen – in whose class during 1941–2 Domar, on his own account, began his 'work on growth', and whom Domar called his 'teacher, supervisor, and friend' – would not have pointed Domar in the direction of Harrod's 1936 book (Harrod, 1936a) at least, if not his 1939 'Essay' (Harrod, 1939a); Hansen having reviewed the former, and was most probably aware of the latter, if he had not read it immediately upon publication himself.[9]

Now, what has further complicated matters is the fact that Harrod was somewhat inconsistent with regard to the importance he placed upon establishing priority in discovery in economics. On the one hand, in his 1959 paper dealing with Domar – which will be discussed in detail below – and in a 1967 essay, Harrod, in effect, dismissed the 'priority issue' in general; in the former saying that the 'date A.D. of a formulation is of no importance', and in the latter, referring to 'the rather boring question of priorities' in economics. On the other hand, however, in the section of his 1938 'Scope and method' paper which dealt with 'dynamic economics', Harrod wrote 'May I be excused for touching on a theory in which I believe – subject, of course, to the eroding researches of historians of thought – that I have certain proprietary rights?'.[10]

Harrod himself probably realised that to criticise Domar's approach on the 'grounds' of precedence would be damaging to his own object of bringing about what he saw as a 'mental revolution' amongst economists regarding economic dynamics. In his paper entitled 'Domar and dynamic economics' (1959), Harrod was, therefore, willing to accept Domar's assertion of independent discovery – noting Domar's own 'statement' with regard to this – of 'an equation, formally identical' with the one Harrod 'had previously furnished', and which he believed 'must remain central to growth theory'. Thus, while Harrod said 'since the date A.D. of a formulation is of no importance, our names have rightly been jointly associated with this equation', he also went on to say that 'the formal identity of the two equations is preserved, owing to Domar's assumption that $\Delta I/I = \Delta Y/Y$. I make no such assumption, and my equation is accordingly more general than his'.[11]

The true relation, in Harrod's own view then, between his equation and that of Domar is as follows – while they are formally identical, Harrod's is the more general, and therefore, as he put it in his book *Economic Dynamics* (1973):

> I should claim for the basic principle, as distinct from the alternative variants, that it has as wide a generality and as high a deductive status as any of the 'laws' of static economics.[12]

Discovery, Formalisation, and Reconstruction

This important area of concern relates to Harrod's own version of the process of discovery of his growth equation system, for here, Harrod was seemingly not consistent over the years. Now, this may be due to the fact that 'memory is treacherous' – as Hicks once put it, albeit in another context. On the other hand, Harrod's 'inconsistency' may have also been due to the difficulty he faced in reconstructing how, when, and where he exactly made his conceptual breakthrough, or as he put it 'mental revolution'.[13]

In my view, however, the actual reason for the variations in his own account of the genesis of his growth equation system, simply resulted from Harrod not making the distinction between the stage of its discovery ('in my head'), and its later formalisation ('written out'), as evident in his letter to Dennis Robertson of 5 July 1938 cited above.

In 1972 Harrod related how he 'continued thinking furiously' after publication of *The Trade Cycle*, while in a letter written in 1964, Harrod told Matthews how he came to discover the equation, as he put it 'just like that!'. In this letter, Harrod remembered 'brooding on it over and over again, thinking that there must be a snag in something seemingly so simple'. Some ten years later, in his book *Economic Dynamics* (1973), Harrod told how 'in the course of my "reflections" I suddenly saw it in a split second'. The problem, however, is exactly when Harrod first made his discovery and when he formalised it. Now, in his 1964 letter to Matthews, Harrod gave the following account. The discovery of 'the so-called Harrod-Domar equation' as he put it 'came into my mind suddenly . . . this was in the Spring of 19*38* [Harrod's emphasis] . . . I worked up the E.J. article during the long vac. [summer vacation] of 1938'. In his book *Economic Dynamics* (1973), however, Harrod wrote that he came upon his growth equation 'not in my Oxford study, but in John Betjeman's cottage in Berkshire, which he lent me in July 1938'. The missing link, then, is Harrod's letter to Robertson of 5 July 1938 in which he wrote 'I have in my head, though not yet written out . . . a fundamental equation governing the normal rate of growth'. It would seem, therefore, that Harrod actually discovered his growth equation in the Spring of 1938, as he himself related in 1964. But, as is evident from his letter to Robertson over 25 years before, Harrod formalised the equation, that is, had it 'written out' only in July 1938, and thus the apparent 'discrepancy' in his own account of its origin.[14]

In my view, the more fundamental issue here, however, relates to whether the GRP as a whole can be considered to have emanated – as Harrod put it in 1964 – from the 'so-called Harrod-Domar equation'. For, in light of the evidence presented above, I would contend that, in fact, the GRP emerged from the approaches developed by Harrod and Meade between 1924 and 1939, and thus should be called the Harrod-Meade growth research programme (GRP) accordingly.

B. HARROD, MEADE, HICKS, AND SOLOW: 1948–63

In his review essay on Jaffé's translation of Walras's *Elements* published in the June 1956 issue of *EJ*, Harrod made the distinction between the formulation of economic concepts – tools for the purpose of clarifying, understanding, classifying, or analysing complex economic data and phenomena; and the construction of an economic model – to represent 'a complex of events and relations constituting something less than the whole economy', or representative 'of the whole economy'.[15]

Harrod went on to say that, when a particular model 'which may have played a great part in the development of economic thought' is assigned 'to a particular economist and thereby claims greatness for him', it frequently occurs 'that various concepts and functional relations, comprised within the model, are found to be attributable to earlier authors' and thus 'the claim for originality on behalf of the economist in question', as he put it, 'is whittled away'. 'But', in his view, 'this may be ill-judged', because, as he asserted, 'it is in the synthesis and the creation of a complete model' that the 'genius' of the economist and his 'claim to greatness' becomes evident. According to Harrod, there was an additional, albeit 'more deceptive' process, the result of which could 'erode' an economist's 'reputation'. On his view, after careful examination 'it may be found . . . that many of the concepts used in the model are ill-defined and many of the relations incorrect'.

In Harrod's view, however, while this would seem to be 'very damaging', it is not necessarily the case, and this, since, for the sake of 'good judgement', as he put it, 'it may be necessary . . . to look beyond the precise features of the model as specified by the author to its *general structure*' [Harrod's emphasis]. This is because, in his view:

> it often happens that various models, differing in many particulars, but having a similar general pattern, are successively presented by economists. If an economist invents a model of a certain general type, which many subsequent economists feel impelled to reconstruct and vary, this constitutes the supreme claim to greatness.

Finally, Harrod said 'even if – in the worst case – every single feature of the original model' has to be specifically changed, such a 'claim to greatness' could still, on his view, be made.[16]

Briefly put, then, what Harrod is saying here, in effect, is that the development of core concepts in economic thought involved, in many cases, a process of exchange and 'cross-fertilisation' of ideas, and what I have called their sequential conceptual synthesis. And the best example of this, in my view, was the development of the Harrod-Meade growth research programme (GRP) itself.

Now, on his own account, Hicks was catalysed into considering the trade cycle in detail by Harrod's 1948 book *Towards a Dynamic Economics*, and went on to publish what could be called a 'suggested interpretation' of Harrod's growth and dynamic theory first, in a review article on Harrods 1948 book in the May 1949 issue of *Economica*. This he subsequently developed, expanded, and published in book form as *A Contribution to the Theory of the Trade Cycle* in 1950. Since I have dealt with the issue of 'Harrodian dynamics and Hicksian diagrammatics' elsewhere in detail, I will not repeat this material here. Harrod, for his part, however, and others, such as Yeager, recognised at the time, that Hick's theory closely resembled that of Harrod, with Harrod himself saying 'Mr. Hicks' theory is identical with mine . . .', and Yeager even going so far as to call Harrod's approach 'the Harrod-Domar-Hicks type of theory'.[17]

More interesting for our purpose here, however, is the exchange between Harrod and Solow on what Harrod called his 'Second essay in dynamic theory', which was published in the June 1960 issue of *EJ*, and the correspondence, a year later, between Harrod and Meade, regarding Meade's 1961 book *A Neo-Classical Theory of Economic Growth*.

In his 1960 'Essay', Harrod presented what he termed a 'second form of equation' which, as he put it, provided 'the inner core of the dynamic theory of an insulated economy'. In his view, the equation he presented in his 1939 'Essay' was a 'dynamic analogue of the static law of demand', while that in his 1960 'Essay' could 'be regarded as an analogue of the static law of supply'. Harrod thought of his 'laws' as 'expressing certain necessary' or, as he also put it 'fundamental' relationships rather than constituting a 'model' as such'; since he believed that a 'model' could be 'distinguished from a set of fundamental laws' by the presence in the former, of certain 'adjustable parameters'.[18]

In his 'second essay', Harrod also clarified, in his view, the distinction between 'dynamics' or 'dynamic theory', as against 'growth theory' or 'the theory of economic growth'. According to Harrod, 'dynamic theory' would be used to describe, as he put it, 'the relations between the rates of increase (or decrease) of certain magnitudes in a growing economy'. In his opinion, 'the theory of economic growth', on the other hand, 'would have a wider ambit, including dynamic theory in this narrow sense'. On this basis, Harrod asserted that 'growth economics would then constitute the "political economy" of growth, while dynamic theory would be its pure economics'.[19]

Harrod then went on to give the rationale for the development of what he called his '"second" fundamental equation'. According to him, the 'natural' rate of growth (G_n) was 'indeterminate unless the (natural) rate of interest is specified' and determined. This 'lacuna in the theory', as he put it, would be filled by the introduction of his '"supply" equation, which should be regarded as determining the natural rate of interest'; the natural rate of interest (r_n), according to Harrod, being 'the rate of interest appropriate to a natural (welfare optimum) rate of growth'.[20]

Harrod then went on to 'set out' his 'second' equation, which, as he put it, 'was derived' from his 'abortive attempt, based on Ramsey, in the lecture on the supply of saving', as given in the second chapter of his 1948 book, *Towards a Dynamic Economics*. In fact, Harrod actually specified an equational system composed of four elements. The first determined the 'natural rate' of interest; the second illustrated the possible – albeit in his view 'slight' – dependence of the 'natural' growth rate upon the 'natural' rate of interest; the third showed the dependence upon the 'natural' interest rate of 'the capital intensity of methods used for increments of production', that is, the optimum amount of capital required (C_r); and the fourth was a 'somewhat different form' of his original natural growth rate equation that is, $s_r = C_r G_n$, in which 'the fraction of income to be saved becomes a desideratum, s_r'.[21]

In Harrod's view, his new equational approach would thus also 'satisfy objectors who complain' that he 'took no account of the substitutability of capital for other factors' in his 'earlier equation'. Harrod concluded his 'second essay' by saying:

> Despite Keynes' disclaimers, I have always held that there is a 'natural' rate of interest implicit in the doctrines of the *General Theory* . . . but the natural rate of interest of the dynamic theory

expounded in this article . . . [and] this dynamic theory is in sharper conflict with Keynes than ever Keynes was with Robertson.[22]

Interestingly enough, Harrod sent a copy of his 'second essay' to Solow. Solow, for his part, initially reacted to it in a letter to Harrod dated 18 August 1960, in which he questioned the nature and characteristics of Harrod's 'new' equation determining the 'natural' rate of interest. According to Solow, Harrod wished his equation to be applicable in the case where the capital coefficient was not necessarily a 'technical constant'. However, on Solow's view, Harrod's equation could have only been derived from, as he later put it 'Ramseyian'-type reasoning if it were assumed that the capital coefficient was, in fact, constant. Solow asserted that if his interpretation was correct, then Harrod's 'new' equation actually determined the 'natural' growth rate of consumption and not the 'natural' interest rate.[23]

Harrod replied to Solow on 30 August 1960. In this letter, he said:

I cannot quite agree with your interpretation. I am afraid that my reference to Ramsey may have misled certain readers. On the first round it so misled Dennis Robertson.

What I said was that in the thinking that led to the formulations which I gave in Chapter 2, *Towards a Dynamic Economics*, I was much influenced by Ramsey.

But in this recent article I stressed that I was breaking away from his line of thought (there must be a remote connection because the equation given in the recent article is very close, yet with all important differences, to that in the book).

I now entirely repudiate the idea that in assessing the optimum rate of saving, or the optimum rate of interest, we have to have any regard to utilities in the state named 'bliss' achievable in the remote future.

Harrod continued:

According to me, the natural rate of growth of output is mainly determined by exogenous factors such as increase of technical know-how, and the rate at which a given population can be adapted to the higher tasks (not only of skill and scientific education, but also of honesty and willingness to cooperate). But it may also be to a minor extent determined by the natural rate of interest.

He went on to say:

> I have explained . . . how, contrary to one's first view, a low
> natural rate might involve a low growth rate in certain circum-
> stances. But it is probable that in any case a lower rate of interest
> would require a higher proportion of saving, that is, a lower level
> of consumption. Thus, the matter is simultaneously determined as
> follows: a high growth rate (mainly owing to rapid technological
> advances etc.) requires a high natural rate of interest. This might
> react back on the natural rate of growth of output . . .

Harrod ended his letter to Solow by saying:

> So long as the fundamental determinants (corresponding to tastes,
> wishes, and resources in static theory) remain the same, the rate of
> growth of consumption will remain the same as the rate of growth
> of output. You may ask whether the proportion of income to be
> saved will be higher when the natural rate of growth was higher.
> Presumably it would be. But there are offsetting factors. The
> saving requirement would be higher because more capital would be
> required to sustain a higher rate of growth. On the other hand, the
> saving required would be lower because a high rate of interest
> would dictate methods of production of lower capital intensity.[24]

Solow replied to Harrod on 23 September 1960. In this letter he
claimed that he was still bothered by Harrod's 'new' equation,
although upon reflection he accepted Harrod's contention that it was
not deduced from 'Ramseyian' principles. However, Solow went on
to assert that on his view, even if Harrod's equation was derived on
another basis, it still depended on the supposition that the marginal
productivity of capital (that is, the 'capital coefficient') was a 'technical constant'. Solow then showed in detail why, in his view, this was
the case. He then said that one could also arrive at Harrod's equation
exactly, via strict 'Ramseyian' logic, if it was assumed that both the
elasticity of the marginal utility curve and the 'capital coefficient'
curve were both constants. Solow maintained that irrespective of how
he viewed it, he still found Harrod's 'new' equation to rely, as he put
it, upon a constant value for capital's 'social yield'.

Solow concluded that if this was accepted as a fact, then it would
prescribe the natural interest rate, as he put it 'inevitably'. However,
he also said that while the natural growth rate may not be dependent
on technical change, skill, and attitudinal factors, and so on, all these

would still influence the yield on capital, the interest rate, and the natural growth rate, and this, immediately after their influence on the technical state of the process of production would be felt.[25]

About a year later, on 25 July 1961, Harrod wrote to Meade thanking him for sending a copy of his book, *A Neo-Classical Theory of Economic Growth*, which Harrod read, as he put it, 'with great interest and zeal and as always, admiration'. Harrod also raised a number of important points in his letter which deserve attention, besides adding the caveat that he was 'not really a mathematician', and thus, when he read his comments, Meade should 'treat them with reserve'. Before dealing with them, and so as to both understand Harrod's view of Meade's book and put it in the perspective of the development of the GRP, however, I will briefly compare Meade's 1961 approach with its earlier 1936 version.[26]

While Meade prefaced his 1961 book with the statement that it made 'little, if any claim to originality', and he mentioned other economists, such as Solow and Swan, who in his view 'made important contributions in showing how a classical system would grow', he also said that 'these contributions are important separate pieces of a general picture', going on to say 'and it is simply this general picture which I have tried to draw'. In this case, however, Meade was, in fact, actually re-discovering an earlier version, or what can be called a 'sketch' of the 'general picture' which he had drawn 25 years before.[27]

Now, with the exception of some minor differences in the mathematical formulations used in his 1961 book, the equational system Meade used there, its derivation, and its focus upon the problem of capital-labour substitution and elasticity of substitution, closely resemble the approach of his unpublished 1936 'Note I' (Meade, 1936a) on Harrod's *Trade Cycle* as reproduced in Chapter 4 above. Moreover, even a number of symbols Meade utilised in 1936 are also found repeated in his later work. However, in his 1961 book Meade also considerably expanded on the themes he originally took up in 1936 as mentioned above. He especially focused on the definitional and conceptual problems of technical 'progress' and 'neutrality', and what he saw as the difficulties in Harrod's definitions and concepts; and this, since he agreed with Hick's position on these issues. And it was to this that Harrod first turned in his long and detailed letter to Meade of 25 July 1961. In Harrod's words:

As regards your treatment of me. Admitting for the moment your first point . . . to which I will return, I feel that the judicious reader might infer, from your clear exposition, that my definition is superior . . . I do stress that the great advantage of my definition is that 'neutrality' can be assessed without reference to the elasticity of substitution of factors. The value of this elasticity in the real world is obscure in the extreme. It is obscure even in relation to the industry or process in which the improvement takes place; how much more obscure in the economy as a whole. And yet, it would be needful to know this.

Harrod continued

Accordingly, a definition that can only be used if there is knowledge of this value is, in practice, wholly unusable. I do not think that the component parts which are necessarily brought into prominence by your definition are of much importance, and one of them, as stated above, would be very difficult even to ascertain. In my view, in most cases, an increase of capital occurring without improvement will rapidly run into diminishing returns while an improvement with no increase of capital to implement it will add little to production.

Harrod then turned to what he called 'a more serious worry' regarding Meade's book. As he put it:

I confess that I find your treatment of technical progress as a factor operating independently on growth . . . uncongenial. From the first I took against this separation. I realized that you make it partly with a view to getting a bridge between statics and dynamics. But I must say that I do not like this bridge any more than I like the 'bridge' in Hicks' book between his theory and the traditional econometric analysis of oscillations in a static economy.

Harrod then voiced his concern with what he saw as an inconsistency between the equation which Meade said expressed the 'basic relationship' in his approach and his diagrammatic representation of it. According to Harrod, the diagram did not agree with the equation, and thus he said:

This leads me to the dilemma. Let us suppose that there is no technical progress and that the increase of incomes is entirely due to the increase in the quantity of factors. Thus we have your equation without the *r* term [growth rate of technical progress]. Is it not very strange that one and the same equation determines the marginal product of factors in a static equilibrium and also the rate of growth? I cannot resist thinking that there is something wrong with this.

Harrod went on to say:

In growth theory, we may be concerned with a finite time, as presumable, in your diagram. You're very familiar with the point that, the increase of income is equal to the sum of the effects on income of increases in the factors taken separately, applies only to infinitesimal quantities, and is wrong if we take finite amounts. That was the substance of Edgeworth's rebuke to JA Hobson on the marginal productivity theory, so that if we are considering a finite time, your equation does not hold, and your own diagram . . . is correct.

He continued:

But you might argue that we are interested in the rate of growth at a particular point of time, and indeed I have stressed that in my own writing. But here again, there is an objection to your treatment. I would say that your equation is valid only if the factors are growing at the same rate, i.e. if the factor mix is not changing. Then, assuming constant returns to scale etc. (you have yourself dealt with what happens if that does not hold), the marginal productivity equation will hold for the finite increases of factors also. We get the same equilibrium as before, but at a higher rate of output. But if the factor mix is changing, e.g. owing to a growth of capital, with labour remaining constant, then the marginal productivity of capital and labour are changing. They both have a certain *rate* of changing at a single point of time.

Harrod then said:

The rate of growth at a single point of time – I am no longer talking about the lapse of a finite period, assuming no technical progress – is equal to the rate of growth of the amount of capital multiplied by the rate of decline in the marginal productivity of capital, this product being weighted, as you have weighted the increment of capital, plus the rate of increase of the marginal productivity of capital, this again being weighted as you have weighted it. If the rate of change of factors mix must be included when, say, capital increases but not labour, this rate of change must be included in the equation that determines the growth of income at a single point of time.

Harrod then returned to the first point made by Meade in the paragraph of his book which criticised the approach to 'neutral' technical progress he had taken. In Harrod's words:

> Now I come back to your first point in the criticism of me . . . I think that this paragraph contains a point of the utmost import-ance; in fact one of the most important points in the whole of dynamic theory that badly needs bringing into the limelight. But I do not feel it is a criticism of my definition. Incidentally, the way in which I like to express my definition is that an improvement is 'neutral' if at a constant rate of interest, it does not cause entrepre-neurs to alter the length of the production process.

He went to say:

> I do not see that it need be against this definition that there may simultaneously be causes other than technical progress that are altering the length of the production process. It would seem to me that this was a legitimate use of *ceterus paribus*. Improvement is neutral if it does not cause the length of the production process to be different from what it would be in the absence of the improve-ment, assuming the correct rate of increase of capital to be normal in some sense.

Harrod continued:

> But what I think important in that paragraph is that it hints at the effects of changes in the quantities of non-capital factors on the length of the production process. I am convinced that the reason why the capital-labour ratio is so much higher in the US than here [UK] has nothing to do with the more abundant supply of saving in the former country. If that had been the operating case, we should have expected a lower rate of interest to have obtained in the US than here during the period in which their capital-labour ratio was rising so strongly above ours. But in fact the rate of interest there was no lower but rather higher.

He concluded by saying:

> In my view, the *true* cause was the more abundant supply of land, *including natural resources*, relatively to labour there, than here. Consequently, the price of labour rose relatively to raw materials. The entrepreneur, seeking the cheapest method of production, was more anxious to economize the use of labour relatively to raw materials than we would here. It was profitable to reduce the proportion of labour to raw materials in the factor mix that produced a commodity as much as possible. How can you reduce the proportion of labour in the factor mix? By giving labour as much assistance in the way of power and equipment as possible. That means that the product contains a larger quantity of raw material including power per unit of labour there [US] than here [UK]. It is true,of course, that this more power-aided and mechanized method of production requires more capital disposal. But capital disposal there, as here, was to be had for the asking. More capital disposal was not applied there *because* it was cheaper, for it was *not* any cheaper. More capital disposal was applied, i.e. the production process was lengthened, *because* raw material and power, basically land, was not so scarce as labour.

Finally, Harrod ended his letter of 25 July 1961 to Meade by saying 'I need hardly add that I have learnt a good deal from your book'.[28]

Meade replied to Harrod on 19 August 1961. He opened his letter by thanking Harrod 'for taking so much trouble in commenting on' his book and then said 'I would like to put down my reactions to your three main points'. With regard to Harrod's first point, Meade said:

> I grant that if the rate of interest (rate of profit) *happens to be constant*, then with your definition, one can say whether inventions have been neutral or not without regard to the ease of substitution between factors. One has simply to ask whether the capital-output ratio has changed or not.

He continued:

> But if the rate of interest *has* changed, one cannot say whether inventions have been neutral or not *without* knowing the elasticity of substitution. If the rate of interest *has* gone up, and the capital-output ratio down, one must determine *how much* the capital-output ratio *would* have changed in the *absence* of the bias of inventions.

Meade went on to say:

> With my definition, one can tell whether inventions are biased or not without knowing the elasticity of substitution in those cases where the stock of capital has grown at the same rate as the working population, ignoring the third factor, land. For, in that case, one has only to ask whether the rate of interest has grown in the same ratio as the real wage rate.

Meade concluded his reply to Harrod's first point by saying:

> Your definition probably has the net advantage . . . and in any case, I had the problem of the existence of the third factor, land. I think that my real reason for using the Hicksian rather than the Harrodian definition was that it made the link with the static theory more obvious. I am all the time more anxious to show the student how the static ideas show themselves in growth.

Meade then turned to Harrod's second point and said:

> My equations . . . are all concerned with the rate of growth *at a moment of time*. The diagrams show the change over *a finite period of time*. The two can only be reconciled by making the finite period small and then saying that in *that* case, the diagrams will show relationships which are very close to those written down in the equations. I ought to have said this clearly at some point. I don't believe that I have mentioned it at all in the book, but what I am *really concerned with is the rate of change at a point of time*. I venture, however, to suggest that my equation . . . is correct, whether the factor mix is constant or changing.

He went to say:

> Take as a *special* case the case which you consider in your letter, namely that when there is no technical progress and when the population is constant, so that my equation is reduced to $Y = uK$. This, in turn, can be written as:

$$\frac{dY}{dt} = \frac{\partial Y}{\partial K}\frac{dK}{dt}$$

which states simply that the arithmetic rate of increase in the output, dY/dt, at any one point of time, will be equal to the arithmetic rate of increase of the capital stock, dK/dt, at that point of time multiplied by the marginal product of capital, $\partial Y/\partial K$ at that point in time. This is surely true, and is true whether the marginal product of capital is falling, rising, or stationary.

Meade continued:

By making my point of time short enough, I can make the change in the marginal product of capital negligible from the point of view of the growth rate in the national output. That is to say the level of the growth rate of output will be unaffected by the rate of change in the marginal product of capital.

Meade concluded his reply to Harrod's second point by saying:

But the rate at which the growth rate of output is itself rising or falling will, of course, depend entirely on whether the marginal product of capital is rising or falling.

Meade finally turned to Harrod's third point, and wrote:

I agree very fully with you that the last topic which you mention, namely the interaction between the three factors, labour, capital, and natural resources, is of great and neglected importance in growth theory. I do hope that *you* will develop this analysis. Your reference to conditions in the USA compared with the UK is based, is it not, on the assumption that land and capital are bad substitutes for each other, whereas labour is not too bad a substitute for capital and for natural resources.

Meade concluded his letter of 19 August 1961 to Harrod by saying:

In my book I had tried to write the whole thing in terms of three and not of two factors, and I made a small but clumsy *excursus* in my Appendix 1. Before I got your letter I had sent to the publishers some additions to the book to be included in a reprint of it. Some of these are very much concerned to expand the treatment of the interrelations between the three factors, but they do not cover the point made in the last paragraph of your letter.[29]

Two years later, in his presidential address to the Royal Economic Society published in the September 1963 issue of *EJ* (Harrod 1963a) entitled 'Themes in dynamic theory', Harrod returned to these issues. In this, he both replied to his critics at large, and expanded on specific points raised in his private correspondence with Solow in 1960 and Meade in 1961. For example, in his section on 'Regular Advance', Harrod said:

> the analysis of regular advance should precede, if possible, that of an irregular advance . . . if we first concentrate attention on necessary relations in a regular advance we need and should consider *one point of time* only . . . I hold that all the values in a regular advance should be referred to one date only, being governed by determinants operating at that date.[30]

In his section on 'the rate of interest', Harrod said:

> My dynamic equation $G_w = s/C_r$ has been criticised by neo-classicals for implying a rigid capital-output ratio (C_r) although I did say in my first essay that the value of C_r might 'be somewhat dependent on the rate of interest'.

Harrod continued on to say:

> It is proper, of course, to take both s and C_r to be flexible in relation to the rate of interest. The difficulty is to discover the correct theory of interest.

He then said 'in my Second Essay I have an equation for the natural rate of interest which was related to the natural, not to the warranted rate of growth'. Harrod then turned to the criticism of this equation, recalling, as an example, the point Solow had made in his earlier letters, which, as Harrod put it, was that 'namely . . . it should refer to the rate of growth of consumption, rather than to that of income'. In answer to this, Harrod asserted:

> In my Second Essay . . . I affirmed that these rates would be identical in a regular advance. This seems too restrictive, since it implies that the capital-output ratio is not changing. To widen the horizon, one might assume it to be increasing or decreasing at a *steady* rate at any given point of time.[31]

Harrod then went on to represent the determination of the natural rate of interest and the capital-output ratio using what he called 'a familiar-looking' diagram. He maintained that 'by a conceptual stretch one might regard these curves as the dynamic supply and demand curves jointly determining the price of capital disposal and the amount used, to the extent that the latter depends on the capital-output ratio'. He then said that 'in this analysis, unlike that of F.P. Ramsey, the optimum rate of saving is shown as governed by determinants operating at a given *point of time*, without any reference to the future course of events'.[32]

Here again, Harrod was, in effect, re-emphasising points he had made in his earlier exchange of views with Solow and Meade. But, in my view, the most interesting and important 'theme' in Harrod's 1963 presidential address to the Royal Economic Society was his own rediscovery and restatement of the key themes in the central message of his approach, and the core concepts this involved. And it is to this, and the problems of interpreting both what Harrod's central message, in fact, was, and what the core concepts in his approach to growth and dynamics actually were that we now turn.

C. HARROD, MEADE, AND THE GROWTH RESEARCH PROGRAMME IN RETROSPECT: CENTRAL MESSAGE, CORE CONCEPTS, PROBLEMS, AND FUTURE PROSPECTS

'Warranted' and 'Optimum' Growth, Inherent Systemic Instability, and 'Treatise Saving' *v.* the 'Knife-Edge'

Just what constituted Harrod's central message and the core concepts in his approach has been the focus of many economists – including Harrod himself – since the publication of his early work on the trade cycle, growth, and dynamics. Joan Robinson's treatment of Harrod – and Meade, for that matter – exemplifies this, since it can be said that she 'reviewed' Harrod's *Trade Cycle* approach, in effect, three times; first, in 1936, then again in her March 1949 *EJ* critique of Harrod's *Towards a Dynamic Economics*, and then finally, in her article 'Harrod after 21 Years' in the September 1970 issue of *EJ*.[33]

Moreover, Robinson's 1934 *EJ* review of Meade's *Rate of Interest in a Progressive State*, and her later critique of Meade's *A Neo-Classical Theory of Economic Growth* both focus on the same theme, that is, what she saw as his problematic approach to monetary policy, money wages, capital goods, the rate of interest, and the rate of profit.[34]

With regard to Robinson's view of what she took in 1970, at least, to be Harrod's central message, this can be summed up in two words: 'knife-edge' – a term which Harrod objected to strongly in his 'comment' on her 1970 paper. Interestingly, in her earlier critiques of Harrod's approach, she had, in fact, focused on what she saw as a fundamental problem in the core concepts of 'steady advance' and the 'warranted rate of growth'; the former, as she said in her 1936 review of *The Trade Cycle* being 'based on unnatural assumptions', the latter, as she put it in her 1949 review essay on *Towards a Dynamic Economics*, being 'baffling and mysterious'. Robinson, then, took the main theme in Harrod's central message to be 'the knife-edge', which, as she put it in her 1970 paper, 'is precarious indeed'; and this, rather than the theme of inherent systemic instability based upon a finite, or 'inertial' reaction time which is, in fact, clearly set out in his 1939 'Essay'. In addition, the 'knife-edge' Robinson took as the main theme in the central message of Harrod's approach, cannot actually be considered to be the 'real' problem of the 'knife-edge', since, as Hahn and Matthews noted in 1964:

> It is important to distinguish clearly between the two quite separate obstacles to steady growth that were considered by Harrod in his pioneering contribution. (1)The warranted rate may be unequal to the natural rate. (2)The warranted rate may itself be unstable, even without reference to the natural rate. The second of these problems is the 'knife-edge' properly so-called, though the term is sometimes used confusingly to refer to the first problem as well.[35]

Now, in her 1949 review essay on Harrod's *Towards a Dynamic Economics*, Robinson outlined what she took to be the 'knife-edge' in Harrod's approach. As she put it:

> It might happen by chance that the relationship between thriftiness and capital requirements was just right, so that the rate of saving corresponding to full employment was continuously equal to the required rate of capital accumulation (in Mr. Harrod's terminology G_n is then equal to G_w) . . . There is then a definite rate of capital accumulation which could be maintained continuously, and which would ensure constant full employment (in the loose sense) and the

growth of national income at the maximum rate made possible by changes in population and technical progress. But even when such a rate of accumulation exists, there is no guarantee that it will be realised. If all entrepreneurs got together and found out what the rate was they might agree to put it into effect, but so long as investment is determined by innumerable private decisions, there is no reason to expect that the right rate will be arrived at. And once the rate of accumulation is off the steady course it can never get on to it, but reels along drunkenly below it.

This, however, corresponds to 'obstacle (1)', as Hahn and Matthews put it, which, as they maintained, was not the actual 'knife-edge' problem *per se*.[36]

In any event, what Harrod himself took to be the key themes in his central message and the core concepts involved is, in my view, quite clear, for he expressed them in concise and lucid terms in a series of papers over the 25 years between the publication of *Towards a Dynamic Economics* (1948) and his book *Economic Dynamics* (1973). But the question still remained: how to get the main themes in his central message across. And, it was clear to him from the beginning that the only way this could be done was by dynamising Keynes – both of the *Treatise* and *General Theory*; but, due to its implicit dynamic qualities, with more emphasis on the former than on the latter.

Thus, in his 1939 'Essay', while Harrod accepted 'Keynes's proposition that savings is necessarily equal to investment' (in the *General Theory* sense of *ex post* investment), he went on to say that 'saving is not necessarily equal to *ex-ante* investment'. He then presented Keynes's *Treatise* approach to saving and investment, or, as he put it, 'if investment exceeded saving, the system would be stimulated to expand and conversely', and said that 'Keynes's proposition of the *Treatise* may still be a useful aid to thinking, if we substitute for "investment" in it *ex-ante* investment . . .'. Interestingly enough, nowhere in Harrod's 1939 'Essay' is Keynes's *General Theory* mentioned, since, as he said, it was '*macrostatics*', and his stated objective was to develop a Keynesian-based '*macrodynamics*'.[37]

Harrod returned to this theme repeatedly. For example, in his 1956 're-appraisal' of Walras, when speaking of Keynes's model, and whether it was possible to 'reconstruct' and thereby 'improve' upon it, Harrod said:

It might plausibly be objected that this is not likely to be so, on the ground that his model is static, while interest in future is likely to be concentrated upon dynamic models. But statics and dynamics must have some concepts in common and some interrelation between their principles. Keynes' model, in this being unlike previous complete models of good standing, lends itself easily to dynamisation, so that the movement of interest towards dynamics, far from being the death knell of the Keynesian system, may serve to give it longevity.[38]

In his 1963 presidential address to the Royal Economic Society entitled 'Themes in dynamic theory', Harrod again repeated the theme that his approach was the macrodynamic analogue of Keynes's macrostatic approach; a theme which, in his view, was a key one in his central message. As he put it: 'Keynes held that natural forces did not necessarily tend to establish full employment. The dynamic analogue of this view is that natural forces may not tend to ensure growth at the optimum rate'.[39]

In the same year Harrod published his 'Retrospect on Keynes'. In this important, yet somewhat overlooked statement of what he 'really thought' of Keynes's works, Harrod said:

Since his death, students of Keynes have tended to focus their attention exclusively on the *General Theory* . . . to the neglect of his *Treatise* . . . which was published a few years earlier. This earlier volume is a much richer storehouse of Keynesian thinking than the later volume, which is now so much better known. . . . One would certainly not wish to belittle the *General Theory*; but many of the doctrines of the *Treatise* have passed from view, and much has been lost thereby. I suspect that, had Keynes had a further span of good health and free time at his disposal, he would have wished to write a still more comprehensive work, bringing back into view some doctrines of the *Treatise*, which are crowded out of the *General Theory*.[40]

Harrod then focused upon what was one of the core concepts in his effort at dynamising Keynes, that is, the notion of 'Treatise Saving' as against the *General Theory* approach to saving. Harrod then dynamised the concept of 'Treatise Saving' itself, thus enabling him to arrive at his Keynesian-based macrodynamics. Now, this is not the place for a detailed discussion of Harrod's approach to the *Treatise* concept of saving or the way in which he 'dynamised' it. Suffice it to say, however, that in his 1963 'Retrospect on Keynes', Harrod defined S_t as 'saving in the sense in which it is used in the *Treatise*'. Furthermore, Harrod's S_t was not equal to I (investment). And this, because saving out of corporate profit – whether in excess of, at, or below the normal level – was not included on Harrod's S, or as he put it, 'bookkeeping saving', which *is* equal to I. But, according to Harrod, Keynes's definition of 'normal profit' was 'static'. It thus needed to be 'dynamised', something to which, in his opinion, 'it lends itself easily', and which brings about the transition from Keynesian 'macro-statics' to 'macrodynamics' accordingly.[41]

In fact, in his 1963 presidential address to the Royal Economic Society, Harrod not only focused on 'Treatise Saving', but actually constructed and presented a statistical series representing what he took to be 'Treatise Saving' in the post-Second World War period. After providing what he called his 'dynamic definition' of 'normal profit', he went on to say:

> Total *Treatise* saving is equal to *normal* business saving plus personal saving plus governmental saving. This may, of course, be unequal to total investment. It is the relation between total *Treatise* saving and investment that generates forces of inflation or recession. If investment is greater than *Treatise* saving, actual business saving will exceed normal business saving, and conversely.

Harrod then suggested that his notion of *Treatise* saving was, in fact, valid for both economic analysts and policy-makers alike. In his words:

> I put it to you that there is truth in the *Treatise* doctrine that the forces making for expansion or contraction are related to the balance between saving (in some sense) and investment requirements. If this is so, it is important that policy makers should be able to take cognisance of the current trend in this balance. If the book-keeping proposition that savings is always equal to investment is stressed, and nothing further is vouchsafed, that suggests that policy-makers can get no guidance for policy by looking at the relation between recorded saving and investment, and they are thereby driven to look around for other indicators of economic trends, which may be less valid. If they would look at recorded *Treatise* saving they could get better guidance.[42]

Harrod again returned to these themes in both his book *Money* (1969) and *Economic Dynamics* (1973). It is not surprising, therefore, that in the view of those who knew him well, Harrod was always considered to be a '*Treatise* man', rather than a '*General Theory* man'.[43]

Problems in, and Future Prospects of, the Growth Research Programme

In the retrospective part of their 1964 survey of growth theory, Hahn and Matthews presented a number of issues that emanated from what I have called the growth research programme (GRP) up to that point. The section that dealt with 'theoretical controversies' focused on those issues that emerged, as they put it, from 'the rather extreme level of abstraction employed and the very artificial nature of the problems considered'. The first of these issues related to what they called 'the rather unfortunate dichotomisation between "Keynesian" and "Neo-Classical" growth models'. As they wrote:

> It is perfectly possible to have coherent growth models which employ a classical savings function but postulate a neo-classical production function. Conversely it is easy to analyse a model where there is 'learning by doing' and an absence of perfect competition and yet savings are proportional to income. The question, which kind of savings hypothesis is appropriate is not one of belief and dogma but of fact . . . The real problem here is to find theoretical constructs which, without being downright misleading, are crude enough to bear the weight of the crude evidence . . . We want theories that can be used as plumbers use a spanner – not simply abstract systems.[44]

Moreover, in their section on future prospects, Hahn and Matthews stated:

> while not disparaging the insights that have been gained, we feel that in these areas the point of diminishing returns may have been reached. Nothing is easier than to ring the changes on more and more complicated models, without bringing in any really new ideas and without bringing the theory any nearer to casting light on the causes of the wealth of nations. The problems posed may well have

intellectual fascination. But it is essentially a frivolous occupation to take a chain with links of very uneven strength and devote one's energies to strengthening and polishing the links that are already relatively strong.[45]

In my view, what Hahn and Matthews were, in effect, saying here was that the GRP had, in fact, reached its 'degenerative' phase, and thus was in need of redirection to a 'progressive' one, or 'positive heuristic', to use the Lakatosian terminology. In this regard, Hahn and Matthews concluded that to put the GRP onto what they considered the 'right' track:

> Two aspects may be singled out as requiring more attention in future work (without implying that there are not others). The motivation of economic agents needs analysis in a way that avoids the twin dangers of empty formalism and inconclusive anecdote. And more thought should be given to the concept of the world as a whole as an underdeveloped economy, in which even the evolution of the advanced sectors may be impossible to understand properly in isolation from the sectors that are less developed.

Interestingly enough, in his review of Hicks's book *Capital and Growth* (1965) in the March 1966 issue of *EJ*, Hahn repeated this theme when he said, in effect, that 'current growth theory . . . may yet prove abortive'.[46]

Two decades after presenting what could be taken as the problems inherent in the GRP, Hahn again returned to this theme, albeit in another context. In his 1984 'Discussion' paper, entitled 'Economic Theory and Keynes's Insights', among other things, he also focused upon the limitations of extending the GRP – both its 'Keynesian' and 'Neo-Classical' branches – into areas of economic inquiry for which it was, as Hahn put it, theoretically 'inadequate'. Now, this is not the place for a detailed discussion of Hahn's treatment of Harrod (1939a) and Solow (1956) in his 1984 paper. Suffice it to say, however, that in his 1984 paper, Hahn implicitly showed that the 'old', and by then somewhat 'degenerative', GRP of Harrod-Solow vintage needed to be complemented by a 'new' and 'progressive' GRP which would take into account, in Hahn's view, the following results:

(i) that depending upon the case, there could be many ('indeed a continuum') equilibrium growth paths, as Hahn (1966) showed;

(ii) that the 'saddle-point in phase space' property of the 'steady state' – which, as Hahn put it, was thought to be the only 'feasible' expectation-fulfilling equilibrium growth path – is a 'very special' one indeed, and that there may indeed exist, as Hahn said 'a continuum of expectation-fulfilling' equilibrium growth paths seeking the 'steady-state', as shown by Calvo (1979), and also in the context of an overlapping generations model by Hahn (1982); and

(iii) that as Grandmont (1983) has 'established', an economy 'can possess a countable infinity of cyclical expectation-fulfilling equilibrium' growth paths.[47]

To sum up, then, the Harrod-Meade GRP has indeed come a long way since the halcyon days of Harrod and his *Trade Cycle* group. Moreover, the contribution of the Harrod-Meade GRP to the understanding of economic processes was of fundamental importance, and it paved the way for much new knowledge in economics. And it was Roy Harrod's contributions, along with those of James Meade, that enabled the growth research programme to attain the results it did. But whether this included the 'mental revolution' amongst economists regarding economic dynamics that Harrod had hoped for, however, is another matter indeed. For, as Hahn noted in concise and lucid terms in his 1984 'Discussion' paper, one of the more 'unwelcome' outcomes of the Harrod-Meade GRP was the opening it gave to, as Hahn put it, 'the Lucasians and others', who don't differentiate 'actual and equilibrium growth paths', thus enabling them to reduce economic theory, in effect, as Hahn said, into 'three log-linear equations'.[48]

But let us leave the last word on Harrod's contributions to Professor Sir John Hicks, who, in a letter to Harrod dated 5 January 1973, wrote:[49]

Dear Roy,

You may have heard that the SubFaculty [of Economics, Oxford University] is giving a dinner to celebrate my Nobel Prize on Jan. 24th. I wonder if I dare ask you if you could come. I have felt that we were competitors for this, as in a way on other occasions: Harrod-Domar [sic] would really have been much more suitable than Hicks-Arrow! I hope it will not be long before that comes round.

I shall, however, have to make some remarks and I want to make them rather Oxford remarks. I would do that much better if I could include a tribute to you and you were there to receive it. Would you consider it? It may, I fear, be awkward for you to come then, but I hope not.

Yours ever,
John Hicks

Notes

Introduction: Key Questions and Issues, Myths and Missing Links

1. See Harrod (1964) p. 903.
2. See, for example, Johnson (1971) pp. 49–51; Branson (1972) pp. 375–9; Kregel (1972) pp. 36–44; Jones (1975) pp. 43–68; Venieris and Sebold (1977) pp. 571–601; Levačic and Rebmann (1982) pp. 265–87.
3. See Harrod (1934g) p. 477, (1936a) p. 39, (1968) p. 183; also see Leontieff (1937).
4. See Harrod (1956a) pp. 136–7; also see Hutchison (1935) p. 159.
5. See Harrod (1936a) pp. 166–7.
6. See Harrod (1936a) p. 166; also see Harrod (1939a) in Sen (1970) pp. 44–5. All page references to Harrod (1939a) will be to the reprint in Sen (1970) accordingly.
7. On this, see Kaldor (1986) p. 17; also see Harrod (1939a). For Harrod's view of 'models', also see (1964) p. 903, note 2, where he said 'Incidentally, I am not sure that the word "model" is the right description of what is often cited as the "Harrod-Domar Equation". The nature and proper function of "models" raises wider issues', which Harrod took up in his essay 'What is a model?'. On this, see Harrod (1968) pp. 173–91, especially pp. 176–80ff.
8. See, for example, Meade (1933).
9. See Harrod (1963b) p. 140; also see Keynes (1923, 1930, 1936).
10. Harrod (1936a) p. 150, (1937a) p. 604; JMK (XIV) p. 165; Harrod (1934d) in Harrod (1972) p. 221; also see Young (1987).
11. See, for example, Asimakopulos (1986) p. 278; Kregel (1980). Also see Harrod (1948) pp. 10–18, 72–5, (1963b) pp. 141–3, (1969) pp. 164–6, (1972) pp. x, 260–1, (1973) pp. 29, 31, 56, 68–9, 86–7.
12. See, for example, Goodwin (1982) pp. vii–viii; also see Harrod (1948, 1973) and Riley-Smith (1982).
13. Harrod (1951a) p. 339.
14. Ibid., pp. 339–53, esp. p. 350; Hawtrey (1951) p. 375.
15. See Riley-Smith (1982).
16. Harrod (1951b) p. 261.
17. As reprinted in Harrod (1972) p. 316.
18. Kregel (1980) p. 98, (1985) pp. 66–7.
19. On this, see JMK (XIV) pp. 301, 304–5; also see Tinbergen (1937), Goodwin (1982) pp. vii–viii, Young (1987).
20. Harrod (1959) p. 451, (1971) p. 77, (1972) pp. 221, 317.
21. Kregel (1980) p. 98, (1985) p. 66.
22. On these points, see Harrod (1938) pp. 402–12, esp. p. 410; (1948) pp. 10–12, 18, (1969) pp. 164–5, 191, (1972) pp. 260–1, 286, (1973) pp. 11, 86–7.
23. See, for example, Brems (1986); Domar (1946, 1947, 1952) reprinted in Domar (1957); especially Domar (1952) in Domar (1957) pp. 17–18.

24. Harrod (1948) p. 15, (1968) p. 189, (1971) p. 77.
25. On this, see Harrod (1960); also see Harrod (1939a).

1 Harrod's Early Activities, 1924–34

1. Harrod to Robertson, 18 May 1926, in Harrod papers, file IV–990–1069d; also see Riley-Smith (1982) and Robertson (1926).
2. See Riley-Smith (1982) p. 121. Harrod papers, files V–105; V–108; V–110; V–112; also see Harrod (1933a). On these points, see also, Keynes (1923, 1930).
3. On this, see JMK (XIII) p. 354, and Keynes (1923) pp. 82–3, 188.
4. Harrod (1924) pp. 1–2, in Harrod papers, file V–105; all page references here to unpublished essay.
5. Ibid., pp. 2–3.
6. Ibid., pp. 3–10.
7. Ibid., pp. 10–11.
8. Ibid., pp. 13–14.
9. On this, see Keynes (1923) pp. 188–9.
10. Harrod (1924) pp. 14a–15, in Harrod papers, file V–105.
11. On these points, see Baumol and Turvey (1959) pp. 14–15; Harrod (1933a) p. 160, (1934d) in Harrod (1972) p. 223, (1936a) p. 89; Also see Bertalanffy (1968) p. 138.
12. Harrod (1936a) pp. 88–90, (1939a) in Sen (1970) p. 47.
13. Harrod (1926b) p. 4, in Harrod papers, file V–110; page references to unpublished essay; also see file V–108 and Riley-Smith (1982).
14. Ibid., p. 8.
15. Ibid.
16. On this, see Keynes (1923) pp. 38, 188–9.
17. Harrod (1934d) in Harrod (1972) pp. 230–2, (1936a) pp. 90, 167.
18. Harrod (1927) pp. 224–32; Harrod to Robertson, 18 May 1926, file IV–990–1069d, in Harrod papers.
19. Ibid.
20. Ibid.
21. Ibid.
22. Ibid.
23. Harrod (1927) p. 224.
24. Ibid., p. 225.
25. Ibid., pp. 225–6.
26. Ibid., p. 232.
27. Ibid., p. 226; also see Tappan (1928) pp. 95–109.
28. Harrod (1933a, 1936a) (1971) p. 77; Harrod papers, file V–112 contains his 1933 essay.
29. Harrod papers, file V–112; also see Riley-Smith (1982) p. 121.
30. Harrod (1936a) pp. 159–232, esp. pp. 191ff.
31. Harrod (1933a) pp. 127–36, 160–3, 170.
32. See Haberler (1936).
33. Robertson to Harrod, 6 April 1932, in Harrod papers, file IV–990–1069.
34. Robertson to Harrod, 26 April 1932, in Harrod papers, file IV–990–1069.

35. Harrod to Robertson, 13 October 1932, in Harrod papers, file IV–990–1069; Harrod to Robertson, 29 April 1933, original in the Robertson collection. I am grateful to Professor S. Dennison for sending me a photocopy of this letter and to Lady Harrod for permission to cite it here.
36. Harrod to Robertson, 29 April 1933.
37. Harrod (1933a) pp. 131–2.
38. Harrod to Meade, 25 November 1932. The original letter is in the Meade papers held at the British Library of Economics (LSE) Special Collection; Meade papers file 2/4/4. I am again grateful to Lady Harrod for permission to cite it here and to Professor Meade for allowing me to study his papers.
39. Meade to Harrod, 30 November 1932; in Harrod papers, file IV–745–67. I am very grateful to Professor Meade for permission to cite it here.
40. Meade (1933).
41. Haberler (1934a) p. 100, (1936).
42. Harrod (1934a); Pigou (1933).
43. Keynes to Harrod, 10 October 1933; in Harrod papers, file II–34.
44. Keynes to Harrod, 27 October 1933; in Harrod papers, file II–34.
45. Keynes to Harrod, 30 December 1933; in Harrod papers, file II–34; also see Keynes (1936) pp. 272–9.
46. Harrod (1934a) pp. 19–20, 32; Keynes (1936) pp. 275–7.
47. Harrod (1934a) pp. 22, 25, 29.
48. Keynes (1936) p. 275.
49. Harrod (1934a) pp. 21–2, 31.
50. Ibid., pp. 29–30; Harrod to Meade, 4 January 1933; original in Meade papers file 2/4/5. I am grateful to Lady Harrod for permission to cite it here.
51. Harrod (1934a) pp. 31–2; Patinkin (1976) p. 132, note 17.
52. Harrod (1934a) p. 31. On the notions of 'complementarity' and 'relativity', see Feuer (1974), Holton (1970) and Snow (1982).
53. See Young (1987).
54. Harrod (1956b); also see Harrod (1938).
55. See Harrod (1956b) p. 471.
56. Keynes (1936) pp. vi–vii; Young (1987).
57. On this, see Patinkin (1976) p. 33.
58. For example, Harrod's effort at dynamising the notion of '*Treatise* Saving' – see chapter 6.
59. See Harrod (1934g, 1968).
60. Patinkin (1976) pp. 27–8.

2 Individuals and Groups in Oxbridge, 1930–39

1. On this, see Riley-Smith (1982) p. 104; also see Shackle (1967).
2. See JMK (XIII) p. 342.
3. Meade (1932) p. 433.
4. See Solow (1987); also see Meade (1933) p. viii.
5. See J. Robinson (1934) pp. 282, 284–5; also see Meade (1933) p. vii.

6. Harrod to Meade, 4 January 1933, original in Meade papers, file 2/4/5.
7. Harrod to Meade, 13 November 1933, original in Meade papers, file 2/4/7. I am very grateful to Lady Harrod for allowing me to cite these letters here; also see Meade (1933) p. 1; and J. Robinson (1934) p. 284.
8. See Meade (1933) pp. 48–56.
9. Ibid., pp. 48–50.
10. Ibid., pp. 52–5.
11. Ibid., pp. 55–6, especially p. 56, footnote 1.
12. Harrod to Meade, 13 November 1933 cited above (Meade papers, file 2/4/7).
13. A similar process also occurred regarding Meade's 1936 textbook, *Economic Analysis and Policy*, as will be seen below.
14. See Robertson (1933) p. 407, (1934b) p. 656; also see JMK (XXIX) p. 23. Maurice Allen, who, as Kaldor recalled, was 'under the influence of Robertson and Harrod' (Kaldor, 1986) p. 7, also proved to be an objective – albeit in Harrod's view sometimes overcritical – 'sounding-board'. Thus, although in a letter to Meade dated 6 March 1935 (Meade papers, file 2/4/23), Harrod disagreed with and complained to Meade about Allen's criticism of his note 'The Equilibrium of Duopoly' (Harrod, 1934c), Harrod still sent Allen the draft manuscript of his book *The Trade Cycle* (Harrod, 1936a) for critical evaluation and comment. Moreover, Harrod even incorporated some of Allen's comments in the book itself, as will be seen below.

This is not the place for a detailed treatment of Maurice Allen's contributions to economic inquiry and analysis. Suffice it to say, as I have already pointed out elsewhere (Young, 1987), that a study of his role in the development of modern economics is long overdue, and his contributions deserve both the attention and recognition of historians of economic thought and the economics profession as a whole.
15. Robertson (1934b); Kaldor (1951) reprinted in Kaldor (1960) p. 193, footnote 2.
16. Young (1987); Harrod (1937a); Harrod papers, Robertson-Harrod correspondence, file IV–990–1069.
17. Harrod to Robertson, 11 November 1935 in Harrod papers, file IV–990–1069; also see JMK (XIII) pp. 548–53, 557.
18. Harrod to Robertson 18 May 1936; in Harrod papers, file IV–990–1069.
19. Robertson to Harrod, 28 October 1936; in Harrod papers, file IV–990–1069; also see Young (1987).
20. Robertson to Harrod, 9 November 1936; in Harrod papers, file IV–990–1069; also see Young (1987).
21. See Harrod (1937a); Young (1987).
22. Harrod to Robertson, 9 December 1936; in Harrod papers, file IV–990–1069.
23. See Harrod (1938) pp. 384–6, 402, 403, note 1, 405; also see Fraser (1937) and Robbins (1932).
24. Fraser (1932) p. 560.
25. Ibid., pp. 564–5.
26. Ibid., p. 566.
27. Ibid.

28. Ibid., pp. 569–70.
29. Fraser (1937); McCloskey (1985); Machlup (1958).
30. Fraser (1937) p. 375, note 1.
31. Harrod (1936a) p. 39.
32. Harrod (1938) p. 396.
33. Ibid., pp. 406–7.
34. Ibid., p. 407.
35. Meade (1936b, 1937, 1938, p. ix). The dissemination of Keynes's *General Theory* and the IS–LM approach to it in this context is discussed in Young (1987). What is interesting to also note here is that Harrod's approach to 'dynamic analysis' entered the sphere of Oxford undergraduate final examinations as early as the Trinity term 1940, when in question 10 on the BA 'Honours School' economic theory exam, the student was asked: 'What is dynamic analysis. Has it substantially modified any economic doctrines?'. Now, while the student could choose to answer this question or not, it is most likely that those who had attended Harrod's lectures or talks to the Oxford Political Economy Club would answer it, since it was most probably set and marked by Harrod himself.
36. Meade (1936b, 1937, 1938); also see Young (1987).
37. Meade (1937) p. 69, (1938) pp. 77–8.
38. Meade (1937) pp. 71–3, (1938) pp. 80–1.
39. Meade (1938) p. vi.
40. See Young (1987).
41. On the 'Circus', see, for example Kahn (1984, 1985) and A. Robinson (1985); on the '*General Theory* group', see Young (1987). For a survey of what occurred at the LSE, see Robbins (1971); also see Coats (1982) and Coase (1982), for their impressions and recollections of this period.
42. See Young (1987).
43. See chapter 4.
44. Ibid.
45. Harrod to Meade, 4 October 1934; original in Meade papers file 2/4/12. I am again grateful to Lady Harrod for permission to cite it here.
46. See Lee (1981); also see Harrod (1939b); I also wish to again thank Dr Charles Hitch for pointing out to me the importance of Harrod's activities in the OERG and also the crucial significance of Meade's early works – both published and unpublished.
47. Harrod to Meade, 4 October 1934, op. cit. (Meade papers, file 2/4/12).

3 Towards the Trade Cycle, 1934–35

1. Harrod (1934b, 1934d) both reprinted in Harrod (1972).
2. Haberler (1937).
3. Robertson (1934a); Harrod (1934g); Haberler and Bode (1935); Harrod (1935a).
4. Harrod (1934e, 1934f); Haberler (1934b); Kaldor (1934).
5. Harrod (1934d) reprinted in Harrod (1972) pp. 230–2.
6. Ibid., pp. 232–4.
7. Ibid., pp. 230, 235.

8. Robertson to Harrod, 27 September 1934; in Harrod papers, file IV–990–1069.
9. Robertson to Harrod, 4 October 1934; in Harrod papers, file IV–990–1069.
10. Ibid.
11. Robertson to Harrod, 6 October 1934; in Harrod papers, file IV–990–1069.
12. Robertson (1934a) p. 473.
13. Ibid., pp. 473–4
14. Ibid., pp. 474–5.
15. Harrod (1934g) p. 478.
16. Harrod to Robertson, 3 October 1935; in Harrod papers, file IV–990–1069.
17. Harrod (1935b) pp. 725–9.
18. Harrod (1952), reprinted in Harrod (1972) p. 221, note 1.
19. Haberler to Harrod, 3 September 1934; in Harrod papers, file IV–395–422.
20. Ibid.; also see Harrod (1934b, 1934d).
21. Harrod to Haberler, 19 October 1934; in Harrod papers, file IV–395–422.
22. Harrod (1934e); Haberler (1934b).
23. Harrod to Haberler, 19 and 21 October 1934; in Harrod papers, file IV–395–422; Haberler to Harrod, 25 October 1934, in same file.
24. Harrod (1934f) p. 8; Haberler and Bode (1935) p. 81.
25. Haberler to Harrod, 2 November 1934; in Harrod papers, file IV–395–422; Harrod to Haberler, 5 November 1934, in same file.
26. Ibid.
27. Ibid.; also see Hayek (1933).
28. Haberler to Harrod, 12 November 1934; in Harrod papers, file IV–395–422.
29. Haberler and Bode (1935); Harrod (1935a).
30. Bode to Harrod, 7 and 15 January 1935; in Harrod papers, file IV–114–15. Interestingly enough, Bode became a research student at St John's College, Cambridge, working under the supervision of Professor Dennis Robertson. His chosen topic was entitled 'The monetary problems of investment with special reference to the natural rate of interest'. On this, see the Annual Report of the Board of Research Students, 10 March 1936, in the Cambridge University *Reporter*, v. 66, 21 April 1936, pp. 870ff.
31. See Harrod papers, file IV–395–422.
32. Haberler to Harrod, 7 February 1935; in Harrod papers, file IV–395–422.
33. Harrod to Haberler, 28 February 1935; in Harrod papers, file IV–395–422.
34. Haberler and Bode (1935) pp. 80–1; Harrod (1935a) p. 84.
35. On this correspondence, see Riley-Smith (1982) pp. 89–91; also see Harrod papers, Kahn-Harrod correspondence file in file IV.
36. Ibid.
37. Ibid.

38. Ibid.
39. Haberler (1938) p. 325; also see Kahn (1937) and Harrod (1937c).
40. Haberler to Harrod, 20 August 1934; in Harrod papers, file IV–395–422.
41. Haberler to Harrod, 3 September 1934; in Harrod papers, file IV–395–422.
42. Harrod to Haberler, 19 October 1934 and Haberler to Harrod, 25 October 1934; in Harrod papers, file IV–395–422.
43. Haberler to Harrod, 25 October 1934; in Harrod papers, file IV–395–422.
44. Haberler (1936, 1939).
45. Haberler to Harrod, 8 January 1937; in Harrod papers, file IV–395–422; also see Haberler (1937).
46. Haberler to Harrod, 3 January 1937; in Harrod papers, file IV–395–422. On what Haberler called the 'cumulative' or 'Wicksellian process' and Harrod's *Trade Cycle* approach, see Haberler (1936, pp. 82ff, and p. 97, note 1); Haberler's review of Harrod's *Trade Cycle* (Haberler, 1937) pp. 690–1; also see Haberler (1939) chapter 8, and Haberler (1958) p. 487, Appendix I.
47. On these points, see Harrod to Haberler, 19 October 1934, in Harrod papers file IV–395–422 cited above; also see Haberler (1936, 1939, 1958).

4 The Trade Cycle: Group, Critics and Critiques

1. Harrod to Robertson, 18 May 1936; in Harrod papers, file IV–990–1069; also Harrod (1936a) p. 128.
2. Harrod to Robertson, 21 May 1936; in Harrod papers, file IV–990–1069.
3. Harrod to Robertson, 25 December 1936; in Harrod papers, file IV–990–1069; also see Harrod (1938).
4. Harrod to Robertson, 3 April 1937; in Harrod papers, file IV–990–1069; on this see also Robertson (1937); Hawtrey (1937).
5. Harrod to Robertson, 4 October 1937; in Harrod papers, file IV–990–1069.
6. Harrod to Robertson, 8 October 1937; in Harrod papers, file IV–990–1069.
7. Henderson to Harrod: 21, 23, 26 February 1936 and 4, 10 June 1936; in Harrod papers, Henderson-Harrod correspondence, file IV–480–84.
8. Henderson to Harrod, 23 February 1936; file IV–480–84.
9. Henderson to Harrod, 26 February 1936; file IV–480–84.
10. Henderson to Harrod, 4 June 1936; file IV–480–84.
11. Harrod (1936a) p. ix.
12. Young (1987) pp. 126–8.
13. See, for example, J. Robinson (1936) p. 691; also see Harrod (1936a) p. ix; JMK (XIV) pp. 150–83.
14. Also see Haberler (1937) pp. 690–1.
15. See the Harrod-Meade correspondence in the Harrod papers (Meade to Harrod), file IV–745–67; and in the Meade papers (Harrod to Meade), file 2/4.
16. Also see Meade (1961).

17. Harrod to Meade, 13 January 1936; original in Meade papers, file 2/4/24. I am again very grateful to Lady Harrod for allowing this letter to be cited here, and also those below.
18. Meade to Harrod, 14 January 1936; in Harrod papers, file IV–745–67.
19. Harrod to Meade, 16 January 1936; original in Meade papers, file 2/4/28.
20. Meade to Harrod, 16 January 1936; in Harrod papers, file IV–745–67.
21. Harrod to Meade, 19 January 1936; original in Meade papers, file 2/4/29.
22. Meade to Harrod, 1 May 1936; in Harrod papers, file IV–745–67.
23. Harrod to Meade, 4 May 1936; original in Meade papers, file 2/4/32.
24. Allen to Harrod, in Harrod papers, file IV–14–15c. I am very grateful to Maurice Allen for allowing his letters to be cited here.
25. Ibid.
26. Harrod (1936a) p. 51, note 1; Meade (1937) pp. 79–82, (1938) pp. 87–90.
27. Meade (1937) p. 79, (1938) p. 87.
28. Meade (1937) pp. 77, 82–3, (1938) pp. 83–4, 90.
29. On these points, see for example, Blaug (1985) pp. 678–83, especially p. 681, note 1.
30. Meade (1937) pp. 80–2, (1938) pp. 88–90; also see Harrod (1939a) in Sen (1970) p. 64.
31. Meade (1933, 1938, 1961); also see Harrod, ibid., p. 53.
32. See Young (1987).
33. For the list of participants at the Oxford meeting, 25–29 September 1936, see *Econometrica*, April 1937, p. 198.
34. On these points, see Phelps-Brown (1937) pp. 361–83; also see Lutfalla (1937) pp. 423–45, for an additional report on the conference proceedings prepared for French members of the Econometric Society.
35. See Shackle (1967) p. 267; Young (1987) pp. 55–7.
36. Phelps-Brown (1937) pp. 363–6.
37. Ibid., pp. 367–8.
38. Ibid., pp. 375–6.
39. Harrod to Meade, 7 February 1937; original in Meade papers, file 2/4/35. I am again grateful to Lady Harrod for allowing me to cite this letter here.
40. Fraser (1935), (1937) p. 342. It is important to note here that Fraser kept up his correspondence with Harrod after leaving Oxford to take up a Chair at Aberdeen. On this see Riley-Smith (1982) p. 106, and the Harrod papers, file IV–1238–54.
41. For example, not only did Harrod focus upon the problem of growth in many places in *The Trade Cycle*, but he actually posed a question there in which he implicitly outlined the notion of 'warranted growth'. On these points, see, for instance, Harrod (1936a) p. 150.
42. On this, see Young (1987).
43. See J. Robinson (1936) pp. 691–3.
44. Robertson (1937) pp. 124–6.
45. Stafford (1937) pp. 70, 82–3.
46. Wynne (1937) pp. 143–4.
47. Hansen (1937) pp. 510–12, 522–4, 531; (1938).
48. Tinbergen (1937) pp. 89–91.
49. Haberler (1937) pp. 690–5.

50. Gaitskell (1937) pp. 472–6.
51. Hawtrey (1937) pp. 316, 327; Young (1987) pp. 126ff; also see Harrod papers, file IV–446–7 for Hawtrey's letters to Harrod and the Hawtrey papers Churchill College, Cambridge, for Harrod's letters to Hawtrey. For his reaction to Harrod's 'Essay', see Hawtrey (1939).
52. Keynes to Harrod, 18 February 1937; in Harrod papers, file II–67; also see Riley-Smith (1982) p. 24.
53. See JMK (XIV) pp. 163–4.
54. JMK (XIV) p. 165.
55. JMK (XIV) pp. 170–3.
56. JMK (XIV) p. 176.
57. JMK (XIV) p. 179; also see Harrod (1939a) in Sen (1970) p. 45.

5 From the Trade Cycle to the 'Essay', 1935–39

1. Robertson to Harrod, 15 March 1945; in Harrod papers, file IV–990–1069.
2. Harrod to Robertson, 20 March 1945; in Harrod papers, file IV–990–1069.
3. On this, see Brems (1986); Cassel (1918, 1923); Robertson (1926) pp. 1–2, 5, 7, 58, 73, 90, 97; Harrod (1927), (1938) p. 393, note 2, (1956c) p. 311.
4. Cassel (1923) p. 62; Harrod (1938); also see Harrod papers, file V–40.
5. Cassel (1923) p. 62.
6. On Harrod's 's' and for the definitions of the terms he used, see Harrod (1939a) in Sen (1970) pp. 46–7.
7. Kalecki (1935, 1937); Harrod to Robertson, 3 October 1935, in Harrod papers, file IV–990–1069.
8. See JMK (XIV) p. 304.
9. See Tinbergen (1935, 1938); Young (1987) pp. 90–3.
10. Harrod to Keynes, 6 July 1938; in Harrod papers, file II–34; also see JMK (XIV) p. 299.
11. JMK (XIV) pp. 301, 304.
12. Keynes to Harrod, 11 August 1938; in Harrod papers, file II–34.
13. Tinbergen (1938) pp. 164, 176.
14. In light of Harrod's later remarks regarding Frank Ramsey's influence on him, Ramsey's 1928 paper and the notion of 'optimal' growth and saving it contains must also be taken as a possible additional source of Harrod's ideas. On this, see Ramsey (1928) reprinted in Sen (1970).
15. Lange (1938a) p. 32.
16. Lange (1938b); Harrod (1937c).
17. Harrod (1939a) in Sen (1970) pp. 47–8; Harrod (1973) p. 41.
18. Lange (1945); Harrod (1946) p. 107.
19. Durbin (1935); Harrod (1935b) pp. 725–9; Robertson to Durbin, 29 July 1935; original in the papers of the late Evan Durbin. I want to thank Professor Liz Durbin for sending me copies of the Robertson-Durbin and Harrod-Durbin correspondence cited here; also see Harrod papers, file IV–293–5 for additional examples of the Harrod-Durbin correspondence.

20. Durbin to Harrod, 15 June 1937; original C11–14 in Durbin papers. I want to again thank Professor Liz Durbin for allowing me to cite from this letter here.
21. Harrod (1937b) p. 330.
22. Harrod to Robertson, 22 January 1938; original in Robertson papers. I am very grateful to Professor S. Dennison for sending me a copy of this letter and to Lady Harrod for permission to cite it here.
23. Harrod (1937c) pp. 495–6.
24. Ibid., p. 495; Lange (1938b) p. 247.
25. Harrod (1937c) p. 495.
26. Ibid., pp. 496, 498.
27. Ibid., p. 496.
28. Ibid., pp. 496–7.
29. This material was originally presented in a paper entitled 'Lundberg and the Growth Research Program in Economics', given at the Conference on the Stockholm School after 50 years, Saltsjöbaden, Sweden, 31 August–1 September 1987.
30. Harrod to Robertson, 5 July 1938; in Harrod papers, file IV–990–1069; also see JMK (XIV) p. 298.
31. JMK (XIV) p. 301.
32. Harrod to Robertson, 3 August 1938; in Harrod papers, file IV–990–1069.
33. See, for example, Young (1975); Kregel (1980, 1985).
34. Keynes to Harrod, 26 September 1938 in JMK (XIV) pp. 349–50. There would seem to be a misprint in the letter as originally published in JMK (XIV) p. 349, where the symbol 'a' appears. From the context of the letter, Keynes was referring here to the propensity to save, which he designated as 's', and thus my correction here; on this, see Young (1975).
35. JMK (XIV) pp. 345–6, 349.
36. Harrod (1939a) in Sen (1970) p. 47.
37. On this, see Harrod papers, file V–113a; also see Riley-Smith (1982) p. 121, and Young (1987) p. 193, note 25.

6 Overview and Conclusions – Harrod, Meade, and the Growth Research Programme

1. Solow (1956); Swan (1956); both reprinted in Sen (1970).
2. Domar (1957) pp. 17–18.
3. Cassel (1923, 1932); Brems (1986).
4. See chapter 5, note 3; also see Lundberg (1937) pp. 138, 255, where Cassel (1923) is cited, for example, Cassel (1923) p. 61.
5. Domar (1946, 1947), reprinted in Domar (1957).
6. See Domar (1957) pp. 70, 76ff, 79–80, 89ff, 91; Cassel (1918, 1923) p. 62; Lundberg (1937) pp. 183–5, 240.
7. Asimakopulos (1986) p. 275.
8. Perhaps the best bibliographical listing of works undertaken during this period is to be found in Samuelson (1947).
9. Domar (1957) p. vii.

10. Harrod (1938) p. 405, (1959) p. 451, (1967) in Harrod (1972) p. 304.
11. Harrod (1959) pp. 452–3.
12. Harrod (1973) p. 286.
13. Hicks (1973) p. 2; Harrod (1939) in Sen (1970) p. 45.
14. Harrod (1972) p. x, (1973) p. 41; Young (1987) pp. 91–2.
15. Harrod (1956c) pp. 307–8.
16. Ibid., p. 308.
17. Harrod (1948) (1951a) p. 264; Hicks (1949, 1950); Yeager (1954) p. 61; Young (1987) pp. 145–51.
18. Harrod (1960) p. 277; Meade (1961).
19. Harrod (1960) pp. 277, 288.
20. Ibid., pp. 279, 281, 285.
21. Ibid., pp. 281, 285.
22. Ibid., pp. 285, 291–2.
23. Solow to Harrod, 18 August 1960; original in Harrod papers, file IV–1158–64.
24. Harrod to Solow, 30 August 1960; in Harrod papers, file IV–1158–64.
25. Solow to Harrod, 23 September 1960; original in Harrod papers, file IV–1158–64.
26. Meade (1961); Harrod to Meade, 25 July 1961; in Harrod papers, file IV–745–67.
27. Meade (1961) p. v.
28. See, for example, Appendix I in Meade (1961) pp. 77–82; Harrod to Meade, 25 July 1961; in Harrod papers, file IV–745–67.
29. Meade to Harrod, 19 August 1961; in Harrod papers, file IV–745–67. Harrod returned to some of these themes in *Economic Dynamics* (1973).
30. Harrod (1963a) pp. 402–3.
31. Ibid., pp. 404–5.
32. Ibid., p. 406.
33. J. Robinson (1936, 1949, 1970).
34. Robinson (1934) pp. 282–5; Robinson (1962) reprinted in Sen (1970) p. 139 (page reference to reprint).
35. J. Robinson (1936) p. 692, (1949) p. 80, (1970) pp. 734–5; Harrod (1939a) in Sen (1970) pp. 55–7, 59, 63; Hahn and Matthews (1964) p. 27, note 2, reprinted in *IEA* (1967) (page references to reprint).
36. Robinson (1949) p. 77; Hahn and Matthews (1964) ibid.
37. Harrod (1939a) in Sen (1970) p. 49.
38. Harrod (1956c) p. 309.
39. Harrod (1963a) p. 407.
40. Harrod (1963b) pp. 140–1.
41. Ibid., pp. 141–2.
42. Harrod (1963a) p. 413.
43. Harrod (1969) pp. 162–6, (1973) pp. 86–7.
44. Hahn and Matthews (1964) p. 110.
45. Ibid., p. 112.
46. Ibid., pp. 112–13; Hahn (1966) p. 87; Lakatos (1970) pp. 118, 132, 137; also see McMahon (1982) for an example of the application of the Lakatosian framework to the 'business cycle research program'.

47. Hahn (1984) pp. 6–7; also see Calvo (1979); Hahn (1966); and a personal communication to Hahn from Grandmont (1983) as cited in Hahn (1984) p. 7.
48. Hahn (1984) pp. 6, 23.
49. Hicks to Harrod, 5 January 1973; original in Harrod papers, file IV–485–501. Harrod did not attend the dinner, but in 1973 – the same year as Hicks got his Nobel prize – he published a completely rewritten version of his 1948 book, *Towards a Dynamic Economics* called *Economic Dynamics*, which he hoped would fill, as he put it, 'a great gap in all modern economics' (1973, p. vii). However, this book was somewhat overtaken by the events of the 1970s, and their ostensible implications for both Keynesian economics and the Harrodian (Keynesian) branch of the growth research programme, as Hahn (1984) pp. 21–2, duly noted. Thus, as Hahn said, 'so really what one must look at is dynamics and it is an unfortunate fact than economic theory is [still] ill equipped to do so' (Hahn, 1984) p. 17.

Bibliography

Abbreviations

This bibliography encompasses the articles, books, and other material cited in the text and notes. The abbreviations used are as follows:

AEJ	*Atlantic Economic Journal*
AER	*American Economic Review*
BLQR	*Banca Nazionale del Lavoro Quarterly Review*
CJEP	*Canadian Journal of Economics and Political Science*
EC	*Econometrica*
Econ (n.s.)	*Economica* (new series)
Econ (o.s.)	*Economica* (old series)
EJ	*Economic Journal*
ER	*Economic Record*
HOPE	*History of Political Economy*
IER	*International Economic Review*
JMK	*Collected Writings* of John Maynard Keynes, with volume number
JPE	*Journal of Political Economy*
MS	*Manchester School*
OEP	*Oxford Economic Papers*
QJE	*Quarterly Journal of Economics*
REP	*Revue d'économie politique*
RES	*Review of Economic Studies*
REcon.Stat	*Review of Economics and Statistics*
Welt.Arch.	*Weltwirtschaftliches Archiv*
ZFN	*Zeitschrift für Nationalökonomie*

References

ASIMAKOPULOS, A. (1985) 'Harrod on Harrod: the evolution of a line of steady growth', *HOPE*, vol. 17 (Winter).

ASIMAKOPULOS, A. (1986) 'Harrod and Domar on dynamic economics', *BLQR*, vol. 39 (September).

BAUMOL, W. and TURVEY, R. (1959) *Economic Dynamics*, 2nd edn (New York: Macmillan).

BERTALANFFY, L. von (1968) *General System Theory* (Harmondsworth: Penguin).

BLAKE, R. (1970) 'A personal memoir', in W. Eltis (ed.) *Induction, Growth, and Trade: essays in honour of Roy Harrod* (Oxford: Oxford University Press).

BLAUG, M. (1985) *Economic Theory in Retrospect*, 4th edn (Cambridge: Cambridge University Press).

BRANSON, W. (1972) *Macroeconomic Theory and Policy* (New York: Harper & Row).

BREMS, H. (1986) *Pioneering Economic Theory 1630–1980: a mathematical restatement* (Baltimore: The Johns Hopkins University Press).

CALVO, G. (1979) 'On Models of Money and Perfect Foresight', *IER*, vol. 20 (February).

CASSEL, G. (1903) *Nature and Necessity of Interest* (London: Macmillan).

CASSEL, G. (1918) *The Theory of Social Economy* (trans. 1923, J. McCabe) (London: T. Fisher Unwin).

CASSEL, G. (1925) *Fundamental Thoughts on Economics* (New York: Harcourt Brace).

CASSEL, G. (1932) *The Theory of Social Economy* (trans. S. Barron) (New York: Harcourt Brace).

COASE, R. (1982) 'Economics at LSE in the 1930's: a personal view', *AEJ*, vol. 10 (March).

COATS, A. (1982) 'The distinctive LSE ethos in the inter-war years', *AEJ*, vol. 10 (March).

DOMAR, E. (1946) 'Capital expansion, rate of growth, and employment', *EC*, vol. 14 (April).

DOMAR, E. (1947) 'Expansion and employment', *AER*, vol. 37 (March).

DOMAR, E. (1952) 'Economic growth: an econometric approach', *AER*, papers and proceeding, vol. 42 (May).

DOMAR, E. (1957) *Essays in the Theory of Economic Growth* (New York: Oxford University Press).

DURBIN, E. (1935) *The Problem of Credit Policy* (London: Chapman and Hall).

FEUER, L. (1974) *Einstein and the Generations of Science* (New York: Basic Books).

FRASER, L. (1932) 'How do we want economists to behave?', *EJ*, vol. 42 (December).

FRASER, L. (1935) 'Review of Macfie's *Theories of the Trade Cycle*', *EJ*, vol. 45 (June).

FRASER, L. (1937) *Economic Thought and Language* (London: Black).

FRASER, L. (1938) 'Economists and their critics', *EJ*, vol. 48 (June).

GAITSKELL, H.M (1937) 'Review of Harrod's *Trade Cycle*', *Econ* (n.s.), vol. 4 (November).

GOODWIN, R. (1982) *Essays in Economic Dynamics* (London: Macmillan).

HABERLER, G. (1934a) 'Review of Harrod's *International Economics*', *Econ* (n.s.), vol. 1 (February).

HABERLER, G. (1934b) Letter to the Editor of *The Economist* on 'Banking policy and stable prices', 10 November 1934.

HABERLER, G. (1936) *Prosperity and Depression* (Geneva: League of Nations).

HABERLER, G. (1937) 'Review of Harrod's *Trade Cycle*', *JPE*, vol. 45 (October).

HABERLER, G. (1938) 'Some comments on Mr. Kahn's review of *Prosperity and Depression*', *EJ*, vol. 48 (June).

HABERLER, G. (1939) *Prosperity and Depression*, 2nd edn (Geneva: League of Nations).

HABERLER, G. (1958) *Prosperity and Depression*, 4th edn (London: Allen & Unwin).

216   *Bibliography*

HABERLER, G. and BODE, K. (1935) 'Monetary equilibrium and the price level in a progressive economy', *Econ* (n.s.), vol. 2 (February).

HAHN, F. (1966) 'Review of Hicks' *Capital and Growth*', *EJ*, vol. 76 (March).

HAHN, F. (1984) 'Economic theory and Keynes's insights', *Economic Theory Discussion Paper*, no. 72 (Research Project on Risk, Information, and Quantity Signals) (University of Cambridge, Dept. of Applied Economics, January).

HAHN, F. and MATTHEWS, R. (1964) 'The theory of economic growth: a survey', *EJ*, vol. 74 (December); reprinted in International Economic Association (1967) *Surveys of Economic Theory: growth and development* (New York: St Martin's Press).

HANSEN, A. (1937) 'Harrod on the trade cycle', *QJE*, vol. 51 (May).

HANSEN, A. (1938) 'Harrod on the trade cycle', in *Full Recovery or Stagnation?* (London: Black).

HARROD, R. (1924) 'The trade cycle and the theory of distribution' (unpublished); in Harrod papers, file V–105.

HARROD, R. (1926a), 'The effect of falling prices on employment' (unpublished); in Harrod papers, file V–108.

HARROD, R. (1926b) 'The trade cycle' (unpublished); in Harrod papers, file V–110.

HARROD, R. (1927) 'Mr. Robertson's views on Banking Policy', *Econ* (o.s), vol. 7 (June).

HARROD, R. (1933a) *International Economics* (Cambridge: Cambridge University Press).

HARROD, R. (1933b) 'On the political economy of the trade cycle' (unpublished); in Harrod papers, file V–112.

HARROD, R. (1934a) 'Prof. Pigou's *Theory of Unemployment*', *EJ*, vol. 44 (March).

HARROD, R. (1934b) 'Doctrines of imperfect competition', *QJE*, vol. 48 (May).

HARROD, R. (1934c) 'The equilibrium of duopoly', *EJ*, vol. 44 (June).

HARROD, R. (1934d) 'The expansion of credit in an advancing community', *Econ* (n.s.), vol. 1 (August); reprinted in Harrod (1972).

HARROD, R. (1934e) 'Banking policy and stable prices', letter to the editor of *The Economist*, 6 October 1934.

HARROD, R. (1934f) 'Reply to critics', letter to the editor of *The Economist*, 10 November 1934.

HARROD, R. (1934g) 'Rejoinder to Mr. Robertson', *Econ* (n.s.), vol. 1 (November).

HARROD, R., (1935a) 'Rejoinder to Drs. Haberler and Bode', *Econ* (n.s.), vol. 2 (February).

HARROD, R. (1935b) 'Review of Durbin's *Problem of Credit Policy*', *EJ*, vol. 45 (December).

HARROD, R. (1936a) *The Trade Cycle: an essay* (Oxford: Clarendon Press).

HARROD, R. (1936b) 'Imperfect Competition and the Trade Cycle', *REcon.Stat*, vol. 18 (May).

HARROD, R. (1937a) 'Mr. Keynes and traditional theory', *EC*, vol. 5

(January); reprinted in S. Harris (ed.) (1948) *The New Economics: Keynes' Influence on Theory and Public Policy* (London: Dennis Dobson).

HARROD, R. (1937b) 'Review of Joan Robinson's *Essays in the Theory of Employment*', *EJ*, vol. 47 (June).

HARROD, R. (1937c) 'Review of Lundberg's *Studies in the Theory of Economic Expansion*', *ZFN*, vol. 8 (August).

HARROD, R. (1938) 'Scope and method of economics', *EJ*, vol. 48 (September).

HARROD, R. (1939a) 'An essay in dynamic theory', *EJ*, vol. 49 (March); reprinted in A. Sen (ed.) (1970) *Growth Economics: selected readings* (Harmondsworth: Penguin).

HARROD, R. (1939b) 'Price and cost in entrepreneurs policy', *OEP*, vol. 2 (May).

HARROD, R. (1946) 'Review of Lange's *Price Flexibility and Employment*', *EJ*, vol. 56 (March).

HARROD, R. (1948) *Towards a Dynamic Economics* (London: Macmillan).

HARROD, R. (1951a) *The Life of John Maynard Keynes* (London: Macmillan).

HARROD, R. (1951b) 'Notes on trade cycle theory', *EJ*, vol. 61 (June).

HARROD, R. (1952) 'Addendum note' to Harrod (1934d) in Harrod (1972).

HARROD, R. (1956a) *Foundations of Inductive Logic* (London: Macmillan).

HARROD, R. (1956b) 'Economics, 1900–1950', in A. Pryce-Jones (ed.) *The New Outline of Modern Knowledge* (London: Gollancz).

HARROD, R. (1956c) 'Walras: a re-appraisal', *EJ*, vol. 66 (June).

HARROD, R. (1959) 'Domar and dynamic economics', *EJ*, vol. 69 (September).

HARROD, R. (1960) 'Second essay in dynamic theory', *EJ*, vol. 70 (June).

HARROD, R. (1963a) 'Themes in dynamic theory', *EJ*, vol. 73 (September).

HARROD, R. (1963b) 'Retrospect on Keynes' in R. Lekachman (ed.) (1964) *Keynes General Theory: Reports of Three Decades* (London: Macmillan).

HARROD, R. (1964) 'Are monetary and fiscal policies enough?', *EJ*, vol. 74 (December).

HARROD, R. (1967) 'Increasing Returns', in R. Kuenne (ed.) *Monopolistic Competition Theory: essays in honour of Edward Chamberlain* (New York: John Wiley).

HARROD, R, (1968) 'What is a model?', in J. Wolfe (ed.) *Value, Capital, and Growth: essays in honour of John Hicks* (Edinburgh: Edinburgh University Press).

HARROD, R. (1969) *Money* (London: Macmillan).

HARROD, R. (1971) *Sociology, Morals, and Mystery: the Chichele Lectures* (London: Macmillan).

HARROD, R. (1972) *Economic Essays*, 2nd edn (1st edn 1952) (London: Macmillan).

HARROD, R. (1973) *Economic Dynamics* (London: Macmillan).

HAWTREY, R. (1937) *Capital and Employment*, 1st edn (London: Longman).

HAWTREY, R. (1939) 'Mr. Harrod's essay in dynamic theory', *EJ*, vol. 49 (September).

HAWTREY, R. (1951) 'Review of Harrod's *Life of John Maynard Keynes*', *EJ*, vol. 61 (June).

HAYEK, F. (1933) *Monetary Theory and the Trade Cycle* (trans. by Kaldor and Croome) (London: Jonathan Cape).

HICKS, J. (1939) *Value and Capital* (Oxford: Clarendon Press).

HICKS, J. (1949) 'Mr. Harrod's dynamic theory', *Econ* (n.s.), vol. 16 (May).

HICKS, J. (1950) *A Contribution to the Theory of the Trade Cycle* (Oxford: Oxford University Press).

HICKS, J. (1965) *Capital and Growth* (Oxford: Clarendon Press).

HICKS, J. (1973) 'Recollections and documents', *Econ* (n.s.), vol. 40 (February).

HOLTON, G. (1970) 'The roots of complementarity', *Daedalus*, vol. 99. (Autumn).

HUTCHISON, T. (1935) 'A Note on tautologies and the nature of economic theory', *RES*, vol. 2 (February).

JOHNSON, H. (1971) *Macroeconomics and Monetary Theory* (London: Gray-Mills).

JONES, H. (1975) *An Introduction to Modern Theories of Economic Growth* (London: Nelson).

KAHN, R. (1937) 'The League of Nations enquiry into the trade cycle', *EJ*, vol. 47 (December).

KAHN, R. (1938) 'Review of Lundberg', *EJ*, vol. 48 (June).

KAHN, R. (1984) *The Making of Keynes's General Theory* (Cambridge: Cambridge University Press).

KAHN, R. (1985) 'The Cambridge "Circus" (1)', in G. Harcourt (ed.) *Keynes and his Contemporaries* (London: Macmillan).

KALDOR, N. (1934), Letter to the editor of *The Economist* on Banking policy and stable prices, 10 November 1934.

KALDOR, N. (1951) 'Hicks on the trade cycle', *EJ*, vol. 61 (December); reprinted in Kaldor (1960) *Essays on Economic Stability and Growth* (London: Duckworth).

KALDOR, N. (1986) 'Recollections of an economist', *BLQR*, vol. 39 (March).

KALECKI, M. (1935), 'A macrodynamic theory of business cycles', *EC*, vol. 3 (July).

KALECKI, M. (1937) 'A theory of the business cycle', *RES*, vol. 4 (February).

KEYNES, J.M. (1923) *A Tract on Monetary Reform* (London: Macmillan).

KEYNES, J.M. (1930) *A Treatise on Money* (London: Macmillan).

KEYNES, J.M. (1936) *The General Theory of Employment, Interest and Money* (London: Macmillan).

KEYNES, J.M. (1939) 'Review of Tinbergen', *EJ*, vol. 49 (September).

KEYNES, J.M. (1971–82) *Collected Writings*, D. Moggridge (ed.) (London: Macmillan); cited as JMK with volume number.

KREGEL, J. (1972) *The Theory of Economic Growth* (London: Macmillan).

KREGEL, J. (1980) 'Economic dynamics and the theory of steady growth: an historical essay on Harrod's "knife-edge"', *HOPE*, vol. 12 (Spring).

KREGEL, J. (1985) 'Harrod and Keynes: increasing returns, the theory of employment, and dynamic economics', in G. Harcourt (ed.) *Keynes and his Contemporaries* (London: Macmillan).

LAKATOS, I. (1970) 'Falsification and the methodology of scientific research programs', in I. Lakatos and A. Musgrave (eds) *Criticism and the Growth of Knowledge* (Cambridge: Cambridge University Press).

LANGE, O. (1938a) 'The rate of interest and the optimum propensity to consume', *Econ* (n.s.), vol. 5 (February).

LANGE, O. (1938b) 'Review of Lundberg's *Studies in the Theory of Economic Expansion*', *Econ* (n.s.), vol. 5 (May).

LANGE, O. (1945) *Price Flexibility and Employment* (Bloomington, Ind.: Principia Press).

LEE, F. (1981) 'The Oxford challenge to Marshallian supply and demand: the history of the Oxford Economists' Research Group', *OEP*, vol. 33 (November).

LEKACHMAN, R. (ed.) (1964) *Keynes General Theory: Reports of Three Decades* (London: Macmillan).

LEONTIEFF, W. (1937) 'Implicit theorizing: a methodological criticism of the neo-Cambridge school', *QJE*, vol. 51 (February); reprinted in Leontieff (1966) *Essays in Economics* (New York: Oxford University Press).

LEVAČIC, R. and REBMANN, A. (1982) *Macro-economics: an Introduction to Keynesian-Neoclassical Controversies*, 2nd edn (London: Macmillan).

LUNDBERG, E. (1937) *Studies in the Theory of Economic Expansion*, Stockholm Economic Studies, no. 6, (London: P.S. King).

LUTFALLA, G. (1937) 'Compte rendu des travaux de la VI réunion européene de la societé internationale d'econométrie', *REP*, vol. 51 (notes et memoranda).

MACHLUP, F. (1958) 'Equilibrium and disequilibrium: misplaced concreteness and disguised politics', *EJ*, vol. 68 (March).

MARSCHAK, J. (1939) 'Remarks to R.F.H's "Essay in Dynamic Theory"' (unpublished); in Harrod papers, file V–113a.

McCLOSKEY, D. (1985) *The Rhetoric of Economics* (Madison: University of Wisconsin Press).

McMAHON, M. (1982) 'Methodology and the equilibrium approach to business cycles', *AEJ*, vol. 10 (September).

MEADE, J. (1932) 'Review of Akerman's *Economic Progress and Economic Crises*', *EJ*, vol. 42 (September).

MEADE, J. (1933) *The Rate of Interest in a Progressive State* (London: Macmillan).

MEADE, J. (1936a) 'Note I' on the draft manuscript of Harrod's *The Trade Cycle* (12 January 1936, unpublished); in Harrod papers, file IV–745–67.

MEADE, J. (1936b) *An Introduction to Economic Analysis and Policy* (Oxford: Oxford University Press).

MEADE, J. (1937) *An Introduction to Economic Analysis and Policy*, 2nd edn (Oxford: Oxford University Press).

MEADE, J. (1938) (American edited by C. Hitch) *An Introduction to*

Economic Analysis and Policy (New York: Oxford University Press); with an introduction by A. Hansen.

MEADE, J. (1961) *A Neo-Classical Theory of Economic Growth* (London: Allen & Unwin).

MODIGLIANI, F. (1944) 'Liquidity Preference and the Theory of Interest of Money', *EC*, vol. 12 (January).

NEUMANN, J. von and MORGENSTERN, O. (1944) *Theory of Games and Economic Behaviour* (Princeton: Princeton University Press).

PATINKIN, D. (1976) *Keynes' Monetary Thought: a study of its development* (Durham: Duke University Press).

PHELPS-BROWN, H. (1937) 'Report of the Oxford meeting, 25–29 September, 1936', *EC*, vol. 5 (October).

PHELPS-BROWN, H. (1980) 'Sir Roy Harrod: a biographical memoir', *EJ*, vol. 90 (March).

PIGOU, A. (1933) *The Theory of Unemployment* (London: Macmillan).

PRESLEY, J. (1979) *Robertsonian Economics* (London: Macmillan).

RAMSEY, F. (1928) 'A mathematical theory of savings', *EJ*, vol. 38; reprinted in A. Sen (ed.) (1970) *Growth Economics* (Harmondsworth: Penguin).

RILEY-SMITH, H. (1982) *Catalogue of the Papers of Sir Roy Harrod* (Norfolk: Riley-Smith Booksellers).

ROBBINS, L. (1932) *The Nature and Significance of Economic Science* (London: Macmillan).

ROBBINS, L. (1971) *Autobiography of an Economist* (London: Macmillan).

ROBERTSON, D. (1926) *Banking Policy and the Price Level: an essay in the theory of the trade cycle* (London: P.S. King).

ROBERTSON, D. (1933) 'Saving and hoarding', *EJ*, vol. 43 (September).

ROBERTSON, D. (1934a) 'Mr. Harrod and the expansion of credit', *Econ* (n.s.), vol. 1 (November).

ROBERTSON, D. (1934b) 'Industrial fluctuation and the natural rate of interest', *EJ*, vol. 44 (December).

ROBERTSON, D. (1937) 'Review of Harrod's *Trade Cycle*', *CJEP* vol. 3 (February).

ROBINSON, A. (1985), 'The Cambridge "Circus" (2)', in G. Harcourt (ed.) *Keynes and his Contemporaries* (London: Macmillan).

ROBINSON, J. (1934) 'Review of Meade's *Rate of Interest in a Progressive State*', *EJ*, vol. 44 (June).

ROBINSON, J. (1936) 'Review of Harrod's *Trade Cycle*', *EJ*, vol. 46 (December).

ROBINSON, J. (1937) *Essays in the Theory of Employment* (London: Macmillan).

ROBINSON, J. (1949) 'Mr. Harrod's Dynamics', *EJ*, vol. 59 (March).

ROBINSON, J. (1962) 'A model of accumulation', in *Essays in the Theory of Economic Growth* (London: Macmillan) reprinted in A. Sen (ed.) (1970) *Growth Economics* (Harmondsworth: Penguin).

ROBINSON, J. (1970) 'Harrod after twenty-one years', *EJ*, vol. 80 (September).

SAMUELSON, P. (1939) 'Interactions between the Multiplier Analysis and the Principle of Acceleration', *REconStat*, vol. 21 (May).

SAMUELSON, P. (1947) *Foundations of Economic Analysis* (Cambridge, Mass.: Harvard University Press).

SEN, A. (ed.) (1970) *Growth Economics: selected readings* (Harmondsworth: Penguin).

SHACKLE, G. (1967) *The Years of High Theory* (Cambridge: Cambridge University Press).

SOLOW, R. (1956) 'A contribution to the theory of economic growth', *QJE*, vol. 70 (February); reprinted in A. Sen (ed.) (1970) *Growth Economics* (Harmondsworth: Penguin).

SOLOW, R. (1987) 'James Meade at 80', *EJ*, vol. 97 (December).

SNOW, C.P. (1982) *The Physicists* (London: Macmillan).

STAFFORD, J. (1937) 'Review of Harrod's *Trade Cycle*', *MS*, vol. 8 (January).

SWAN, T. (1956) 'Economic growth and capital accumulation', *ER*, vol. 32 (November).

TAPPAN, M. (1928) 'Mr. Robertson's views on banking policy: a reply to Mr. Harrod', *Econ* (o.s.), vol. 8 (March).

TINBERGEN, J. (1935) 'Suggestions on Quantitative Business Cycle Theory', *EC*, vol. 3 (July).

TINBERGEN, J. (1937) 'Review of Harrod's *Trade Cycle*', *Welt.Arch.* vol. 45 (May).

TINBERGEN, J. (1938) 'Statistical evidence on the acceleration principle', *Econ* (n.s.), vol. 5 (May).

VENIERIS, Y. and SEBOLD, F. (1977) *Macroeconomic Models and Policy* (New York: Wiley).

WYNNE, W. (1937) 'Review of Harrod's *Trade Cycle*' *AER*, vol. 27 (March).

YEAGER, L. (1954) 'Some questions about growth economics', *AER*, vol. 44, (March).

YOUNG, W. (1975) 'Harrod, Keynes, and the fundamental relationship', *AEJ*, vol. 3 (November).

YOUNG, W. (1987) *Interpreting Mr Keynes: the IS–LM Enigma* (Oxford: Polity Press).

Index